University and College Women's and Gender Equity Centers

University and College Women's and Gender Equity Centers examines the new institutional contexts surrounding women's centers. It looks at the possibilities for, as well as the challenges to, advocating for gender equity in higher education, and the ways in which women's and gender equity centers contribute to and lead that work.

The book first describes the landscape of women's centers in higher education and explores the structures within which the centers are situated. In doing so, the book shows the ways in which many women's centers have expanded their work to include working with athletics, Greek life, men, transgender students, international students, student parents, veterans, etc. Contributors then delve into the profession of women's center work itself, and ask how women's center work has become "professionalized." Threats and challenges to women's and gender equity centers are also explored, as contributors look at how threats and challenges have helped or complicated the role of centers. The collection concludes by highlighting current successes and forward-thinking approaches in women's centers and asking how gender equity centers can best prepare for the future.

Through narratives, case studies, and by offering strategies and best practice, *University and College Women's and Gender Equity Centers* will engage emerging and existing equity center professionals and women's and gender studies faculty and students and help them to move the work of gender equity forward in the next decade.

Brenda Bethman is the Director of the Women's Center and Women's, Gender, and Sexuality Studies Program at the University of Missouri–Kansas City, USA. She also holds appointments as Affiliated Faculty in German and Coordinator of the General Education Program.

Anitra Cottledge is the Director of the Women's Center at the University of Minnesota (UMN), USA. Previously, she served as the Director of Communications in the UMN Office for Equity and Diversity and as the Assistant Director of the UMN Women's Center for several years.

Donna M. Bickford is the Director of the Women's and Gender Resource Center at Dickinson College in Carlisle, Pennsylvania, USA. Previously she served as Director of the Carolina Women's Center and then Associate Director of the Office for Undergraduate Research at UNC–Chapel Hill, USA.

University and College Women's and Gender Equity Centers

The Changing Landscape

Edited by Brenda Bethman,
Anitra Cottledge, and
Donna M. Bickford

Routledge
Taylor & Francis Group

LONDON AND NEW YORK

First published 2019
by Routledge
2 Park Square, Milton Park, Abingdon, Oxon OX14 4RN

and by Routledge
711 Third Avenue, New York, NY 10017

Routledge is an imprint of the Taylor & Francis Group, an informa business

British Library Cataloguing-in-Publication Data
A catalogue record for this book is available from the British Library

Library of Congress Cataloging-in-Publication Data
A catalog record has been requested for this book

ISBN: 978-0-8153-8681-0 (hbk)
ISBN: 978-1-351-17470-1 (ebk)

Typeset in Goudy
by Apex CoVantage, LLC

Contents

Contributors

Sharalle V. Arnold is the Associate Director of the Center for Women and Gender Equity at Grand Valley State University.

Susannah Bartlow is a writer, educator, yoga practitioner, social worker, and recovering academic currently based in Memphis, Tennessee.

Brenda Bethman is the Director of the Women's Center and Women's, Gender, and Sexuality Studies Program at the University of Missouri–Kansas City. She also holds appointments as Affiliated Faculty in German and Coordinator of the General Education Program.

Donna M. Bickford serves as the Director of the Women's and Gender Resource Center at Dickinson College in Carlisle, Pennsylvania. Previously she served as Director of the Carolina Women's Center and then Associate Director of the Office for Undergraduate Research at UNC–Chapel Hill.

Nicole Carter is the Director of the Wright State University Women's Center in Dayton, Ohio.

Erin Chapman is a Clinical Associate Professor in Child, Family & Consumer Studies at the University of Idaho and is passionate about comprehensive, sex-positive sexuality and healthy relationship education for all.

Anitra Cottledge is the Director of the Women's Center at the University of Minnesota (UMN). Previously, she served as the Director of Communications in the UMN Office for Equity and Diversity and as the Assistant Director of the UMN Women's Center for several years.

Karlyn Crowley is Founding Director of the Cassandra Voss Center and Professor of English and Women's and Gender Studies at St. Norbert College, De Pere, Wisconsin.

Emelyn dela Peña is a second generation Filipina-American from Los Angeles, California, who is currently serving as Associate Vice Chancellor for Student Affairs and Dean of the Center for Diversity & Inclusion at Washington University in St. Louis.

Melanie DeMaeyer is a lifelong southern queer feminist and currently serves as the Assistant Director of the Women's Resource Center at Georgia Institute of Technology (Georgia Tech).

Susanne B. Dietzel is the Executive Director of Eden House in New Orleans, Louisiana.

Kimberly A. Fulbright is the Interim University Ombudsperson at the University of Cincinnati.

Jane Goettsch is the Director of the Women*s Center at Miami University, Oxford, Ohio.

Brittany Harris is a social justice educator, strategist, and advocate, committed to bringing knowledge and resources into the communities she serves while uplifting historically oppressed and marginalized communities.

Kathleen Holgerson is the Director of the Women's Center at the University of Connecticut.

Amy J. Howton is the former Associate Director of the Women's Center at the University of Cincinnati.

Susan V. Iverson is professor of and program coordinator for the doctoral concentration in Higher Education Leadership at Manhattanville College.

Jessica Jennrich is the Director of the Gayle R. Davis Center for Women and Gender Equity at Grand Valley State University.

Rita M. Jones is the Director of the Center for Gender Equity and Affiliate Faculty in Women, Gender & Sexuality Studies at Lehigh University.

Julia Keleher is the Director of the LGBTQA Office at the University of Idaho.

Ann Linden is an Associate Professor in the Department of English & Humanities and former Women's Center Director at Shawnee State University in Ohio.

Heather C. Lou is an angry Gemini earth dragon; multiracial, Asian, queer, cisgender womxn of color; multimedia artist; and postsecondary education administrator based in Minneapolis, Minnesota.

Susan B. Marine is Associate Professor of Higher Education at Merrimack College.

Marci McCaulay is the former (retired) Director of the Center for Women and Gender Action at Denison University in Granville, Ohio.

Rebekah MillerMacPhee is the Office of Violence Against Women Project Director at the University of Idaho Women's Center.

Uyenthi Tran Myhre is the Assistant Director of the Women's Center at the University of Minnesota, Twin Cities.

Jessica Nare is a Lecturer in the Department of Women's Studies and manages the Women's Resource Center at San Diego State University.

Juli Parker is the Assistant Dean of Students and Director of the Center for Women, Gender & Sexuality at the University of Massachusetts–Dartmouth.

Purvi Patel is the Assistant Director of the Center for Diversity & Inclusion at Washington University in St. Louis, Missouri.

Cassie Pegg-Kirby is the Director of the Women's Center at Kent State University.

Colleen Riggle is Assistant Dean of Students and Director of the Women's Resource Center at the Georgia Institute of Technology.

Lisa Rismiller, formerly the Founding Director of the University of Dayton (Ohio) Women's Center, is the Secretary of UD's Board of Trustees.

Allison C. Roman is the Director for Diversity and Inclusion at Trinity University.

Lysa Salsbury is the Director of the Women's Center at the University of Idaho–Moscow.

Hannah Thompson is the Associate Director for the LGBTQ+ Center in the Department of Student Diversity, Equity and Inclusion at Miami University in Oxford, Ohio, and a Licensed Professional Counselor.

Cindy Vanzant is the Assistant Director of the Women's Center at Wright State University.

Pattie Waugh was the Programming Coordinator for the University of Dayton Women's Center in Dayton, Ohio, until her retirement, and is a lifelong activist for social justice.

Raquel Wright-Mair is Assistant Professor of Higher Education and Student Affairs Leadership at the University of Northern Colorado.

Acknowledgments

Co-editors: We would like to acknowledge each other as co-editors. The idea for this book has been germinating for a long time, but it took all of us working together to bring it into fruition. We are so grateful for our partnership and look forward to more collaborations in the future! We would also like to thank all of the contributors who shared their ideas, research, and wisdom in this book; there literally would be no book without all of you.

Brenda Bethman: Thanks, as always, to Larson Powell for his support and cooking.

Donna M. Bickford: I would like to also thank my family, friends, and colleagues for their interest and support.

Anitra Cottledge: Lastly, thank you to my partner and our two weird cats for always supporting me, making me laugh, and sharing a life that's full of love.

Susannah Bartlow (Chapter 8): Very little work is actually the sole product of its author; a number of people have contributed to the perspective and growth discussed here. Particular thanks to Lee Abbott, Andrew Anastasia, Shelby L. Crosby, Ava Hernandez, Irna Landrum, Sheltreese McCoy, Sameena Mulla, Neeve Neevel, Jardana Peacock, Julie Perini, Stephanie Roades, and Cathy Seasholes for conversations since 2015 that helped shape this chapter. Thanks also to Ex Fabula's fall 2016 storytelling fellowship cohort, especially coach Destinny Fletcher aka Deolinda Abstrac.

Introduction

Donna M. Bickford

It's been nearly 15 years since Sharon Davie published the landmark volume *University and College Women's Centers: A Journey toward Equity* (2002), and, although the body of literature about women's centers has grown, Davie's remains the only book about women's and gender equity centers in US higher education. In the ensuing years since the publication of *University and College Women's Centers*, how has the work of women's centers shifted and expanded to include new ways of thinking, being, and doing? Where do gaps still exist and what is on the horizon?

Since the first campus-based women's center was founded at the University of Minnesota in 1960, women's centers have worked to respond to the ever-evolving needs related to women's and gender equity. While early centers may have focused on the continuing education needs of 1950s married women (Opitz), women's centers throughout the last 50+ years have employed a great deal of flexibility in their responses to national gender equity issues. As a result, centers have taken on issues like violence against women; pay and salary equity; body image and body positivity; and issues of diversity, inclusion, and intersectionality (Bonebright et al. 81–3). The populations many women's centers serve has also changed and now might include pregnant and parenting students; veterans; trans*[1] students; non-traditional age students; and larger populations of students of color, international students, and first-generation students.

In Davie's list of campus-based women's centers, included as an appendix in her book, the names of women's centers were fairly consistent and were variations on Women's Center, Women's Programs, or Women's Resource Center. In the current list compiled by the National Women's Studies Association (NWSA) Women's Centers Committee, we see more variety in center names (A Women's and Gender Centers List). From the Gender Equity Resource Center at UC–Berkeley to the Women's and Gender Resource Center at Dickinson College to The Center for Women, Gender & Sexuality at the University of Massachusetts–Dartmouth, the name changes reflect an expanded sense of the work of centers.

The phenomenon of women's centers changing their name to reflect the need to serve expanded populations or to reflect the development of their work parallels the change in many academic departments as they, too, respond to a changing environment. In addition to Women's Studies Departments, we see Women's and

Gender Studies Departments, Women's, Gender and Sexuality Studies Departments, or Departments of Feminist Studies. Some have argued that the expansion of the name is a "disservice" to the history of women's studies, which began because of the need to focus on the "experiences of women that have been largely silenced within the dominant historical discourse" (Feminist Fatale). Alice E. Ginsberg suggests instead that:

> Perhaps the most compelling argument for changing the name to gender studies is that it invites men to look at their experiences in American culture, as well as how they may be complicit in the continuation of systems of power and privilege. It also compels men to see themselves not as the "norm" but as gendered human beings.
>
> (Jaschik)

Some women's and gender centers have also begun to address the need to explore the ways in which cultural representations of masculinity negatively impact men, to help men explore their masculinity, and to catalyze a shift from toxic to healthy masculinity. See, for example, the Duke Men's Project (housed in the Duke Women's Center) or the Masculinity Project at Westchester University (housed in the Center for Women and Gender Equity).

Davie closes her book with some thoughts about future directions for women's centers at that time, focusing on three areas: leadership, internationalization, and technology (448). She is thinking here about leadership both institutionally and individually, as well as how feminist approaches to leadership might build new capacities and new relationships. And, indeed, women's centers are certainly engaged in developing and supporting leaders. One current example is the Young Women Leaders Program at the Maxine Platzer Lynn Women's Center at the University of Virginia (where Davie herself was the director for many years), a program which pairs undergraduate women with girls from local middle schools for mentoring and which aims to empower the girls as leaders. The Women's Leadership Institute at the Women's Center at the University of Minnesota provides leadership development for women faculty and staff. The Women's Center at the University of Cincinnati hosts WILL: Women in Leadership and Learning, a three-year leadership development program for undergraduate women. These are just a few examples of the range of approaches to leadership and leadership development provided in women's centers today.

Davie imagines internationalization as building relationships with women's centers around the world and strengthening global women's networks. We might also think of the development of intercultural competency, the impact of gender on study abroad programs, the recruitment of international women faculty and staff, the creation of resources and support for female international students, and the development of co-curricular programming on global gender issues. The Women's Center at Ohio University hosts a monthly International Women's Coffee Hour, an opportunity for international students to build community and practice English. Co-sponsored by International Student and Faculty Services, this provides an opportunity to collaborate with campus units that might otherwise not have much opportunity to interact. The Women's Center at the University of Louisville, housed in the Office of Diversity and International Affairs, takes students on an annual global trip with a woman's perspective, designed to learn about and from women in other areas of the world. The Women's Resource Center at Texas A&M hosts an annual International Women's Day Conference focused on a different theme each year.

When Davie named technology as an area of development for women's centers, the most common uses were in email listservs (like WRAC-L) and websites for individual women's centers. Those continue to be common, but Davie could not have predicted the substantial increase in the use of technology by women's centers with the advent of social media. Now it is a rare women's center whose web presence is limited to their website. Women's centers are using Facebook, Twitter, Instagram, Snapchat, YouTube, and blogs to publicize their events, provide students with opportunities to share their feminist analysis and build communication skills, maintain connections with alumni, and build connections between centers.

The majority of institutions of higher education enroll more women undergraduates than men. This has led some to question whether there is still a need for women's centers, or whether they continue to serve an important purpose. In fact, these attitudes are so common that many women's centers have engaged directly with the question on their websites (see Frequently Asked Questions on the websites of the Women's Center at the University of Rhode Island or the Women's Center at Western Illinois University for examples). Some campuses have put together material documenting the continuing inequity women face (see "Why We Still Need Women's Centers: 40 Facts You Never Knew About Gender Inequity"). These are powerful rebuttals to the implication that work on gender and gender equity issues are no longer necessary.

Increased representation does not necessarily equal equity, and certainly not in the case of higher education. Corrie Martin argues that "the increase in and dominance of women students earning all degrees belie entrenched inequities and roadblocks to actual equity in higher education for women" (Santovec 7). We know that women continue to have a different experience on most campuses than men. Although there are certainly male and gender nonbinary victims of sexual violence, women continue to be victimized at higher rates. Women are often treated differently in class discussions; they are interrupted more often and their comments get uptake less often. Women continue to be discouraged from declaring certain majors, particularly in STEM fields. Despite Title IX, in some institutions, women's athletics are not funded at the same rate as men's, or they have fewer opportunities to play competitive sports. The existence of a gendered wage gap is something about which our students need to be aware. Many women's centers offer workshops in salary negotiation as one avenue of response.

Women's centers are intentionally deploying an intersectional lens in their work. Still, many centers struggle to respond to the diversity of social identity locations on their campuses, and, in particular, race and ethnicity. Although women's centers at historically black colleges and universities (HBCUs), Hispanic-serving institutions (HSI), and tribal colleges are specifically designed to serve women of color, women's centers on predominantly white institutions (PWI) must be vigilant and intentional. Elena Marie DiLapi and Gloria M. Gay note that despite our best efforts, too often women's centers are "utilized by, and perceived to be a space for, white women only" (204). In some ways this is reflective of the history of feminist struggle in the US. Although "the women's movement has made some strides in understanding the diversity of all women" (DiLapi and Gay 204), it has struggled to practice inclusion and intersectionality in a consistent and meaningful way. Structural and systematic racism continue to impact the experiences of our students of color, which means we must develop ways to support and provide resources to them, including making sure that our women's centers are places where they feel welcomed and included. A range of strategies is being deployed in centers across the US. The Women's Center at the University of Maryland, Baltimore County, hosts biweekly Women of Color Coalition meetings to provide space for conversation and community building. At Wake Forest University, the Intercultural Center and Women's Center collaborate to offer a peer-facilitated Women of Color discussion twice each semester. The Flora Stone Mather Center for Women at Case Western Reserve University offers a Woman of Color discussion series intended to build a community able to advocate for equity for all women.

This anthology picks up where Davie left off, and examines the new institutional contexts surrounding women's centers, the possibilities as well as the challenges to advocating for gender equity in higher education, and the ways in which women's and gender equity centers contribute to and lead that work. The book is divided into four sections. The first section examines the landscape of women's centers in higher education and explores the structures within which centers live. Who do women's centers serve, and how? What reporting structures do centers belong to, and what resources are available to them? How have social and political forces shaped contemporary centers? Have they shifted to center the experiences of marginalized and underrepresented voices, including those of women of color and American Indian women? Finally, this section explores the ways in which many women's centers have expanded their work to include working with athletics, Greek life, men, transgender students, international students, student parents, veterans, etc. Chapters in this section include Jane Goettsch et al.'s *Positioning Campus Women's and Gender Equity Centers for Success: Structural Issues and Trends*, which explores a range of structural issues impacting today's campus women's and gender equity centers, and highlights the recent interconnected trends of incorporating inclusion and intersectionality principles and (re) naming centers. Rita M. Jones examines an under-discussed connection on campuses in her chapter, *Beyond Parties and PNMs: An Integrated Model for Women's and*

Gender Centers and Sororities, which focuses on the relationships between women's centers and sororities. Jones's analysis and model provides a path for centers to consider the possibilities and pitfalls of building collaborative relationships with campus organizations that represent a large body of women. Jane Goettsch et al.'s *Exploring the Relationships between Campus Women's Centers and LGBTQ+ Centers and Initiatives* includes a discussion of the challenges and opportunities that these relationships represent, including examples of possible collaborations and funding and staffing considerations. Lysa Salsbury and Rebekah MillerMacPhee examine how women's centers function to resist and dismantle institutionalized sexism and racism in *Solidarity Is for All: Women's Centers Serving Women of Color*. The final chapter in this section is *Late to the Game: The Politics of Opening a Women's Center in 2015*, in which Jessica Nare explores the political opportunities and challenges of opening a women's center in 2015.

Section two delves into the profession of women's center work itself, and asks how women's center work has become "professionalized." What does it mean to require a PhD for some center director positions? Is there a value conflict in this? What are the implications of "credentialization" on access and succession? What competencies and credentials do women's center staff truly need in order to be effective? Is it still important to be/label oneself a feminist in order to work in a women's center? How does intersectionality trouble the notion of "feminist" identity as a requirement for women's center work? In *Where Do We Enter? How Do We Stay? The Role of Consciousness-Raising in Developing Women's Center Professionals*, Kathleen Holgerson and Juli Parker explore how women's centers have modeled consciousness-raising as a professional development strategy within and outside of formal organizations and associations, and reflect on the "credentialing" now often required for women's center staff positions. *Experiences of Women's Center Directors in Student Affairs*, a contribution from Colleen Riggle and Melanie DeMaeyer, highlights the findings of their qualitative study that investigates the work experiences of women's center professionals in a director role in a student affairs division. In *On Trauma, Ambivalence, and Trying Too Hard* by Susannah Bartlow, the author analyzes her experiences working as a white activist-director of two gender-based centers and explores questions related to issues of mental health, leadership, and power encountered by women's center employees. Brenda Bethman and Anitra Cottledge explore the importance of intersectionality in reframing self and community care in the context of women's and gender equity centers as well as practical strategies for women's center staff to prevent burnout, particularly in environments that do not prioritize self and community care and institutions that value productivity over sustainability in *Putting Our Oxygen Masks on First: Women's Center Staff and Self-Care*.

Our third section addresses some of the threats and challenges to women's and gender equity centers. As centers have expanded their work to include many populations, how has resource allocation aligned with that expansion? How does that expansion help and complicate the possibility of collaboration with other offices/departments that share a social justice agenda? How have centers engaged in cultural and climate change in the face of institutional resistance? Susan V. Iverson and Cassie Pegg-Kirby examine questions surrounding whether and how women's centers can unite across differences in their chapter *Seeking Relevance in an Age of Inequity: A Case Study of the Identity Struggle of One Women's Center*. In *"Blue" Language in a Red State: Inclusive Sexuality Education in a Conservative Climate*, Lysa Salsbury and her co-authors explore the evolution of a comprehensive campus sexual health education forum and share the challenges of and techniques for addressing the controversy that often surrounds these efforts. At a moment of increased focus on assessment, Nicole Carter et al. provide ways to engage in successful models of assessment and evaluation that attend to processes, participation, and a grounding in the experiences of women in their essay, *Ohio Women's Centers' Reflections on Evaluation and Assessment: Revisited*.

The fourth and final section of this collection highlights current successes and forward-thinking approaches in women's centers. How are centers being nimble in the face of changing landscapes and shifting priorities? What creative solutions have women's centers been able to employ? What programs could serve as exemplars for other centers to adapt to their contexts and communities? How have partnerships with not-just-the-usual suspects helped centers to transform, thrive, and evolve? How are women's centers looking toward and preparing for the future? Emelyn dela Peña et al. explore the possibilities for women's centers within new university structures more broadly defined under equity, diversity, and inclusion in *Paying Homage to College and University Women's Centers: Gender Justice Work in the Center for Diversity and Inclusion*. In a climate where access to financial resources continues to be constrained, Uyenthi Tran Myhre's *Beyond the Label: Leveraging the Iconography of "Feminist" from Moments to Movements* is a timely description of efforts to connect the iconography of "feminist" to fundraising efforts. Jessica Jennrich and her co-authors blend intersectionality, postmodernism, critical race theory, and disability studies to frame a radically inclusive gender justice approach in *The Personal and the Professional: Intersectional Experiences in Gender Justice Work*. In *Addressing and Dismantling Cisgenderism in Womxn's Centers: Reframing Womxn's Centers Work Toward an Intersectional Critical Trans Politic*, Heather C. Lou utilizes critical trans politic to provide tools and tactics for womxn's center administrators to address and dismantle cisgender privilege. Karlyn Crowley stresses the importance of strategic planning and examines strategies for aligning women's center's visions and goals to initiatives and programming in, *Vision to Action: Inside Out Strategic Planning*. And, finally, Raquel Wright-Mair and Susan B. Marine close the volume with their contribution, *Setting a Transformative Agenda for the Next Era: Research on Women's and Gender Centers*, in which they call for education researchers and WGC practitioners to produce collaborative research responding to the research questions that will move forward the work of women's centers.

We hope this book is useful to women's and gender center directors and other staff members in moving the work of gender equity forward in the next decade.

Note

1 Trans* is an umbrella term referring to the range of transgender, gender non-binary, and gender diverse identities.

Works cited

Bonebright, Denise A., et al. "Developing Women Leaders on Campus: A Human Resources – Women's Center Partnership at the University of Minnesota." *Advances in Developing Human Resources*, vol. 14, no. 1, 2012, pp. 79–95.

Davie, Sharon L. *University and College Women's Centers: A Journey toward Equity*. Greenwood P, 2002.

DiLapi, Elena Marie, and Gloria M. Gay. "Women's Centers Responding to Racism." In Davie, pp. 203–26.

"Frequently Asked Questions." *Women's Center, The University of Rhode Island*, web.uri.edu/womenscenter/faq. Accessed 28 Mar. 2018.

"Frequently Asked Questions." *Women's Center, Western Illinois University*, www.wiu.edu/student_services/womens_center/faq.php. Accessed 28 Mar. 2018.

Jaschik, Scott. "The Evolution of American Women's Studies." *Inside Higher Education*, 27 Mar. 2009, www.insidehighered.com/news/2009/03/27/women. Accessed 20 Feb. 2018.

Opitz, Donald L. *Three Generations in the Life of the Minnesota Women's Center: A History, 1960–2000*. Minnesota Women's Center, 1999.

Santovec, Mary Lou. "Women's Centers: Even More Relevant and Necessary Today." *Women in Higher Education*, vol. 21, no. 10, Oct. 2012, p. 7.

"What's in a Name? Is 'Gender Studies' More Inclusive?" *Feminist Fatale*, 6 July 2013, www.feministfatale.com/2013/07/whats-in-a-name-is-gender-studies-more-inclusive. Accessed 20 Feb. 2018.

"Why We Still Need Women's Centers: 40 Facts You Never Knew about Gender Inequity." *Women's Center, University of Minnesota*, diversity.umn.edu/women/40facts. Accessed 20 Feb. 2018.

"A Women's and Gender Centers List." *NWSA Women's Centers Committee*, nwsawcc.wordpress.com/womens-and-gender-centers-list. Accessed 26 Jan. 2018.

"WRAC-L." *NWSA Women's Centers Committee*, nwsawcc.wordpress.com/wrac-l. Accessed 5 Jan. 2018.

1 Positioning campus women's and gender equity centers for success

Structural issues and trends

Jane Goettsch, Ann Linden, Cindy Vanzant, and Pattie Waugh

The continuing relevance of women's and gender equity centers

Gender demographics of students at US colleges and universities have changed in recent decades. By 1980 women had overtaken men as the majority of undergraduates, and by 2006 women were earning more degrees than men at every level except professional (where their representation almost equaled men's) (Touchton et al. 11). For some, these factors alone prompt questions about whether campus women's centers are still relevant. In addition, recent political, economic, and social conditions have heightened scrutiny of higher education and the continuing need for units like women's centers.

While the first campus women's centers were founded in the 1960s, they emerged in large numbers in the 1970s and 1980s, often alongside women's studies programs, to address gender inequities experienced by women, including unequal access to higher education. Now that women outnumber men on most college campuses, is access still an issue? For whom? And what of other gender inequities? Vlasnik notes that gender inequity is still a concern despite women's growing numbers, and she offers these cautions:

> First, we must identify which women and men we are discussing and attend to how intersecting identities change access and equity in higher education; second, the "quantity" of women in higher education is a different discussion than the "quality" of their experiences, and; third, the many histories of women's access to higher education are critical to understanding their current status, opportunities, and challenges.
>
> (24)

In addition to issues of access, many of the other inequities that led to the establishment of women's centers decades ago also remain, contributing to such ongoing, serious campus problems as sexual harassment and assault, chilly classroom climate, and other barriers to student success that disproportionately affect women and shape their experience following graduation through the continuing gender wage gap, family/work integration challenges, and underrepresentation of women in leadership and in certain professions.

Research by Sax found that women enter college with lower levels of academic self-confidence (25), higher levels of self-reported stress (33), and lower ratings of their physical and emotional health (34) than those of men. This gender gap remains significant over the college years. As Marine notes, women's centers continue to play an important role in "extending support, and creating spaces for quiet comfort and fortitude for boundary pushing" (19), as well as educating their campus communities about gender equity.

Despite evidence of continuing inequities, some in higher education believe that gender equity has been achieved. This belief presents challenges for women's centers attempting to engage students and other members of the campus community with ongoing women's and gender issues. In her study of 75 campus women's centers, Kasper notes obstacles mentioned by women's center directors in running their centers, including "the notion that special attention to women's issues isn't 'necessary' anymore," negative attitudes toward feminism, and general apathy toward women's issues (498). Campbell observes that "programs and pedagogies that engage directly with questions of gender and sexuality may be located at the edges of the curriculum [and, by implication, co-curriculum], implicitly marginalizing the issues and people they address" (1). This marginalization further challenges women's centers.

An additional concern for women's centers – and certainly not a new issue – is lack of funds. Thirty years ago Clevenger found that, regardless of institutional demographic categories, lack of funding was the most significant constraint on the operation of women's centers (6). Marine's research confirms that this is an ongoing, serious challenge (22).

In the context of changing student demographics, the belief that gender equity has been achieved, continued marginalization of gender-related work, and serious economic challenges facing colleges and universities, campus women's centers must be strategic to thrive now and in the future. Strategic planning requires consideration of structural factors shaping campus women's and gender equity centers.

Structural issues for campus women's and gender equity centers

Organizational configurations

Several types of women's and gender equity centers exist on college campuses:

- *Community activist/action centers*. Often staffed by volunteers, including students, or by part-time staff, such centers provide places to meet, find support, organize, and take action for social change.
- *Student services/resource centers*. Often led by a master's-level professional director, though increasingly led by doctoral-level directors, these

student-focused centers are typically located in student affairs divisions. They are generally strong on programs and services and less focused on influencing or setting institutional policy.

- *Synthesis centers.* Often led by professional directors with doctorates or by faculty, these centers are more likely to be housed in academic affairs or institutional diversity divisions and to serve a broad constituency. They also play a role in curriculum and policy transformation as well as offer programs and services.
- *Hybrid centers.* Typically staffed by a faculty member, these combined academic and administrative centers offer coursework in Women's, Gender, and Sexuality Studies along with student services such as community space, programming, and student organization advising.
- *Research centers.* Staffed primarily by faculty, these centers focus on research and publication of scholarly reports on gender issues.

The word *center* has symbolic value in naming women as the "center" of inquiry and action. According to the data compiled by the National Women's Studies Association Women's Centers Committee, of the approximately 500 campus women's program and service units in the US, almost 75% include the term *center* in their title. However, campus sites for work on women's and gender issues are not always called women's centers. While the term *women's center* is used throughout this chapter, the authors intend for this chapter to be applicable to and useful for all configurations.

The remainder of this chapter focuses on the most common types of women's center configurations – student services/resource centers and synthesis centers serving faculty and staff as well as students. It is important to note that the faculty and staff women who advocated for creation of women's and gender equity centers in the 1960s, 1970s, and 1980s are retiring and younger people are taking their place. The entrance of young, increasingly doctoral-level professionals into the field is reshaping women's center work.

Divisional placement and reporting line

The women's centers literature clearly documents that centers vary widely across institutional types, needs, and histories. According to Marine, the type of women's center an institution establishes is shaped by "the specific institutional context, the attendant political milieu, and the relative weight/importance of student, faculty and staff needs and concerns" (19).

Since a center's divisional placement helps determine its constituents, mission, and activities, it is important to be strategic about organizational location and reporting line when centers are being established or when organizational changes are being considered. Decisions about reporting line should take into account a center's mission and constituent base as well as how the reporting line will be perceived. If the women's center exists to serve students, a reporting line through student affairs makes sense. Conversely, if the center serves faculty and staff as well as students, reporting to an entity that has responsibility for all of these constituencies (e.g., academic affairs/provost or an institutional office of equity/diversity/inclusion) may be more effective. A center's organizational placement and reporting line within a division (e.g., health/wellness unit, student leadership unit, or diversity unit) can also impact the focus of a center's work.

Finally, given the hierarchical nature of colleges and universities, placement within the reporting line hierarchy is important. In general, the closer one is to senior decision makers, the better. Of the 124 campus women's centers featured in Clevenger's study, "respondents who were separated from the office of president by two or more hierarchical levels (particularly four or more levels) were more likely to express that their center was constrained by lack of institutional commitment" (5). This affects not only the staff's ability to advocate for change but also the public's perceptions of the center's effectiveness as a change agent. If constituents perceive that their women's center has little power to bring about institutional change, they may be less likely to bring campus-wide issues (e.g., harassment or gender bias in policies and practices) to the attention of the center. Center staff cannot act on issues of which they are unaware. Consequently, problematic policies and practices persist, and the center continues to be perceived as ineffective in influencing institutional change.

Space issues

Women's centers are more likely than offices of women's programs/services to be allocated gathering space that is separate from staff offices. Such space highlights the value of dedicated areas for group work and community building.

Some women's centers are located in stand-alone houses; others in suites within administrative, academic, or residential buildings. Each type of location has merits and disadvantages. A house often provides more space but may be an older building in need of repair. A house also typically seems more "homey," but may be perceived as a place where support is plentiful but education is not. Women's centers located within administrative, academic, or residential buildings are often cramped but more likely to be modernized as part of building renovations. They may also be perceived as less "homey" but more educational in function.

Some women's centers are located in basements, on the fringes of campuses, or in spaces that are hard to find or difficult to access. And some women's centers are co-located with other identity centers, either as distinct areas within a shared space or blended into a common area. Co-location with distinct spatial areas can promote collaborative working relationships among staff and students while retaining space for various constituency groups. Co-location that blurs the identity-based nature of identity centers' work can increase confusion about who the space serves, who is welcome, and how various constituencies "claim" space.

Where a center is located and how much and what kind of space it has been allocated say a lot about how the center and its constituents are valued by the institution. It is important for decision makers to think strategically when considering space issues, particularly when women's centers are being established or when location changes are being considered.

Trends for campus women's centers

Incorporating inclusivity, intersectionality, and social justice principles

Feminism, foundational to women's center work, has become more inclusive, intersectional, and social justice oriented as women's centers draw on the interdisciplinary work of their academic colleagues. Further, students, increasingly exposed to these concepts in classes, bring an interest in and familiarity with these principles as tools of analysis.

Jennrich and Kowalski-Braun note that "As the landscape of higher education has continued to evolve and change, identity-based centers have been encouraged to be less singularly focused and be able to articulate the tensions among and amongst the groups which they serve" (202). They suggest that:

> The movement towards an intersectional approach requires a shift of centers' self-concept. Instead of assuming an identity group has a universal experience of oppression based on race, gender, sexuality, and/or the combinations of these identities, intersectionality imposes no limits to the numbers or types of intersected identity experiences.
>
> (204)

Marine highlights "the importance of inviting others into the work remaining to be done around gender equity," including men and transgender individuals, and the need for authentic engagement with "other forms of anti-oppression work" (26). There is now more focus within women's centers on explicitly anti-racist/anti-oppression work and the broader category of gender and its fluidity. Such work requires a supportive, collaborative relationship with multicultural and LGBTQ+ centers and diversity affairs offices. Additionally, women's centers' social justice efforts can benefit from partnerships with programs that focus on community service and service learning. Jennrich and Kowalski-Braun call on centers "to move beyond identity work to engagement in authentic social justice work, undergirded by intersectionality theory" (200).

The incorporation of principles of inclusivity, intersectionality, and social justice require alliances with other campus units. Working to build alliances and coalitions across campus and in the local community is often the way women's centers accomplish their work. Alliances allow for resource sharing, helping the typically small staffs of women's centers accomplish more with less. Allies also provide support in difficult times.

Women's centers often find value in building partnerships with academic programs (e.g., women's/gender/sexuality studies programs), institutional commissions on women, and campus LGBTQ+ and diversity/inclusion offices. When such units work together as equals to address an issue, the results are often exponentially larger than if the women's center addressed an issue alone. Building alliances helps not just across campus but also in the community (Marine 24), which enhances women's centers' relevance to the institutional mission. Doing women's center work within the framework of the university mission, as noted by Marine, "is not something that a women's center can afford to be casual about" (24). Alliances make particular sense for women's centers in an era of shrinking resources and significant institutional change.

Merging identity centers

Another trend is the merging of distinct identity centers into a combined center. This trend may reflect the move toward inclusivity, intersectionality, and social justice principles. It may also reflect fiscal challenges within an institution and the increasing corporatization of higher education in general.

There are advantages to a combined center in terms of ability of team members to support each other in what is often emotionally difficult work, ease of collaborating, and ability to do truly intersectional work. There are also potential drawbacks to combining identity centers. Merging can result in a department that is so diffuse that the original identity centers lose their distinctness and their attractiveness as safe spaces for minoritized groups. In addition, merging can mean that identity center directors lose access to decision makers and communication channels. On the other hand, Jennrich and Kowalski-Braun remind us that "intersectionality (does) not function to eradicate difference, but to illuminate the potential interactions among identity groups and to uncover how we are oppressed by the same systems" (205).

(Re)naming women's centers

When women's centers are brought together with other identity centers, renaming may be part of the merger process. If the women's center retains its distinctiveness as an entity within the combined unit or shared space, it may be able to keep its name or choose a new name that recognizes the collaborative work that the merger encourages. If the merger is complete and the women's center loses its distinct identity, the combined department should adopt a name that clearly recognizes gender or equity as a key identity category or goal.

Even when a merger is not planned, women's centers may wish to consider a name change. In discussing the trend in the late 1990s of women's studies programs being renamed gender studies, Yee states,

> The act of naming has a particular strategic value for women's studies and other historically marginalized areas such as ethnic studies. It encourages participation by certain populations of students and attention in scholarship and teaching to the very systems of inequality that make the issue of access

a critical one in the lives of students and scholars who have stood at the margins of university life and scholarly discourse.

(48)

Reasons for name changes are varied and range from reflecting new alliances and organizational structures to reconsiderations of services and constituents. Regardless of the motivation, the act of naming has significant implications for women's centers as well as women's studies programs so must be carefully considered.

Some name choices are motivated by practical as much as ideological issues. A women's center whose primary mission involves support of feminist scholarship, sponsorship of educational programming, and distribution of information and referrals may choose to call itself a women's resource center, emphasizing its role as a campus resource. Similarly, some campus organizations use the term *office* rather than *center* in their names. In many cases, such offices arose from recommendations of commissions or task forces charged with studying the climate and conditions of women on campus. The term *office* reflects their administrative roots and original emphasis on addressing inequities in work and learning environments for women faculty, staff, and students.

In recent years, the rise of gender studies as an academic discipline and methodological approach has influenced many women's studies programs to rename themselves gender studies or at least include gender, and in some cases also sexuality, in their designations. Sometimes, the changes are motivated by the desire to be more inclusive of the field's expanding scholarship and to create space for "those interested in researching and teaching gender who do not identify as feminists and/or reject feminist theory and methodology as a framework" (Yee 49). Given the historically close connections between women's studies programs and campus women's centers, it is not surprising that many women's centers are considering similar name changes.

While renaming women's centers to women's and gender centers, women's and gender equity centers, or simply gender centers is sometimes prompted by challenges (e.g., poor event attendance, lack of funding or administrative support, negative attitudes toward feminism), name changes may also be a response to evolving definitions of feminism and emergent forms of feminist activism.

Others assert that use of the term women reproduces an essentialist framework that privileges a monolithic category of women while the term gender (as in gender studies and gender equity center) is more inclusive of all individuals and their diverse experiences of gender, and of gender-based inequality and discrimination. For some, the term gender in program names also more explicitly draws attention to masculinities and services for men and gender diverse individuals, which women's centers have provided to varying degrees.

(Goettsch et al. 489)

Data compiled by the National Women's Studies Association Women's Centers Committee in 2016 indicate that about 350 of the approximately 500 campus centers listed are still called women's centers, women's resource centers, or a variation that includes the words *women* and *center*. The remaining 150 use other names, though most retain the word *women*. Approximately 30 centers include gender and/or sexuality in their name.

In 2015, the Council for the Advancement of Standards in Higher Education (CAS) issued its 9th edition of the CAS *Professional Standards for Higher Education*, which includes revisions to the Women Student Programs and Services functional area. CAS changed the name of the functional area to Women's and Gender Programs and Services in recognition of the expanded and intersectional work women's centers are undertaking and the fact that these programs often serve a broader constituency.

There are benefits to replacing the word *women* with *gender* in a center's name, but there are also potential challenges. In her consideration of women's studies programs being renamed gender studies, Yee points out that, although both disciplines "focus on gender and identity as socially constructed categories and both foster interdisciplinary scholarship," gender studies "may or may not focus on women" and may reject the use of feminist theories and methodologies (49). Yee concludes, "The 'women' in women's studies, then, functions in part as a symbol of the continued existence of unequal power and access to resources in society" (61).

Like women's studies, women's centers serve as a centralized location for information and programming on a multitude of women's issues and feminist concerns. In their sincere desire to mark their inclusiveness with the use of the word *gender*, women's centers could conceivably be requested to provide programming and resources that actually exclude women's experiences and/or feminist perspectives. Particularly in the context of resource limitations, a transition to the word *gender* may increase the possibility that resources are shifted away from efforts to address the status of women. It is worth noting that "There is a similarly complex dialogue regarding the naming, configuration, and delivery of programs and services at the intersection of gender and sexuality" (Goettsch et al. 489).

In summary, there are many important factors to consider when naming or renaming a women's (or other identity) center. Centers may want to fully consider the implications and strategic value of naming and not be swayed by political or budgetary pressures. There is real strategic value in a name. Chosen carefully, a center's name indicates its affiliations, mission, services, and constituents and reflects its continued efforts to remain relevant, inclusive, and vital to the communities it serves.

Final thoughts

This chapter offers considerations for positioning campus women's and gender equity centers to continue their important work in the years to come. If women's centers are to thrive in these challenging times, they must understand their institution's current and projected context and politics as well as the current and future needs and concerns of their constituents (broadly defined). To secure their place in the changing landscape of higher education, women's and gender equity centers must articulate their continued value to the institution through a clear mission, objectives, and activities that align with current and future institutional priorities. They need to forge strategic alliances across campus and in the community and advocate for organizational configurations, locations, and names that best reflect their evolving work and contributions to their institution's mission. If they are successful, women's and gender equity centers can look forward to a bright future within higher education.

Note

1 This chapter updates and expands on a 2012 issue brief written as a collaborative project of The Southwestern Ohio Council for Higher Education's Women's Centers Committee.

Works cited

Campbell, Kathryn P. "Making Excellence Inclusive: Higher Education's LGBTQ Contexts." *Diversity and Democracy: Civic Learning for Shared Futures*, vol. 15, no. 1, 2012, p. 1.

Clevenger, Bonnie M. "Women's Centers on Campus: A Profile." *Initiatives*, vol. 51, no. 2/3, 1988, pp. 3–9.

Goettsch, Jane, et al. "Women's and Gender Programs and Services." *CAS Professional Standards for Higher Education.* 9th ed., Council for the Advancement of Standards in Higher Education, 2015, pp. 489–501.

Jennrich, Jessica, and Marlene Kowalski-Braun. "My Head Is Spinning: Doing Authentic Intersectional Work in Identity Centers." *Journal of Progressive Policy & Practice*, vol. 2, no. 3, 2014, pp. 199–212.

Kasper, Barbara. "Campus-based Women's Centers: Administration, Structure, and Resources." *NASPA Journal*, vol. 41, no. 3, Spring 2004, pp. 487–99.

Marine, Susan. "Reflections from 'Professional Feminists' in Higher Education: Women's and Gender Centers at the Start of the Twenty-First Century." *Empowering Women in Higher Education and Student Affairs: Theory, Research, Narratives, and Practice from Feminist Perspectives*, edited by Penny A. Pasque and Shelley Errington Nicholson, Stylus Publishing, 2011, pp. 15–31.

Sax, Linda J. *The Gender Gap in College: Maximizing the Developmental Potential of Women and Men.* Jossey-Bass, 2008.

Touchton, Judy, et al. *A Measure of Equity: Women's Progress in Higher Education.* Association of American Colleges and Universities, 2008.

Vlasnik, Amber L. "Historical Constructs of Gender and Work: Informing Access and Equity in U.S. Higher Education." *Women as Leaders in Education: Succeeding Despite Inequity, Discrimination, and Other Challenges. Volume 1: Women's Leadership in Higher Education*, edited by J.L. Martin, Praeger, 2011, pp. 23–44.

Yee, Shirley J. "The 'Women' in Women's Studies." *Differences*, vol. 9, no. 3, 1997, pp. 46–64.

2 Beyond parties and PNMs

An integrated model for women's and gender centers and sororities

Rita M. Jones

Mutually beneficial and sustainable relationships between women's and gender centers (WGC) and Panhellenic sororities have the potential to create significant positive changes toward gender equity on college campuses. For ten years, I have directed the Center for Gender Equity at Lehigh University, consistently engaging sorority women in gender equity work. I continue this work for many reasons, not the least of which is that nearly 40% of our undergraduate women are part of Panhellenic sororities, and those women, therefore, represent the largest organized group of women on our campus ("Fraternity & Sorority"). Though organized, they are certainly not homogenous, and moving past stereotypes creates opportunities for members to participate in gender equity on campuses. Put another way, groups tend to play to the options provided them, and WGCs can provide an additional identity – one of intersectionality and inclusion – for sorority women. WGCs cannot complete their missions of creating gender equity on campus without working with all identities and groups on campus, and the Panhellenic Council and affiliated sororities exist as spaces that provide support to women. WGCs can help sororities move beyond simple support and into feminist praxis-based change.

Creating a successful relationship requires long-term commitment, mutually beneficial goals, and understanding that the two organizations will not always agree on topics and methods. From different frames, both bell hooks and Chandra Talpade Mohanty talk about how organizations can build solidarity, and in the case of the CGE's approach, a feminist one. hooks asserts that "sisterhood goes beyond positive recognition of the experiences of women and even shared sympathy for common suffering. Feminist Sisterhood is rooted in shared commitment to struggle against patriarchal injustice, no matter the form that injustice takes" (15). While Mohanty prefers "solidarity" to "sisterhood," she similarly understands that women can come together "in terms of mutuality, accountability, and the recognition of common interests as the basis for relationships among diverse communities . . . of people who have chosen to work and fight together" (7). These forms of feminist-informed alliances create part of the foundation of the CGE's approach to working with others. Rather than assume all women want to participate in our work, we find ways to educate everyone and learn who shares our goals, which means we often look in unlikely places. We are also here to support all students in creating equity on campus, which means a large amount of our time is spent reaching those who do not understand or see sexism as a problem. Although sororities may not define themselves as feminist or as overtly participating in the struggle against patriarchal oppression, they do share our goal of empowering women. I once surveyed the council members, asking what they would like people outside of sororities to say about them, and 74% said "exemplary women who empower other women." Many of these women come from environments where they were told they could be and do anything, that girls were as good as boys. Once they leave the confines of those spaces, they encounter more challenging beliefs and structures of sexism, and many turn to sororities that emphasize women's leadership and power as sources of comfort and support. Some even join the sorority seeking a space of feminist-informed empowerment. As Jessica Bennett pointed out in a provocative *New York Times* article in 2016, several Ivy League women in sororities identified as feminists, who actively critiqued rape culture and sought to empower themselves and their sisters. And even the National Panhellenic Conference, the national governing body of Panhellenic sororities, includes a section entitled, "Sorority Women Are Feminists, Too" in their marketing materials.

WGCs are well-equipped to work with *all* of these women, since WGCs already simultaneously mobilize self-identified feminist activists and educate the rest of campus about sexism. Sorority members already have common bonds with one another, enabling them to have tough conversations with each other, and WGCs can make sure one of those conversations is about the oppression that the sorority, as an institution, participates in and may perpetuate. Neglecting these women ignores a potentially powerful group of women who are eager to explore their identities. As Faith Kurtyka notes, "Because sororities are and have long been and continue to be an important site of identity formation for many college women . . . it is time to re-consider the kinds of experiences college women have as a part of sororities" (41). Sororities continue to recruit strong numbers of women (Bennett; Heyboer), even as their actions as institutionalized organizations often re-inscribe heterosexist, racist, and classist notions of femininity and womanhood. Rolnik, Engeln-Maddox, and Miller accurately note that "[a] lthough sororities provide college women with a number of opportunities for personal growth and enrichment . . . they have been criticized for their potential to engender an excessive focus on appearance in their members" (7). The emphasis on appearance often stems from sororities that root their sense of success or desirability in attention from men in fraternities. As Lisa Handler argues, fraternities often determine the "top" sororities by the appearance and party-willingness of the members. She accurately points to a tension in sororities: helping women navigate pressures of being a woman even as they reaffirm the primacy of heterosexual connections (238). WGC staff can call attention to this tension, and create space for women to name issues, recognize why those issues exist, and co-create alternatives.

Operating within spaces of tension to build equity, or what I refer to as Inclusive Relationship Building, is a core concept of our CGE, and fundamentally connected to feminist praxis, where we learn about issues, seek models and methods of making change, try out those changes through action, and take the learnings back to the learning; we create a sustained, researched form of activism. These relationships require continual work, on the part of all involved in the relationship, and require time. My concept of Inclusive Relationships rests upon Audre Lorde's concepts of imagining difference as creative potential. She explains that we have all been socialized to respond to difference in one of four ways: ignore, neutralize, copy, or destroy. Rather than follow these four practices, Lorde urges people to acknowledge difference and allow the community or person who is deemed "different" to define themselves and their own difference. She explains,

> If you allow your difference, whatever it might be, to be defined for you by imposed externals, then it will be defined to your detriment, always. . . . But as you acknowledge your difference and examine how you wish to use it and for what – the creative power of difference explored – then you can focus it toward a future which we must each commit ourselves to in some particular way if it is to come to pass at all.
>
> (Lorde 203–4)

Lorde urges people to self-author their lives and identities, and, in turn, demands that we listen for self-authorship of others. Instead of looking at women in sororities and categorizing their difference as anti-feminist, shallow (only focused on looking attractive and recruiting other attractive PNMs (potential new members)), and raging party-goers, I realized the many sorority women I met were different from my CGE student staff members but not always in these stereotyped ways. If I was really going to practice Lorde's ideas of finding the creative potential in difference, I needed to learn what differences – if any – the sorority women saw between themselves and the CGE.

The only way to learn more about the community and the individuals who composed it was to listen. Informed through Inclusive Relationships, I put my assumptions on the back burner, recognized but was not handcuffed to history, and listened to sorority chapters and individuals. Having never been a member of a sorority, I started this work with my own personal experiences with sororities – which were pretty positive as an undergraduate – and theoretical and researched knowledge of sororities – which was disconcerting. Because our culturally based sorority chapters are small, both in number and size, our connection to them has been stronger than with the larger, Panhellenic chapters. I realized that because I knew less of the latter, I needed to learn. I listened as I had coffee with chapter presidents early on in my tenure at Lehigh. I listened when chapters came to ask for workshops. I listened to sorority representatives in our Sorority Liaison meetings. And then a council member met with me to talk about forging a stronger connection between our spaces and invited me to attend their council meetings regularly. Because I took with me all my feminist theoretical teachings – don't be the great white rescuer, you don't know the circumstances of other women's

lives, let women define themselves – I was welcomed into the community's discussions. I listened a lot in the first few weeks, making notes when I didn't understand something and doing research outside the meetings to learn the answers.
I realized how much of their lives are dominated by recruitment-related issues. In
many ways, their emphasis comes from their nationals, the National Panhellenic
Conference, and on-campus oversight, all of whom have ideas about "successful"
recruitment of PNMs. I learned the women quickly switch from academic and
career-bound success to a social life that often included their participation in
their own trafficking (Mears). I started offering some observations here and there,
and, suddenly, I had a spot on the agenda; they implemented a form of Inclusive
Relationships by wanting to listen to me and the differences I brought into the
space. I have been participating for four years now, using both a rant/rave/reflect
about what I am seeing and also a semester-based curriculum. I provide content
and skills to help them understand how sexism may be influencing some of their
decisions and how their internalized biases often get in the way of creating the
inclusive community they often say they want.

Working with the council, however, is not the only – or, sometimes, the best –
way to create change, and WGC staff should implement strategies that engage
sorority women on multiple levels. Our collaborative approach comes in three
main levels: individual (sorority members on the CGE staff or workshops and
consultations I do with specific chapters), group outreach (Sorority Liaison program), and institutional (CGE director as an active member in weekly Panhellenic Council meetings and partnering with the Office of Fraternity and Sorority
Affairs). Typically, the women who choose to become staff members are already
active in feminist work and women's issues. Sorority women who are on our staff
reaffirm what Susan Marine and Ruth Lewis find among college student feminists. They point out that feminist community, such as one in a WGC, is particularly important for young feminists where "[a]spects of themselves that fit
awkwardly on campus and may be silenced are, in these communities, validated
and acknowledged" (9). For many sorority women, expressing feminist principles
within the sorority may not be acceptable. As Alan D. DeSantis finds in his study
of gender within fraternity and sorority life, these spaces "proudly and fiercely
reproduce *many* of the most traditional and harmful ideas about gender" and create a "subculture where deviant performances – performances that are potentially liberating because of their ability to expand brothers' and sisters' gendered
repertoire – are prohibited" (27). When women within sororities want to push
against strict gender roles, particularly the roles they find oppressive and hierarchical, they find places to create community with like-minded people. Sometimes that happens to be their sorority, and sometimes it is the CGE. When we
support these women's feminist pursuits, we help them live holistic lives and
create a path for them to take the ideas back to their chapters.

Beyond a one-to-one approach, our outreach to sororities also occurs on a
peer-led group level in a program we call Sorority Liaisons. As her parting "gift"
to Lehigh, sororities, and the CGE, one of our former staff members, who was

also a sorority member, created the program, a monthly meeting of one or two representatives of the nine Panhellenic sororities on campus and led by a CGE student staff member, who is also a sorority member. This group functions as a way to reach out to sorority members who know they want more feminist or women's issues-based conversations as well as members who do not. Importantly, these representatives often are what I would term "general members"; they do not aspire to major leadership roles and joined their sororities for the social benefits. The Panhellenic Council members on our campus include the executive board, chapter presidents, and chapter delegates. The first two sought out the leadership roles and strive for unity and seek to make the Panhellenic community inclusive. General members, alternatively, are still processing what it means to be in a sorority. In the conversations, the women learn how different chapters tackle challenges or respond to university policies and also learn some of the issues of being a sorority woman are not just limited to their own chapter. They find they are part of a larger community and can seek advice and support from women outside their chapters. Reaching general members within sororities is particularly important since they are least likely to be reached by or reach out to other spaces, departments, and individuals on campus. Many women in sorority leadership positions have some kind of interaction with professional staff members on their campus or alumnae advisors from Nationals. Lehigh has been willing and able to support professional staff engagement with sororities and fraternities, and our Panhellenic Council members receive time-intensive support from OFSA assistant directors who challenge and support the leaders to create inclusive communities within their chapters. Because campuses often partner chapters with professional staff – or even faculty or staff who volunteer time to advise – who have expertise in Greek life, these advisors do not often have expertise in gender equity, opening an important connection point for WGCs. WGCs can work with these groups of women who seek out other women to share successes and struggles, but do not always have the language or tools not only to understand why they may have negative experiences outside the chapter (through institutionalized sexism) but also the tools to respond.

Part of my role in connecting with Panhellenic Council, at the institutional level, is to help them understand and talk about their own internalized sexism, not as some kind of failure on their part but as an opportunity to understand their – and most every American woman's – socialized experience. hooks sees examining one's own internalized sexism as a crucial starting point for feminist work, and in examining the sexism, people also start to come to terms with other internalized oppressions as well as internalized biases based upon race, class, sexual identity, and ability (14). In some ways, my participation in Panhellenic Council meetings is a form of large-scale consciousness raising, and two different examples on our campus highlight the positive potential in this collaboration. As with many campuses, parties between fraternities and sororities on our campus are frequent, particularly in the spring. Our campus has around twice as many Interfraternity Council fraternities as Panhellenic sororities: thus while the fraternities may only have three parties per week, the sororities often have five, because of the imbalance in numbers. One year, the women decided enough was enough and rather than party every Tuesday through Saturday, they canceled all Wednesday parties in order to give their members a much-needed and much-desired night off. After announcing this decision to fraternities, fraternity representatives appeared at the Panhellenic Council meeting to state their frustration with this policy, explaining how it hurt their members and disproportionately affected the lower tier fraternities. The women had worked long and hard to create this policy, earning unanimous support from all chapters. However, once the men complained, the women reverted to apologizing to them, questioning their own policy, and asking the men what they could do to make things better. When my place on the agenda came, I told them to stop apologizing to the patriarchy and explained how I saw power operating within the discussion.

My comment marked a turning point in the relationship between the communities. I named for them a behavior they knew was familiar and contextualized that behavior as a form of women's internalized sexist response to patriarchy. I gave them a "what" and a "why" and opened space for them to stop feeling guilty and start taking steps to strengthen their community of women. Because this instance occurred at the council level, I could point out how sexism is a systemic not just an individual behavior one or two people need to fix within themselves. In another instance, I led them in an activity about likeability and leadership, where nearly 90% of the council members indicated the need to be liked overwhelmed their ability to be leaders. Following that conversation, one of the members wrote an op-ed in the university student newspaper, drawing attention to the activity and urging all women on campus to rethink what it means to lead and feel confident in their own decision-making process as leaders. A WGC staff member certainly is not the only person who can facilitate these kinds of dialogues or awareness-raisings, but they are particularly *well-suited* as the content and skill experts to do so.

Successful collaboration requires a clear working relationship with the campus department that advises or supports the Panhellenic community, in our case, the OFSA. Because the latter may be in student affairs while the WGC may not be, WGC staff can reach out to their colleagues to let them know about ideas and request feedback before beginning a large-scale relationship. Like WGCs, sorority and fraternity affairs departments may or may not exist on campuses, have various staffing structures, and may have high volumes of staff turnover. WGC staff can sometimes be the one, consistent university administrator to whom the council can turn. In my case, I was invited by the students to participate in council meetings, and on campuses where the relationship between sorority affairs and WGCs may be nonexistent or strained, letting students make the connection can be helpful. Depending upon strategic plans and long-term goals of each department, both departments might reinforce the other's approach. The WGC staff can also learn more about any requirements the sorority affairs office is placing upon sororities. Understanding the policies and mandated meetings from the OFSA, the chapter's nationals, and the sorority's own goals and plans can create a huge shift in how the WGC connects with sororities. In addition to the time requirements of sorority life, these women are also successful academically and often involved in several other clubs and extracurriculars. They have very little "free" time to add new programs or meetings to their calendars; consequently, our approach is based upon infusing inclusion and gender equity into the preexisting sorority format.

Working with the institutional, group, and individual levels helps WGCs call out institutionalized forms of sexism and move beyond feminism as a kind of lifestyle that only individuals, rather than communities, participate in. Rosalind Gill speaks of how "postfeminism" operates within contemporary culture and astutely points out that, within this postfeminist moment, "the impression given of feminism . . . sits comfortably with neoliberal capitalism" (623), with the rhetorical emphasis on "choice" and "empowerment" that "repeatedly turn attention away from social transformation to one of individual entrepreneurialism" (624). Definitely, I have met with many women in Panhellenic sororities who stay focused on self-esteem as an individual pursuit and have little interest in trying to alter the whole system for the betterment of all. At the same time, creating space for the women to see that the individual can go further to transform the organization remains a useful goal. Indeed, Becker, Ciao, and Smith accurately point out that sororities are "an ideal target for creating positive change on college campuses, particularly when they can be convinced to operate as one larger unit (i.e., the campus sororities) versus multiple smaller organizations (i.e., sorority A, sorority B, etc.)" (19). Helping sororities see and move into joint work to be "exemplary women who empower other women" goes beyond the individual sorority women who can see the value of this project. These women are students, they leave approximately every four years, and they have other things going on in their lives. WGC staff, however, often stay beyond that four-year period and can help one council carry on the work from one year to the next. Rather than simply mobilizing more people to work toward gender equity on campuses, WGC staff can also work to mobilize students who have social capital on campuses to assist in large-scale climate change. And this mobilization may not be all that time consuming or challenging when WGCs create spaces for sorority women to gather and talk more about feminism and women and gender issues. WGCs have often been that kind of "home base" for feminist-identified students on college campuses, and creating a space for students who may be struggling with what Roxane Gay defines as "essential feminism . . . the notion that there are right and wrong ways to be a feminist and that there are consequences for doing feminism wrong" (304) is something WGCs are uniquely poised to provide. Women within sororities do desire to learn more about feminist spaces, seek out empowered communities of women, and want to work with others to create gender equity on campus. Without the support of women's and gender centers, their desires will simply remain in a space of hope rather than move into a space of action.

Works cited

Becker, Carolyn Black, et al. "Moving from Efficacy to Effectiveness in Eating Disorders Prevention: The Sorority Body Image Program." *Cognitive and Behavioral Practice*, vol. 15, 2008, pp. 18–27. Print.

Bennett, Jessica. "When a Feminist Pledges a Sorority." *The New York Times*, 9 Apr. 2016. Online.

DeSantis, Alan D. *Inside Greek U: Fraternities, Sororities, and the Pursuit of Pleasure, Power, and Prestige*. Lexington, KY: U Kentucky P, 2007.

"Fraternity & Sorority Statistics and Trend Analysis." *Fraternity and Sorority Affairs*, Fraternity and Sorority Affairs at Lehigh U, 2017, Studentaffairs.lehigh.edu. Accessed 13 Oct. 2017.

Gay, Roxane. "Bad Feminist: Take One." *Bad Feminist: Essays*, New York: Harper Perennial, 2014, pp. 303–13. Print.

Gill, Rosalind. "Post-Postfeminism? Ne Feminist Visibilities in Postfeminist Times." *Feminist Media Studies*, vol. 16, no. 4, 2016, pp. 610–30.

Handler, Lisa. "In the Fraternal Sisterhood: Sororities as Gender Strategy." *Gender and Society*, vol. 9, no. 2, 1995, pp. 236–55.

Heyboer, Kelly. "Fraternity and Sorority Numbers Climbing Amid Concerns about Bad Publicity." *NJ.com*, 29 Mar. 2015. Online.

hooks, bell. *Feminism Is for Everybody: Passionate Politics*. Cambridge, MA: South End P, 2000. Print.

Kurtyka, Faith. "We're Crafting Ourselves Now: Crafting as Feminist Rhetoric in a Social Sorority." *Peitho Journal*, vol. 18, no. 2, 2016, pp. 25–44. Print.

Lorde, Audre. "Difference and Survival: An Address at Hunter College." *I Am Your Sister: Collected and Unpublished Writings of Audre Lorde*, edited by Rudolph P. Byrd, Johnnetta Betsch Cole, and Beverly Guy-Sheftall, New York: Oxford UP, 2009.

Marine, Susan, and Ruth Lewis. "Mutuality without Alliance: The Roles of Community in Becoming a College Student Feminist." *Gender and Education*, 2017, pp. 1–17. Print.

Mears, Ashley. "Who Runs the Girls?" *nytimes.com*, 20 Sept. 2014. Online.

Mohanty, Chandra Talpade. *Feminism without Borders: Decolonizing Theory, Practicing Solidarity*. Durham, NC: Duke UP, 2003. Print.

Rolnik, Ashley Marie, et al. "'Here's Looking at You': Self-objectification, Body Image Disturbance, and Sorority Rush." *Sex Roles*, vol. 63, 2010, pp. 6–17. Print.

"Sorority Women Are Feminists Too." *National Panhellenic Conference 2015–2016 Annual Report*, Npcwomen.org. Online.

3 Exploring the relationships between campus women's centers and LGBTQ+ centers and initiatives

Jane Goettsch, Marci McCaulay, and Hannah Thompson

This chapter is intended to provide a framework that campuses can use to explore the connections between the work of women's centers and LGBTQ+ centers and initiatives. It poses questions and provides suggestions for things for campuses to consider in approaching this work. For the purposes of this chapter, the term "women's and LGBTQ+ centers" is used as a shorthand to refer to the many different types of women's centers and LGBTQ+ centers and initiatives that exist at colleges and universities in the United States. Addressing all of the different types of programs and initiatives, and the variation in the institutional environments in which they exist, is beyond the scope of this chapter. We recognize that this may affect the applicability of some of the examples to individual campus situations.

Factors that shape the relationship between women's and LGBTQ+ centers

There are a number of factors that shape the relationship between women's and LGBTQ+ centers, including philosophical, structural, and institutional. The degree to which these factors are present will vary depending on the structures and histories of these centers.

Philosophical factors

At the core of the work of women's and LGBTQ+ centers are the values, visions, and missions that guide their work. One of the values that these centers share is a commitment to social justice work. Their work typically includes educational and advocacy efforts directed at identifying and addressing oppression and discrimination and their causes. Many centers share a commitment to empowerment in the work that they do. These centers sometimes differ in the extent to which feminism and feminist principles frame their work and play a role in establishing policies and priorities. In addition to having an impact on the focus of their work, feminist principles frequently guide the ways that women's centers operate and inform the leadership models that are used (Marine 21). While a commitment to gender justice is certainly a part of social justice work, not all social justice work places a focus on feminist principles in the ways that women's center work does.

The evolution and expansion of our thinking about gender and gender identity has had a significant impact on gender work on campuses (Marine et al. 50). Historically, women's centers' work related to sexual orientation focused primarily on women's heterosexual, lesbian, and bisexual identities (Firestein 233). With changes in our understanding of gender, there has been a growing focus on programs and services that are inclusive of trans and queer identities. This has contributed to changes in how women's and LGBTQ+ centers address the relationships among gender identity, gender expression, and sexuality.

The educational, outreach, and advocacy efforts of women's and LGBTQ+ centers often reflect the value of inclusivity. How inclusivity is interpreted and how it is represented in the missions and work of these centers can vary. The extent to which centers take an intersectional approach to their work can have significant implications for their relationships and their work on campus. Recognizing the multiple and intersecting aspects of individuals' identities is an important step. Understanding and exploring the interlocking systems of oppressions that are associated with these identities is a more complex process.

Structural factors

Structural factors such as divisional placement and status, reporting lines, and resource allocation shape the relationship between women's and LGBTQ+ centers. Each institution is, of course, unique, and the structural factors identified in this section will play out differently on each campus.

Divisional placement within an institution can impact the relationship between women's centers and LGBTQ+ centers. Generally, when centers are located within the same division or department, relationships are easier to create and maintain.

Women's center and LGBTQ+ center staff work within hierarchical institutions. Hierarchy shapes opportunities and support for relationship building. Staff with equal status in an institution (for example, through similar job titles and reporting lines) are more likely to be brought together to connect their work. Likewise, when the two centers occupy an equal organizational status, they are more likely to have a productive relationship.

Organizational status is also reflected through resource allocation. Resources include budget, staffing, space, and campus location. Women's and LGBTQ+ centers that are allocated similar space in equally desirable locations on campus are perceived to be of equal status, which may facilitate collaboration. Likewise, centers that have similar budgets and numbers and levels of staff can offer programming and organize staff responsibilities in comparable ways, facilitating collaboration. In fact, an organizational emphasis on collaboration can alter and perhaps align duties of staff within identity centers.

Some women's and LGBTQ+ centers are less organizationally discrete. They may be housed in one department and share staff and financial resources. This structure can promote a close relationship between the two centers, particularly when the centers are located close to each other. Some centers are colocated in a space, making it easier to build relationships. Staff can meet and retreat regularly together and discuss opportunities for complementary mission statements as well as collaborative programming that makes efficient use of often limited resources and reduces the likelihood of overlapping programs.

Institutional factors

Similar to philosophical and structural factors, institutional factors play a large role in how women's and LGBTQ+ centers are related and function within the higher education system. Institutional factors such as existing academic programs, student organizations, and other departments doing identity-based work (i.e., offices concerning diversity, equity, and inclusion efforts) shape how women's and LGBTQ+ centers have historically been linked and how they continue to interplay. Academic programs such as queer studies historically grew out of women's and ethnic and race-related studies that were (and still are) exploring social constructs, gender and sexuality, and systems of oppression. In addition, women's studies programs have been at the forefront of gender equity work, which often paved the way for gender and sexuality programs and/or served as a preexisting program to absorb such programs. Although queer studies is still a relatively young, emerging field, it has been gaining momentum and prestige over the last two decades in part by joining established academic programs, such as women's studies. The intrinsic and historic link between gender and sexuality programs and women's studies programs can also be seen within how women's and LGBTQ+ centers have similarly functioned. For instance, some LGBTQ+ centers have developed from women's centers or been placed within the center's existing structure due to overlapping work and/or as a preexisting center to absorb or expand offerings.

In addition to academia's influence on the work of women's and LGBTQ+ centers, student organizations have played a role in shaping the relationship between the two. Student organizations are student-driven, student-led organizations that function within the university context as a representation of various student populations, as well as their unique needs. Due to still so few dedicated LGBTQ+ centers with full-time staff within colleges and universities, the work to serve this population often relies on student organizations and student activism. The natural link between who is already doing gender equity and identity work is reinforced in the absence of institutionalized support for LGBTQ+ initiatives. This relationship can frequently be seen in the way of faculty and staff advisors for student organizations, meeting locations for student groups, funding sources, etc., due to the ideological similarities of women's centers and LGBTQ+ equity work.

Furthermore, a connection between departments working towards equity and inclusion for marginalized groups is an institutional factor that impacts the work of women's and LGBTQ+ centers. Similar to the intrinsic link between the aforementioned groups, offices working on diversity (or multicultural), equity, and inclusion issues have played a part in promoting women's and LGBTQ+ work due to their identity-based focus and similarities working with minoritized and marginalized populations. If women's and LGBTQ+ centers are not in the same department as these offices, they are often in the same reporting structures and/or are called together in the form of diversity task forces and committees. These relationships ideally allow for synergy and collaborative efforts and the potential to participate in truly intersectional work. However, the structural factors previously explored are a representation of the institutional factors in play at the upper administration level as it relates to institutional priorities and funding.

Challenges and opportunities related to women's centers' work with LGBTQ+ centers

Building on the factors that were identified in the previous section, we turn now to some of the concepts and practices that are central to the work of women's centers. We explore how these concepts and practices represent both challenges and opportunities in women's centers' work with LGBTQ+ centers.

Role of feminism

Many of the first women's centers developed out of feminist activism on their campuses. While not always included explicitly in the mission statements of current women's centers, feminist principles and ideals frequently inform their work. This is reflected in a conscious focus on gender dynamics in not only the content but also the process of women's center work. This can include utilizing different models of leadership and challenging hierarchical structures. One potential challenge women's centers may face in working with LGBTQ+ centers is a lack of a shared understanding of and commitment to feminist principles in terms of establishing priorities and determining decision-making processes. While these two groups share a commitment to social justice work, they may not share a prioritization of gender justice work. While both groups are committed to identifying and challenging discrimination against non-normative identities and gender-based oppression, these points of connections may be less evident when addressing topics like patriarchal oppression and male privilege.

The challenges identified also represent opportunities. Women's center work with LGBTQ+ centers offers the opportunities for engaging in conversations with others about their understandings of feminism and feminist principles. As Marine suggests, "We needn't insist on a false comfort level with the word *feminism* that is often belied by its complicated and exclusionary history" (29). Just as critiques of feminism by women of color helped raise awareness about the limitations of the ways that feminism has been practiced in the United States, expanding conversations about feminism to other groups with marginalized identities can inform and shape the continued evolution of the meanings and understandings of "feminisms."

Women's centers' work with LGBTQ+ centers provides an opportunity to identify and work on common goals and visions while also raising awareness about issues and concerns that may initially be less visible to the other, including recognizing the impact of systems of heteronormativity on individuals and institutions. This can contribute to an expanded recognition of common goals associated with advocating for inclusion, equality, and safety for all individuals.

Understanding of gender

While women's center work has traditionally focused on gender discrimination associated with being a woman, an expanded and evolving understanding of gender and gender identity has brought new opportunities for collaborations with LGBTQ+ centers. This includes developing educational initiatives that recognize gender diversity and affirm all gender identities, working on gender inclusive campus policies, and addressing discrimination based on gender identity and gender expression. As women's centers' work related to gender has expanded, questions about their role in addressing issues related to men and masculinities have also been raised. This represents an additional point of intersection with LGBTQ+ centers. Marine et al. point out that in "(s)triving for gender-inclusivity, some centers may unintentionally reinforce a gender binary system" (54).

With the expansion in understandings of the meanings and experiences of gender, women's centers have increasingly found themselves asking and being asked about not only their missions and the focus of their work but also their names. Centers previously identified as "women's centers" are increasingly exploring and adopting name changes (see Chapter 1, pp. 13–14). Some possibilities that are considered are adding "gender" and/or eliminating "women" from their name. On some campuses, women's and LGBTQ+ centers have been combined to form a Women's, Gender, and Sexuality Center. Name changes have implications for not only the identity and focus of the work of these centers but also for how they are viewed by others on campus (Marine and Nicolazzo 270). Embracing a more inclusive approach to gender may contribute to a loss of distinct focus and identity for women's centers and can lead to questions about who the center is serving.

One of the challenges in embracing an expanded understanding of gender and being more gender inclusive in women's center work is facing the possibility that staffs and programs may be spread too thinly. Without additional resources, women's centers may find themselves facing tough decisions related to establishing priorities for the allocation of time and staff. Another potential challenge is that at the institutional level, the connections and potential overlap between women's and LGBTQ+ centers may be seen as opportunities to combine programs in ways that result in a decrease in the resources allocated to these important issues.

Collaboration and coalition building

Structural factors shape interest in and opportunities for relationships and coalition building between women's centers and LGBTQ+ centers. The closer the centers are organizationally, the easier collaboration may be, particularly if collaboration is a priority within the organization. The farther apart the units are organizationally – for example, when one center is located within academic affairs and the other is in student affairs – the more challenging the relationship can be due to differing divisional priorities, cultures, policies, procedures, constituencies served, and budget models.

Likewise, when women's centers and LGBTQ+ centers are unequal in status within the institution – for example, one center has a longer history with the institution, a stronger reputation, and/or a privileged organizational location (e.g., academic affairs) – the relationship between the centers can be challenging.

Structural challenges to relationship building also include unequal resource allocation. Jennrich and Kowalski-Braun discuss the potentially divisive impact that resource inequities can have on identity centers (207). Even when structural factors would seem to promote a positive relationship between the two identity centers, factors such as the personal relationship between the two identity center heads may get in the way of a positive connection, as Brooks et al. note in discussing collaboration between women's centers and women's studies programs (379).

Assuming mutual interest in, and opportunities for, collaboration and coalition building, much of what passes for collaboration is actually less a true partnership and more a transaction, with partners simply exchanging resources and program ideas but retaining their own sets of goals and responsibilities. Programs may be related but not integrated.

True collaboration requires developing a shared vision and goals, with the partners identifying those goals as important to their own unit and being willing to be held equally accountable for achieving the goals. In this scenario, interaction involves consensus-building among equals where different perspectives are valued and the partners commit to their shared work over time. In developing a truly collaborative approach, it may make sense to begin with a focus on issues rather than programs. Once two units are aligned on an issue, collaborative programming is likely to develop.

In the most recent edition of the CAS Professional Standards for Higher Education, the contributors to the Women's and Gender Programs and Services (WGPS) functional area contextual statement argue that

> Coalition work, which is both integral to WGPS and a method for addressing limited resources, strategically engages partners in WGPS work to dismantle intersecting oppression, deepen the quality and impact of their work, and advance shared priorities and projects that serve their constituents and institutions.
>
> (Goettsch et al. 491)

Intersectionality and identity groups

When exploring the relationship between women's and LGBTQ+ centers, it is imperative to take a closer look into how intersectionality plays a role and presents both opportunities and challenges. Intersectionality has become somewhat of a buzzword within higher education, and the complicated nature and differing (mis)understandings of the theoretical framework is often a challenge within itself. However, Museus and Griffin suggest

> since Crenshaw's illumination of the utility of intersectionality perspectives, scholars have argued that there is a unique experience at the intersection of individuals' identities, and efforts to isolate the influence of any one social identity fails to capture how membership in multiple identity groups can affect how people are perceived, are treated, and experience college and university environments.
>
> (7–8)

If this is the framework within which intersectionality is understood, it is clearly essential to approach women's and LGBTQ+ center work (and other work involving marginalized groups) through an intersectional lens to fully engage and serve these unique populations.

Understanding and addressing interlocking systems of oppression is the main opportunity in incorporating intersectionality into the work. Jennrich and Kowalski-Braun ascertain that "oppression based on gender, race, and sexuality are all intrinsically linked" (202). Centers working with marginalized populations on campuses have historically been in place to address these oppressions and barriers. Therefore, it is crucial for practitioners to look at these intersecting identities and oppressions in order to best understand and serve their constituents regardless of the complicated nature. Jennrich and Kowalski-Braun further state "using a non-intersectional application of social justice has the potential to create spaces where one can engage in efforts to effect change outside but still retain unspoken bias and prejudice within" (203). In other words, to not use an intersectional framework can reinforce and perpetuate the exact thing (bias and prejudice) that women's and LGBTQ+ centers try to diminish. In doing intersectional work, women's and LGBTQ+ centers have the opportunity to confront systems of oppression.

One challenge that centers face is the fear of sharing too much work to the degree that the distinct differences among the groups may be blurred or negated. However, Jennrich and Kowalski-Braun suggest that "intersectionality did not function to eradicate difference, but to illuminate the potential interactions among identity groups and to uncover how we are oppressed by the same systems" (205). Another potential challenge is the concern that already limited resources may be stretched even thinner by conflating two identity-based centers without expanding resources such as funding and staffing. To address this concern, the structural and institutional factors previously explored must be taken into consideration and administration must be willing to prioritize and fund the important work being done by women's and LGBTQ+ centers.

Considerations and suggestions for future directions

The Council for the Improvement of Standards in Higher Education has long included women's programs and services among its functional areas. In 2015 the council updated its contextual statement and professional standards for this area; one of the changes is to the name of the functional area – from Women's Student Programs and Services to Women's and Gender Programs and Services – in recognition of the increasingly intersectional work women's centers are doing to address gender issues as well as the broader constituencies many centers serve (Goettsch et al. 489).

As understandings of gender continue to evolve and women's and LGBTQ+ centers are exploring possibilities for their shared work, Holgerson, et al. invite staff of women's and LGBTQ+ centers to consider their goals related to gender equity and institutional transformation. They suggest this may include deciding whether gender free, gender specific, gender neutral, or gender inclusive is the goal.

In doing our work, it is critical that we develop strategic plans that are based on what is best for the students (and others) we serve, and that are consistent with the institutional priorities where we work. These plans can serve as a framework to help guide and review our work. Just as concepts of gender are expanding and have become more fluid, it may be helpful to adopt an open and fluid approach to our work. That includes listening to the individuals whom we are trying to reach and continuing to review our initiatives and priorities to ensure they are meeting the needs of the students we work with.

Women's and LGBTQ+ centers working together on college campuses provides an opportunity for synergy that may not exist in either separate or combined programs. Having the ability to recognize overlapping goals and objectives can contribute to more inclusive work on the part of both. This will be reflected in their individual and collective initiatives and programs and will benefit the whole campus. As we approach these collaborations, it is important to go beyond engaging in the same work with different people at the table.

While this work may at times be complicated, it may not be necessary to try to resolve these complexities. Rather, it is important to hold space for the tensions and dialogues. While in our various campus roles, there may be a push to solve these perceived conflicts, campus centers' roles may best be envisioned as not trying to "fix" these problems but rather acknowledging them and encouraging and supporting conversations about them. These conversations can inform both programmatic and institutional priorities and decisions.

One of the challenges this presents to those engaging in this work is being comfortable with the ambiguity and resisting the urge to find a solution or develop a formula for how to resolve the tensions. Jennrich and Kowalski-Braun invite us to examine the "invisible boundaries created during the formation of our centers" so that we come to "see our centers as spaces that are inextricably linked" (206). Engaging in this shared work raises the possibility of coalition building rooted in self-awareness and a commitment to common issues and shared values.

Works cited

Brooks, Kathryn H., et al. "Women's Centers and Women's Studies: The Case for Coexistence and Beyond." *University and College Women's Centers: A Journey Toward Equity*, edited by Sharon L. Davie, Greenwood P, 2002, pp. 371–89.

Firestein, Beth A. "Out of the Closet and into the Center: Women's Centers Serve Lesbians and Bisexual Women." *University and College Women's Centers: A Journey Toward Equity*, edited by Sharon L. Davie, Greenwood P, 2002, pp. 227–55.

Goettsch, Jane, et al. "Women's and Gender Programs and Services." *CAS Professional Standards for Higher Education*. 9th ed., Washington, DC: Council for the Advancement of Standards in Higher Education, 2015, pp. 489–501.

Holgerson, Kathleen, et al. "Tensions and Opportunities: On Being Gender Free, Gender Inclusive, and Women Centered." Opening Session, Women's Center Summit, 17 Nov. 2017, Baltimore, MD.

Jennrich, Jessica, and Marlene Kowalski-Braun. "My Head Is Spinning: Doing Authentic Intersectional Work in Identity Centers." *Journal of Progressive Policy and Practice*, vol. 2, no. 3, 2014, pp. 199–212, caarpweb.org/wp-content/uploads/2014/12/Jennrich-Kowalski-Braun-2014.pdf.

Marine, Susan B. "Reflections from 'Professional Feminists' in Higher Education: Women's and Gender Centers at the Start of the 21st Century." *Empowering Women in Higher Education and Student Affairs: Theory, Research, Narratives, and Practice from Feminist Perspectives*, edited by Penny A. Pasque and Shelley Errington Nicholson, Stylus Publishing, 2011, pp. 15–31.

Marine, Susan B., et al. "Gender-inclusive Practices in Campus Women's and Gender Centers: Benefits, Challenges, and Future Prospects." *NASPA Journal about Women in Higher Education*, vol. 10, no. 1, 2017, pp. 45–63, doi:10.1080/19407882.2017.1280054.

Marine, Susan B., and Nicolazzo, Z "Names That Matter: Exploring the Tensions of Campus LGBTQ Centers and Trans* Inclusion." *Journal of Diversity in Higher Education*, vol. 7, no. 4, 2014, pp. 265–81, doi:10.1037/a0037990.

Museus, Samuel D., and Kimberly A. Griffin. "Mapping the Margins in Higher Education: On the Promise of Intersectionality Frameworks in Research and Discourse." *New Directions for Institutional Research*, vol. 2011, no. 151, Fall 2011, pp. 5–13, EBSCOhost, doi:10.1002/ir.395.

4 Solidarity is for all

Women's centers serving women of color

Lysa Salsbury and Rebekah MillerMacPhee

Introduction

Campus-based women's centers, founded as sites of institutional resistance, inclusion, and transformation, are uniquely situated to promote greater understanding of the complex interrelationship dynamics of gender, race, ethnicity, class, ability, sexuality, and positionality (Butler para. 4; Marine 15; Zaytoun Byrne 49). These centers, particularly those at predominantly white institutions (PWIs) must continually challenge the historical racism of the women's movement (Hill Collins 7; hooks 3; Lorde 126; Moraga and Anzaldúa 62) to establish a praxis that not only effectively serves the needs and interests of students of color, but also demands that issues of inequality that converge at the intersection of gender, race, class, and other identities be intrinsically interwoven into all programming and support systems offered by these centers.

Women students of color often feel that the "brand" of feminism promoted at campus-based women's centers does not adequately reflect their opinions, beliefs, or value systems, or fully represent the intersecting identities many women of color experience (DiLapi and Gay 204; Marine 21). In order to create and promote an environment of safety and inclusion for students from different backgrounds and identities, we must prioritize the development of programming and support services that are radically inclusive of students of color. Feminist professionals in higher education must encourage and facilitate open dialogue around white privilege and intersectionality; willingly negotiate the tensions between white feminists and feminists of color; and continually question whether we are replicating and perpetuating oppressive systems of power within our institutions, or instead, consciously positioning our work to actively resist and dismantle institutionalized sexism and racism in the academy.

Background

Like many women's and gender equity centers around the country (Kasper 185; Marine 15; Wies 255; Willinger 47), the Women's Center at the University of Idaho (UIWC) was founded in 1972 at the height of the women's movement, in direct response to the troubling attrition rate for women students at the university, and mounting concern over campus climate for women employees. A core group of women faculty and staff took the bold and courageous step of filing a complaint with the Idaho Commission on Human Rights, demanding from the university a number of restitution measures to improve conditions for gender-based educational equity at the institution. In May 1974, the University of Idaho Conciliation Agreement established permanent funding for a director of the UIWC, as well as the hiring of an affirmative action officer and development of an affirmative action plan; job analysis and retroactive equity pay; a mandate for equal starting salaries; a high school relations program to implement good faith efforts to recruit and retain women students; and a female physician for the student health center, among other equality-seeking measures (University of Idaho Conciliation Agreement).

At the time of its founding, the UIWC was serving a campus that was overwhelmingly white. The demographics of the university mirrored those of the state at the time; according to US census data, in 1970, Idaho was a racially and ethnically homogenous state, with 98.1% of residents identifying as white (US Census Bureau). Consequently, when the UIWC opened, support services and programming for women were geared almost exclusively towards the needs of the majority white women on campus. Today, the university serves an increasingly diverse constituency, with growing numbers of Latinx, African American, Native American, Asian and Pacific American, and other multiethnic and multiracial communities. Current institutional data shows that 73.8% of constituents identify as white (University of Idaho Institutional Effectiveness & Accreditation). For an equality-seeking organization such as the UIWC, which offers intentional opportunities for reflection, discussion, and action around identity, privilege, and oppression, there is urgency to more fully understanding and addressing the needs and interests of all campus women to ensure equality of access and opportunity in learning.

Institutional context

In the past decade, the University of Idaho has experienced several racially motivated bias incidents and hate crimes, from vandalism in a Native Hawaiian staff member's office, and racist interruptions of cultural events during Farmworker Awareness Week to acts of microaggression and intimidation against students of color. Ideological conflicts between LGBTQA+ and Latinx students in the Student Diversity Center, coupled with students' general lack of awareness around the social and economic issues facing ethnic minorities in their own state, have combined to create an environment where students of color often have not felt welcome or safe on campus. In 2012, following the appointment of a chief diversity officer and drafting of a new strategic plan for the institution, the university began to show commitment to the concept of Inclusive Excellence (Williams et al.), a retention strategy that the UIWC had already begun to explore via greater collaborative efforts with the Office of Multicultural Affairs and the College Assistance Migrant Program (CAMP) to provide holistic and intersectional support for students from diverse backgrounds.

In 2004, in collaboration with the UIWC, the statewide organization Women of Color Alliance (WOCA) launched a student chapter on the University of Idaho's Moscow campus. WOCA's mission was "to unite women of color in a common bond to achieve social, economic and political justice in Idaho." The new student group was composed of a number of Latina students affiliated with the UIWC, but the chapter disbanded after two years, largely because aspirations for the group's political and social activism on the part of the professional staff at the UIWC and the statewide organization's leadership did not align with the goals of its student members (Harvey). Following the loss of WOCA, the UIWC began intensifying efforts to recruit staff of color, and in 2005, hired a Latina woman as the center's program advisor, as well as several work-study students of color. UIWC staff became advisors for a number of multicultural student organizations, and the university's first ever Step and Stroll[1] competition was developed as a cultural outreach program through the UIWC.

In 2012, the Division of Diversity & Human Rights (DHR) was created. It was composed of the Women's Center, the LGBTQA Office, the Office of Multicultural Affairs, the Native American Student Center, and the College Assistance Migrant Program (CAMP) office, establishing comprehensive administrative support for students from diverse backgrounds and identities. Following additional restructuring, the division was renamed the Equity & Diversity Unit (EDU) in 2016. This strategic alliance, created with the goal of ensuring holistic student-centered advocacy and support, has been instrumental in challenging systemic institutionalized racism and creating programming for questioning and dismantling the identity hierarchies that privilege the white-majority student body. Programs, support services, and cultural competence trainings offered by the EDU are designed to maximize inclusion of intersectional perspectives and provide cross-cultural education for target student populations. In addition, the development of division-wide learning outcomes ensures program integrity across the unit, and a commitment to comprehensive knowledge acquisition and sharing.

Surveying target audiences

In spring 2014, the UIWC embarked on a pilot data collection project to identify the needs of faculty, staff, and students of color, and ways in which the UIWC could begin to better address them. Two focus groups were conducted by volunteer facilitators from outside the UIWC. Participants were recruited via email, social media, and referral by other EDU offices; students of color were interviewed in one group, and faculty and staff of color in another. Data from the focus groups yielded critical information about the barriers that people of color on campus perceived as hindering their access to the UIWC. Five main themes emerged from the focus group conversations:

1   Feminism – participants felt that the Women's Center's "brand" of feminism was not relevant to women of color, and many did not comfortably identify with the label.
2   Visibility – the remote location of the Women's Center was seen as problematic for constituents seeking safe and accessible spaces on campus. Participants also felt the UIWC staff was not often present at multicultural events on campus.
3   Representation – the décor at the UIWC was not appealing to many women of color, and several expressed feeling uncomfortable that most of the professional and student staff were white.
4   Programming – participants cited a lack of intersectionality as the reason why they weren't attending UIWC programs, and urged us to consider topics of greater interest to students of color.
5   Student interaction – focus group data revealed that multicultural student organizations desired more interaction with students and groups affiliated with the UIWC, and were eager to explore feminism through a multicultural lens.

Following review of the focus group data, the UIWC staff developed a comprehensive strategic plan to address each of the concerns expressed, to create a more inclusive and relevant experience for students of color at the center. Some measures were implemented immediately, while others took consistent and sustained efforts over time.

Multiculturalizing our space and outreach efforts

Obtaining feedback from populations underserved by the UIWC reinforced the ongoing need for women's centers to continually evaluate all outreach and programming efforts, and make continual adjustments and changes in order to better serve the needs of constituents (Davie 11; Marine 19). With this in mind, each of the five main themes that emerged from the focus group data was addressed with intention and purpose.

Representation

A critical first step in addressing the perception that the UIWC is primarily for white women was to update the Center's décor. Framed prints of Wonder Woman and other white feminist icons were removed and replaced with art and photography depicting notable women of color. Kasper's research cites having more staff of color as a successful outreach strategy for engaging women of color at women's centers (193): efforts to recruit students of color for work-study positions at the UIWC became more intentional – a new diversity and inclusion programming assistant position was created, position descriptions were rewritten to appeal to a broader student demographic, and job opportunities at the UIWC for new incoming students were more widely disseminated in recruitment efforts by other identity offices. In an effort to diversify the professional staff, the UIWC hired a new office manager with an academic background in intersectional feminism and social justice activism, who identifies as queer, Latina, and first generation.

Visibility

To help students unfamiliar with the UIWC find their way to the space, informational posters were designed featuring quotes by feminists of color and photographs of multicultural students attending programs in the UIWC. These were printed in Spanish and English, and now display prominently in most student services offices and academic departments around campus. Student staff serve as "ambassadors" for the UIWC to actively engage classmates, roommates, student organization members, and other peers in conversation around UIWC services and programs, as well as to directly invite them to our space. The UIWC's promotional brochure in available in Spanish, and will be translated into Mandarin Chinese and Arabic, facilitating access to the UIWC for those whose first language is not English.

Feminism

Much of the literature discusses the reluctance of many students of color to identify with feminism (Marine 21). Increasing the UIWC's appeal to multicultural students in particular has been a focus of recent programming and outreach efforts. For several years now, UIWC student staff have worked together, in consultation with the Office of Multicultural Affairs, to install a traditional Day of the Dead *ofrenda* (altar) in the UIWC's lounge to honor the historical contributions of feminists of color. Other programming incorporating intersectional feminism developed by UIWC student staff includes: *Viva la Feminista*, a program on Chicana feminism; a presentation on sexual assault and migrant farm working women's rights for Farmworker Awareness Week; and a wall display entitled *Así Se Parece Una Feminista* ("This is What a Feminist Looks Like") installed in a central area of campus, featuring photographs of students of color holding signs explaining why they identify as feminist. Recruiting women of color to participate in UIWC internships has been instrumental in showcasing to a wider audience the voices and opinions on feminist issues of women students of color. Two years ago, three students from the College Assistance Migrant Program (CAMP) were cast in the UIWC's production of *The Vagina Monologues*, resulting in significant attendance by CAMP students, and subsequent engagement with UIWC programs throughout the year. UIWC "swag" (buttons and bookmarks created in-house) has undergone some redesign, featuring images of and quotes by feminists of color, in languages other than English, in order to pique the interest of students of color.

Programming

Seeking opportunities to ground the UIWC's educational programming throughout the year in anti-racist work has been critical to creating broader appeal and safer spaces for students of color. New programs have included guests such as Carolyn Finney, an African American writer, performer, and cultural geographer; Denise Sow, co-founder of the Senegalese social movement *Y'En a Marre* ("We've Had Enough"); Dalia Basiouny, an Egyptian playwright and activist; and Luz Rivera Martinez, organizer with the Mexico Solidarity Network. Existing programs, such as the popular sexuality education forum *Got Sex?* have been reconceived with a culturally responsive framework for specific audiences (see Chapter 11 in this book). In addition, the UIWC has worked intentionally with other offices that serve diverse and multicultural students to develop joint programming, such as partnering with the International Programs Office to celebrate International Women's Day, and collaborations with the Office of Multicultural Affairs to showcase the multifaceted lives and experiences of women during National Hispanic Heritage Month, Black History Month, and Asian Pacific American Heritage Month. UIWC staff have also increased their guest lectures on feminist issues in introductory classes for diversity scholars and in American Language & Culture Program (ALCP) classes.

Student interaction

Outreach to multicultural student organizations has increased significantly, resulting in new program collaborations; for example, two recent projects developed with multicultural fraternities: a healthy masculinities workshop with Omega Delta Phi, and creation of a short film featuring members of Sigma Lambda Beta reciting a Spanish-language version of Eve Ensler's "A Man's Prayer." UIWC staff has also facilitated a number of collaborative projects between social justice-oriented student organizations, such as a "Themes of Oppression" workshop presented for members of Lambda Theta Phi, a Latino fraternity, and the university's Gender & Sexuality Alliance. As DiLapi and Gay point out, the creation of such alliances is "critical for challenging systemic racism on campus" (217).

UIWC's professional staff has made greater effort to attend diversity-related events on campus, particularly those hosted by student organizations, and accept as many invitations as possible to speak at annual banquets, rallies, and brown bag programs organized by international and multicultural student organizations. Student staff are required to attend two diversity events per semester hosted by other offices or groups, and to write a short reflection paper about the experience. Free tickets to UIWC events are offered to diversity scholars, CAMP students, and students affiliated with the Native American Student Center and LGBTQA Office. Other outreach efforts include participating in the Friendship Family

Association, a non-residential cultural exchange program run by the International Program Office, and monthly women-only opportunities for informal socializing and exercise co-sponsored by the UIWC.

Negotiating the tension between white feminists and feminists of color

Efforts to create spaces where students of color feel welcome have also focused on interrupting incidents of racism and white supremacy, and helping to guide white students, staff, and faculty in their development as allies. In collaboration with other offices within the Equity & Diversity Unit, the UIWC's professional staff has developed campus-wide trainings and presentations on diversity and inclusion. All incoming students now receive an hour-long diversity and inclusion training as part of new student orientation; in addition, an online training for all university employees, including students, contains a section on cultural competence and antidiscrimination. UIWC student staff receive weekly presentations from other identity offices, and professional staff consistently emphasize the importance of creating a safe and nonjudgmental space to explore issues of race, ethnicity, and class as they intersect with gender. Prospective and current student staff are encouraged to increase their knowledge around the dynamics of white privilege and racism, and examine their complicity, however unintended, in perpetuating these oppressions at a social and institutional level. These lessons are often hard and painful for students, especially when family beliefs, traditions, and value systems are challenged. They are also particularly difficult for students who believe they have a good understanding of the multiple oppressions experienced by women of color, and whose allyship feels called into question when they unintentionally slip up. Identifying microaggressions that occur within the UIWC's space and in classroom settings, and helping students process and separate the impact of their actions from their intent, is an important role for UIWC staff. Acknowledging harm caused and gently redirecting responsible parties to own their actions and make efforts to honor and center the voices of students of color allows for education and healing. UIWC professional staff are trained victim advocates and serve as confidential resources, providing important emotional support for students of color to process the racist experiences they have encountered.

Ongoing challenges

Despite the best efforts of the UIWC and women's centers across the country to create safe and inclusive spaces for students of color, external and structural challenges often complicate the development of racially and ethnically inclusive spaces on campus. Institutional racism is frequently reflected in the allocation of university resources and the composition of the student body leadership. Like many institutions, the University of Idaho is home to a vibrant and predominantly white mainstream Greek system. Students of color are involved in fraternity and sorority life, but Panhellenic (PH) and Interfraternity Council (IFC) organizations, which represent the majority of Greek organizations, often have a predominantly white membership. Membership within these organizations matters, as their involvement and influence within universities' structure and systems is usually significant. PH and IFC members are consistently overrepresented in universities' student governments. In consequence, a small governing body of mostly white students often represents and makes decisions on behalf of all students on campus. At the University of Idaho, though students of color have run for office in student government, they seldom receive the number of votes needed to be elected president or vice president. In addition, PH and IFC organizations are usually highly engaged in the voting process, which results in their members being elected more often into top positions. A largely white student government generally affords white students greater access to universities' upper administration. Thus, the needs, considerations, and interests of students of color often go unheard. This is compounded by the fact that the upper administration at many universities is predominantly white and male. Greater racial, ethnic, and gender diversity among institutions' senior leadership is critical to fully address the broad scope and specific interests and needs of students of color.

Another challenge that many women's centers have faced in trying to create inclusive and welcoming spaces relates to the race and ethnicity of their professional staff. As Kunkel notes, racial and ethnic diversity must be at the forefront of women's centers' commitment to creating a welcoming space inclusive of all women (69). Two of the three professional staff members at the UIWC identify as white, and hold the more senior positions within the center, a staffing structure which is common in women's centers across the country (DiLapi and Gay 206; Grant 193; Marine 23). As women's center professionals engaging in social justice work challenge their colleagues and constituents to examine their biases and prejudices, we must also *do our own work* to examine and disrupt the systems and structures that privilege the leadership of white women. Women's centers fail in their mission to achieve gender equity on campus if they are not inclusive, representative, and supportive of all women.

Conclusion

Future efforts by women's centers to ensure the inclusion of women of color must be highly attuned to the impact of the current social and political climate on the psychological and physical safety and well-being of people of color across the nation. While the development of educational programming and student recruitment strategies by women's centers may be intentional in addressing lack of participation by women of color, there are still areas that require greater effort. The projected future ethnic and racial demographics of our nation indicate that the student population of institutions of higher education will likely only increase in diversity. Land-grant institutions in particular, whose commitment is to provide accessible education to the people of their state, and women's centers, as organizations committed to challenging and dismantling identity-based discrimination and inequalities, must continue to make forward progress in their efforts to ensure a hospitable and supportive climate for students of all identities. As impossible as it may feel to try to meet the needs of all constituents, reconceptualizing all women's center activities within an intersectional framework, in addition to offering programs and services specifically for women of color, may increase the sense of community and connection to women's centers that women students of color may feel is currently lacking.

Potential areas for action for women's centers seeking to further increase participation by women of color in their programs and services might include: rewriting their mission statement and core values to explicitly outline their commitment to serving students of all identities; inviting more women of color to participate on their advisory boards; increasing outreach to and collaboration with faculty and staff of color; and engaging more purposefully in both personal and campus-wide education that promotes the dismantling of practices and attitudes that alienate and marginalize students from diverse backgrounds.

Note

1 Stepping and strolling are dance traditions of historically black Greek organizations that date back to the early 1900s (Figueroa).

Works cited

Butler, Anthea. "Women of Color and Feminism: A History Lesson and Way Forward." *Rewire*, 28 July 2013, https://rewire.news/article/2013/07/28/women-of-color-and-feminism-a-history-lesson-and-way-forward/. Accessed 31 Jan. 2017.

Davie, Sharon L. *University and College Women's Centers: A Journey towards Equity*. Westport, CT: Greenwood P, 2002.

DiLapi, Elena M., and Gloria M. Gay. "Women's Centers Responding to Racism." *University and College Women's Centers: A Journey toward Equity*, Westport, CT: Greenwood P, 2002.

Figueroa, Laura. *MGC 101: A Guide to Multicultural Greek Organizations*. U Florida, Fall 2003, iml.jou.ufl.edu/projects/Fall03/Figueroa/index.htm. Accessed 26 Nov. 2017.

Gibson, Campbell, and Kay Jung. "Historical Census Statistics on Population Totals by Race, 1790 to 1990, and by Hispanic Origin, 1970 to 1990, for the United States, Regions, Divisions, and States." Working Paper Series No. 56, U.S. Census Bureau, Population Division, 2002, www.census.gov/population/www/documentation/twps0056/tab27.pdf. Accessed 26 Nov. 2017.

Grant, Jaime M. "Affirmative Action Reconsidered." *NWSA Journal*, vol. 10, no. 3, 1998, pp. 192–4.

Harvey, Jeannie. Personal interview, 7 Nov. 2017.

Hill Collins, Patricia. *Black Feminist Thought: Knowledge, Consciousness, and the Politics of Empowerment*. New York: Routledge, Chapman and Hall, 1990. Print.

hooks, bell. *Feminist Theory: From Margin to Center*. Boston, MA: South End P, 1984. Print.

Kasper, Barbara. "Campus-based Women's Centers: A Review of Problems and Practices." *AFFILIA*, vol. 19, no. 2, Summer 2004, pp. 185–98.

Kunkel, Charlotte A. "Starting a Women's Center: Key Issues." *University and College Women's Centers: A Journey toward Equity.* Westport, CT: Greenwood P, 2002.

Lorde, Audre. *Sister Outsider: Essays and Speeches.* Trumansburg, NY: Crossing P, 1984.

Marine, Susan. "Reflections from 'Professional Feminists' in Higher Education: Women's and Gender Centers at the Start of the Twenty-first Century." *Empowering Women in Higher Education and Student Affairs: Theory, Research, Narratives, and Practice from Feminist Perspectives,* edited by Penny A. Pasque and Shelley Errington Nicholson, Stylus Publishing, 2011, pp. 15–31.

Moraga, Cherrie, and Gloria Anzaldúa. *This Bridge Called My Back: Writings by Radical Women of Color.* 2nd ed. New York: Kitchen Table: Women of Color P, 1983.

University of Idaho Conciliation Agreement, May 1974. Women's Center Records, UG 59, Special Collections and Archives, U Idaho Library, Moscow, Idaho.

U Idaho Institutional Effectiveness & Accreditation. "University Population by Race/ Ethnicity." Fall 2016.

Wies, Jennifer R. "The Campus Women's Center as Classroom: A Model for Thinking and Action." *Empowering Women in Higher Education and Student Affairs: Theory, Research, Narratives, and Practice from Feminist Perspectives,* edited by Penny A. Pasque and Shelley Errington Nicholson, Stylus Publishing, 2011, pp. 255–269.

Williams, Damon A., et al. *Toward a Model of Inclusive Excellence and Change in Postsecondary Institutions.* Washington, DC: Association of American Colleges and Universities, 2005.

Willinger, Beth. "Women's Centers, Their Missions, and the Process of Change." *University and College Women's Centers: A Journey toward Equity,* Westport, CT: Greenwood P, 2002.

Yuval-Davis, Nira. "Intersectionality and Feminist Politics." *European Journal of Women's Studies,* 1350–5068, vol. 13, no. 3, 2006, pp. 193–209.

Zaytoun Byrne, Kelli. "The Roles of Campus-Based Women's Centers." *Feminist Teacher,* vol. 13, no. 1, 2000, pp. 48–60.

5 Late to the game

The politics of opening a women's center in 2015

Jessica Nare

San Diego State University (SDSU) is home to the oldest women's studies department in the nation, founded in 1970. Despite the long history of feminist scholarship and activism on this particular campus, the university only recently designated funding and space for an institutionally supported "Women's Resource Center" in 2015. The Women's Resource Center (WRC) at SDSU opened decades after most women's centers emerged on college campuses in the 1960s and 1970s. This chapter situates a new Women's Resource Center in relationship to the existing feminist frameworks that created women's studies departments and women's centers 50 years ago as well as to contemporary gender equity efforts.

History of feminist activism at San Diego State University

The history of the Department of Women's Studies is deeply connected to efforts to create a women's center on campus. SDSU has a rich history of bottom-up feminist activism, which resulted in the creation of the first Department of Women's Studies. The original proposal for the Department of Women's Studies in 1969 included both an academic program and a women's center (among other components). The center, however, was never supported by the university and it would take an additional 45 years of student and faculty-led activism for the university to designate funding to support the Women's Resource Center.

In 1969, a network of students from SDSU's Women's Liberation Group (WLG), in collaboration with faculty and community members, formed an ad hoc Committee for Women's Studies. The committee experienced success quickly with the introduction of five unofficial women's studies courses in the spring of 1970. The next step was to propose a full-fledged department. Modeling a proposal after the recently developed Chicano Studies Department, the WLG Committee originally proposed a new division on campus entitled, "The Center for Women's Studies and Services."

The committee recommended the following structure for this new center:

> The Center will be a large, flexible framework encompassing seven essential components. It is designed to provide a complete program of services to

the individual and to the community. All the students of San Diego State College[1] will be served by the Center. This is only natural since all of the students of San Diego State College are in constant, daily contact with women and need to be aware of their struggle. Women students will receive special benefits from the center since their needs are special. A woman *is* different. She has many doubts about herself, her identity, and her relationship in modern society. She needs a program that integrates her life and her education.

(Foulkes 79)

The proposed Center for Women's Studies and Services (CWSS) included seven core components: Women's Studies Program, Research Center, Publication Center, Recruitment and Tutorial Center, Community Center for Women, Child Care Center, and a Cultural Center. According to the proposal, "The Community Center for Women will be a storefront in the community to provide information about services such as birth control information, abortion counseling or referral, library facilities, and Women's Studies extension courses and programs." Further, the Cultural Center was envisioned as a space that "will provide the facilities for the encouragement of artistic expression of women's oppression and liberation. It will include displays and presentations of written works, art, film, music, dance, drama, and other forms of media" (Foulkes 80).

The committee hoped to gain support for their proposal and establish the Center for Women's Studies and Services in the fall of 1970. They soon learned that because of a large budget crisis in California, the proposal would only succeed if it focused exclusively on the Women's Studies Program. To fund the other components of CWSS, the committee would have to secure funds elsewhere. The proposal to create the first formal women's studies department in the United States was approved by the college's faculty senate in May of 1970, offering a total of 11 courses. Members of the Women's Liberation Group were able to initially secure funding from San Diego State College's auxiliary, the Research Foundation, to provide startup funds to create the Center of Women's Studies and Services on campus. The CWSS became quickly controversial for several reasons, one of which was that foundation funds were vested in oil, military technologies, and other conglomerates that were profit-oriented and pro-war. The Women's Liberation Group was staunchly anti-war and their financial ties to the foundation created significant conflicts to the members of the WLG. The CWSS was also controversial because its name overlapped with the Department of Women's Studies.

In 1972, the Dean of Students wrote in a memo to the Vice President of Academic Affairs,

The Women's Studies Program is an official academic department, approved by the college. The Center for Women's Studies and Services is not recognized by the college in any way except that it has support from the

Foundation for its work recruiting women prisoners and holding poetry read-
ings. In view of the confusion, I am requesting formally that the Center for
Women's Studies and Services be enjoined again using a title which includes
Women's Studies.

(Foulkes 118)

Without support from the college, the CWSS moved off campus in 1972,
renaming itself the "Center for Community Solutions," and it is still in operation
today as a nonprofit (unaffiliated from SDSU) that serves the city of San Diego
as a rape and domestic violence crisis center. On campus, feminist student groups
formed a coalition called the "Women's Center" to continue serving students.
Funded, in part, by the Associated Students (student government), the Wom-
en's Center had a small paid student staff, in addition to interns and volunteers.
Eventually, in the 1990s, the student-run women's center lost the physical space
provided by Associated Students and changed their name to the Womyn's Outreach Association (WOA) to highlight the lack of an institutionally supported
women's-centered space on campus.

Feminist student organizations continued to be highly active through the turn
of the century. In November of 2014, several organizations coordinated a march
across campus in protest of several high-profile sexual violence cases that took
place that fall. During the march, students walked down "fraternity row" where a
men's Greek organization taunted marchers with sex toys and dildos leftover from
a party in the fraternity sponsored by *Hustler* magazine. The encounter between
marchers and Greek men was highly covered in local news sources. Consequently,
the fraternity was banned from campus and the Interfraternity Council decided
to suspend all fraternity-related events for the remainder of the semester. As a
result of these incidents, "Concerned Students of SDSU Members" presented a
list of demands to administrators which included:

1   SDSU Police Department must stop victim-blaming messages and racial
    profiling
2   SDSU must take into account Women's Studies Chair's recommendations
    to open a Women's Resource Center and provide ongoing support, including
    funding and staffing to sexual violence programs already underway
3   SDSU must institute a gender/sexuality studies class as part of the General
    Education requirements

(Hernandez, "Students Present Demands")

By winter of 2014, public outcry, pressure from students, and tireless advocacy
from the chair of women's studies, Dr. Huma Ahmed-Ghosh, culminated in the
allocation of university funds to open a Women's Resource Center (WRC). The
WRC joined the Center for Intercultural Relations, the Pride Center in the suite
of identity-based spaces available on campus.

Like many women's centers, the WRC was developed and funded as a result of
feminist activism on campus. This space, however, is unique in that it was opened

several decades after most women's centers, providing the opportunity for reflection on the politics of who is explicitly included in women-centered spaces.

Emerging challenges and opportunities

Reflecting on the role of womanhood in women's centers

One emerging challenge in operating a women's center is negotiating the instability of the category woman. Established gender equity efforts in both women's studies and women's center's programs, "depended on a reading of women's bodies as the natural site of emancipation. In other words, the identity 'woman' was married to the female-sexed body, and the female-sexed body was the central subject of study within Women's Studies" (Boyd 103). As Nan Boyd explains, recent scholarship in queer theory encourages explorations of the incoherent body, unsettling the naturalization or reification of body-based notions of femininity and masculinity, which, as we know, are difficult to sustain in a truly intersectional and global analysis (105). What does it mean to have a women's center that serves women, but also works to destabilize the category of woman in order to be welcoming of folks who identify as trans or nonbinary?

There have been many debates on the merits and limitations of continuing to center the "women" in women's studies. This chapter doesn't seek to further that conversation. Rather, it is important to highlight the ways in which contemporary women's center work is different from the epistemology of women's studies. At SDSU, the Department of Women's Studies has intentionally maintained their name even as other departments nationally have shifted to call themselves Feminist Studies; Women's and Gender Studies; and Women, Gender, Sexuality Studies. As the first Women's Studies Department, they have chosen to continue to center women in both name and curriculum. To this department, naming is particularly important, given its history as the first department in the nation, its role in the founding of a new discipline, and the continued need to highlight the marginalization of women. Women's centers, however, have different responsibilities. Women's centers are immediately responsible for supporting and advocating on behalf of the students who are in front of us. Though the discipline of women's studies seeks to deconstruct both the discursive and material impacts of patriarchy, there is a different urgency to the material experience that exists in women's centers when counseling students in crisis whose identities complicate our singular understandings of womanhood. How do we create room for this in our spaces? For practitioners, the language and symbols used in our centers are more than discourse. Using inclusive rhetoric is paramount to our ability to connect with students who experience the most marginalization and hardship in higher education.

In order for women's centers to be relevant to students and inclusive to the folks who frequent our space, it is important for our space to support women, but also make room for a nuanced discussion of what womanhood means. In the WRC, we use several strategies to work towards these goals. Our working team expectations, written by students, ask that student staff and volunteers avoid essentialist ideas about womanhood and strive to be trans inclusive. In practice, this means asking for gender pronouns and providing critical feedback to student organizations asking for our support on campus. For example, students in the art department asked for the WRC's sponsorship on an event that would lead students to create mini vulva sculptures to send to congress in protest of recent restrictions on women's reproductive freedom. While this noble message had politics that aligned with our mission, we asked the student organization if there could be multiple sculpture options for students to choose from, in recognition that some bodies without vulvas also need access to reproductive freedom, autonomy, and justice. The WRC also strives to ensure that programs and events hosted by our space include content that welcomes a myriad of expressions of femininity. For example, we address various bodies and identities in queer sexualities workshops, pay special attention to the challenges that trans and nonbinary folks face when healing from sexual violence, and explore the role of colonization in the gendered identities and expressions available to us. Finally, language on our marketing materials and in presentations clarify that folks with any gender identity are welcome to participate programs, but our content centers on the experiences of women and those femme of center.

By women, the WRC likes Sara Ahmed's definition, "all who travel under the sign woman." For we believe that it is important to note,

> Part of the difficulty of the category of women is what follows residing in that category as well as what follows not residing in that category because of the body you acquire, the desires you have, the paths you follow or do not follow. There can be violence at stake in being recognizable as women; there can be violence at stake in not being recognizable as women.
>
> (Ahmed, "Living a Feminist Life" 15)

Working in a women's center means holding multiple truths. One such truth is that systems of oppression still exist (and are often a matter of life and death) and make identity-based analysis of lived experiences an important piece of the work we do. The second truth is that trans and nonbinary folks are more visible than ever before and students are increasingly challenging binary understandings of gender. The possibility of operating within these multiple truths is an emerging gender equity strategy in women's centers. We can center the experiences of women, while creating space to also be critical of these categories.

Beyond "white feminism"

While many women's centers were opened in the late 1960s and early 1970s in direct response to the women's movement (Wetzel 11), their "origins can be traced to continuing education for women. Re-entry programs provided an important mechanism for the development of women's centers." Consequently, early women's centers focused on supporting women through the single axis of gender, which subsequently led some spaces to struggle with engaging women of color and queer students. For example, even in 1994, the National Survey of Campus Women's Centers found that only 52% of responding women's centers provide direct programming and services for specific racial, ethnic, or religious groups. Like the women's movement, women's centers have, at times, centered on whiteness and failed to make spaces available and accessible to women of color. According to DiLapi and Gay,

> Feminism and the women's movement hold the promise of addressing the needs and concerns of all women. This promise, however, has not always translated into reality. Racism bars the access of many women to campus-based resources. This dynamic is reflected on white-majority campuses, where women's centers are too often utilized by, and perceived to be a space for, white women only.
>
> (204)

SDSU's Women's Resource Center opened within a very different context in 2016, when 54.5% of undergraduate students on campus identified as students of color. Located in the border city of San Diego, nearly 30% of students identified as Latinx. Historically women's centers operating within primarily white institutions in higher education struggled to center the experiences of women of color. Several unique factors at SDSU in 2016 created a different environment including: the demographics of San Diego State University, its geographic location, long history of activism on campus, and the presence of vibrant identity-based disciplines like Africana studies, Chicano studies, Native American studies, and women's studies. Because of this context, there is a population of students who are very engaged in social justice issues and have a highly developed intersectional feminist lens.

Many women's centers that opened in the 1960s and 1970s had "bottom-up" beginnings rooted in student protest aimed at transforming bureaucratic/patriarchal academic institutions (Willinger 49). Over 40 years later, the Women's Resource Center opened under similar circumstances. Because the space was funded and opened in response to student and faculty demands, many folks on campus were highly invested in the politics of the center from the beginning. Students, in particular, were eager to be involved in the Women's Resource Center. For example, nearly 100 students applied for five paid "feminist peer educator" roles the semester the WRC opened. These highly competitive positions were awarded to students who had experience organizing on campus, were knowledgeable about feminism, and who demonstrated that they could apply an intersectional feminist lens. Our inaugural student assistants were student leaders in organizations on campus including: M.e.Ch.A. (Movimiento Estudiantil Chicanx de Aztlán), A.Ch.A. (Association of Chicana Activists), and the Womyn's Outreach Association. These feminist peer educators laid the foundation for collaborations on campus, priority action areas, and advocated for programs that centered the experiences of women of color and were trans inclusive.

Further, students in the Women's Resource Center resisted mainstream "white feminism" that has become ubiquitous in pop music and the mainstream media in recent years. White celebrities like Taylor Swift, Lena Dunham, Amy Schumer, and Miley Cyrus have been publicly vocal about their support for feminism, while failing to acknowledge the role of race in structuring oppression among women; creating backlash and the critical phrase "white feminism." Many have written about the ways in which white feminism fails to create solidarity among women by solely centering the concerns of white women and is silent about issues related to institutional racism and cultural appropriation in these industries or bigger national issues like police brutality or violence against trans women. While online platforms provide easy access to corporate and commercial versions of feminism, social media sites, like tumblr and Instagram, and websites like everyday feminism, feministing, jezebel, etc., also connect young feminists to thoughtful, intersectional feminism that centers the experiences of queer women and women of color. Today, students who work in women's centers can learn from, and amplify, marginalized women's voices and stories through digital platforms in a way that was much less accessible to women's centers in earlier times.

Using a feminist lens that pays special attention to race and sexual orientation has been a challenge for some women's centers historically. The WRC, however, focused on programs that are facilitated by, and center the experiences of, women of color. In its first two years, students in the Women's Resource Center hosted the following programs:

- Ana Castillo: An Open Letter to Mr. Trump
- Barriers to Access: Placing Sexual Assault and Domestic Violence in the Black Community in a Socio-Historic Context
- Berenice Dimas: Connecting with Ancestral Strength to Heal from Violence
- Black Feminism(s)
- Black Women's Healing Circle (monthly)
- Brown Girls Web Series Screening and Panel Discussion
- Decolonizing Sex Education
- Intersectional Feminism 101
- Les(bi) Honest Discussion Group
- Mujer Mariposa Writing Workshop
- Mujer, Tierra y Poder: Decolonizing Knowledge and Healing through the Female Corporal Narrative
- Nalgona Positivity Pride: Decolonizing Eating Disorders
- No Mas Bebes film screening + Panel
- Queer Latina/Latinx discussion group
- Reproductive Justice 101
- Womyn of Color Cafe (quarterly)

Although student staff and visitors to the space are primarily women of color, some communities are better represented than others. The WRC has been very successful in engaging black and Latinx women, but needs to continue to collaborate and engage API (Asian Pacific Islander) and Muslim women on campus. Though the WRC has intentionally rejected a white feminist lens dispelling stereotypes about women's centers being spaces for white women, we continue to be challenged in reaching a wide array of students on campus.

As a white cisgender woman serving as the first professional staff member in the WRC, I have struggled to contend with the history of women's centers being spaces designed only for white women. Despite our successes in centering the experiences of women of color, the optics of having a white woman in the sole professional leadership role is difficult to overcome. One strategy I've used in an attempt to redress this challenge is to engage students as creators of change to drive the mission and programs of the space. Distributing as much power as possible horizontally in the WRC helps to ensure a diversity of programs, voices, and perspectives. I have also been intentional about designating funds within our operating budget to support women of color initiatives on campus. Collaboration is important, but capital and investment is an important way that white women's center professional staff members can stand in solidarity with students of color. Finally, being attentive, reflective, and vocal about white supremacy within the institution and greater society is important in building relationships with students. In addition to my role in the women's center, I also serve as an adjunct faculty member in the Department of Women's Studies. Students who have taken my academic courses are familiar with my lens on systemic oppression, which helps to support my credibility as an anti-racist feminist. These tactics, however, don't solve the underlying pervasive problem: a lack of women of color in leadership roles in higher education and in women's centers.

Role of sexual violence in women's center work

Though the mission of women's centers has evolved dramatically over the past several decades, sexual violence has long been an issue addressed by women's centers. In fact, feminist students on campus coordinated a campus-wide task force on rape during the 1970s and 1980s. Since the Department of Education issued the Dear Colleague Letter in 2011, women's centers have been asked to play a larger role in these efforts. The Women's Resource Center came into existence right when sexual violence was being discussed in an unprecedented way on a national scale. As discussed earlier, many women's centers were founded to address women's reentry, enrollment and retention in higher education. That focus is different today when more women graduate from college than men. While it is evident that increased graduation rates have not addressed the systemic inequities that women face in institutions of higher learning, the charge of women's centers has changed.

Increasingly, women's centers are seen as hubs for primary and secondary sexual violence prevention work. This work, while so important, and certainly tied to patriarchy, is vast and has the potential to divert time and resources from other important gender equity efforts that are often only provided by women's centers and women's studies departments. Great strides have been made to draw more attention and funding to the critical issue of sexual violence on college campuses. Yet, chronically understaffed women's centers do not always have the resources needed to adequately address sexual violence and other gender equity issues on campus. How will women's centers, particularly those who were founded recently to address sexual violence, balance these demands?

Conclusion

In the world of women's centers, so much has changed since the 1970s, and yet so much remains to be changed. For example, many challenges that women's centers have faced historically continue to exist for new women's centers. Institutions have not historically valued women-centered spaces. At SDSU, bottom-up activism was the catalyst to create the Department of Women's Studies, the Center for Women's Studies and Services, and finally, the Women's Resource Center. Yet, these spaces are charged with the enormous task of supporting marginalized students and advocating for institutional change with limited resources and professional staff. Typically, "Diversity and equality work is less valued by organizations. Then to become responsible for this work can mean to inhabit institutional spaces that are also less valued" (Ahmed, "On Being Included" 4). Women's centers continue to struggle to make institutional changes and to grow beyond tokenized spaces on campus.

Challenges abound in recognizing and legitimizing women's centers on campuses and yet the promise and hope present in these spaces is limitless. Learning from critiques of women's movements, women's centers have the potential to be spaces that are rich with diverse voices, active organizing, and resistance to systems of oppression. Different from women's centers that opened in the 1960s and 1970s, newly opened women's centers can center the experiences of queer women and women of color from their onset. They also have the ability to be on the vanguard of contemporary conversations about gender, which continue to evolve and become more nuanced. Like women's centers that have been in operation for the last 50 years, women's centers continue to be spaces where students can seek refuge, solidarity, and validation for the challenges they face on campus. For,

> To be part of a [feminist] movement requires we find places to gather, meeting places. A movement is also a shelter. . . . A movement needs to take place somewhere. A movement is not just or only a movement; there is something that needs to be kept still, given a place, if we are moved to transform what is.
>
> (Ahmed, "Living a Feminist Life" 3)

Women's centers can be shelter that provides vital support and resources to students who are resisting sexism, attacks on undocumented populations, transmisogyny, racism, homophobia, sexual violence, and other forms of institutional violence directed towards marginalized populations. They can be the home to our campus movements.

Note

1 In 1974, San Diego State College was renamed San Diego State University per California State Senate Bill 381.

Works cited

Ahmed, Sara. *On Being Included.* Duke UP, 2012.

Ahmed, Sara. *Living a Feminist Life.* Duke UP, 2017.

Boyd, Nan Alamilla. "What Does Queer Studies Offer Women's Studies? The Problem and Promise of Instability." *Women's Studies for the Future: Foundations, Interrogation, Politics,* edited by Elizabeth Lapovsky Kennedy and Agatha Beins, Rutgers, 2005, pp. 97–108.

DiLapi, Elena Maria, and Gloria M. Gay. "Women's Centers Responding to Racism." *University and College Women's Centers: A Journey toward Equity,* edited by Sharon L. Davie, Greenwood P, 2001, pp. 203–23.

Foulkes, Sara Beth. "Coalitions, Collaborations, and Conflicts: The History of Women's Studies at San Diego State University from 1969–1974." MA Thesis, San Diego State U, 2007.

Hernandez, David. "Students Present Demands to Prevent Sexual Assault." *Daily Aztec,* 9 Dec. 2014.

"National Survey of Campus Women's Centers. Appendix C." *University and College Women's Centers: A Journey toward Equity,* edited by Sharon L. Davie, Greenwood P, 2001, pp. 493–504.

Wetzel, Jodi. "Women's Centers: The Frameworks." *Initiatives,* vol. 51, no. 2/3, 1988, pp. 11–16.

Willinger, Beth. "Women's Centers, Their Missions, and the Process of Change." *University and College Women's Centers: A Journey toward Equity,* edited by Sharon L. Davie. Greenwood P, 2002, pp. 47–62.

6 Where do we enter? How do we stay?

The role of consciousness-raising in developing women's center professionals

Kathleen Holgerson and Juli Parker

For almost 50 years, women's centers (WC) have existed on college campuses. In that time, WC staff have sought and created opportunities to find one another in a feminist professional setting. This chapter explores how using consciousness-raising as a strategy and a tool for our professional development has shaped the evolution of those opportunities, the challenges within them, and the ways that WC staff support our profession and envision our role in higher education as feminist practitioners.

Seeking the company of women's center professionals

To start, we have to return to our roots at women's centers. As Davie notes, in her landmark anthology *University and College Women's Centers: A Journey Toward Equity*, "Most chapters have at their core an extended narrative about the center that the writer knows best, while some chapters also offer a national overview of the issue under discussion" (2). Our methodology will also offer a national overview, based on the feminist concept of consciousness-raising, using the narratives of two professionals who "grew up" in WCs to tell the parallel story of the development of WC work as a field, one that is situated at the nexus of feminist theory and practice. We juxtapose our collective stories about the experience of professional development to illuminate the narrative of building a field/profession.

Our stories reflect the "personal is political" slogan invoked early on by Gloria Steinem, The Combahee River Collective, and bell hooks, and which was echoed specifically in the WC context by Davie. Instead of focusing on the "diversity of campus women's centers and of the institutions that house them," we will focus on the spaces where WC professionals seek to find common ground and participate in the knowledge production that informs the work across the diversity of issues, organizational structures, and institutional contexts. As noted in the *2015 Contextual Statement for Women's and Gender Programs and Services (WGPS)*, one of the current issues for WCs is "Building the field of WGPS work by focusing on the professional development, preparation, and experiences of WGPS staff" (Marine; Vlasnik and DeButz). This chapter speaks to the implications of "credentialization" by examining the evolution of the two current primary pipelines for women's center staff – Women's, Gender, and Sexualities Studies (WGSS) and Higher Education and Student Affairs (HESA) programs. Diversity and inclusion/multicultural affairs scholars and/or practitioners, often coming from academic disciplines such as women's and/or ethnic studies or student affairs programs, are also entering the WC profession, particularly in light of the growing trend on campuses to house WCs in diversity- and equity-focused divisions. Given these multiple entry points, it is critical to examine how WC professionals develop the competencies needed to effectively carry out the multilayered missions of our centers and how professional development in the field has largely been modeled on consciousness-raising, as well as the resultant successes and challenges of this model.

The early history of WC professional organizing is detailed in Jodi Wetzel's 1988 article "Women's Center: The Frameworks." Twenty-nine years ago, there was no "national organizing agent" (11). At that time, the Women's Centers Caucus of the National Women's Studies Association (NWSA) conducted a survey that sought "both to develop a data base by region on women's centers and services in the United States and to establish professional standards for program administrators" (13). Simultaneously, regional and statewide coalitions of WC professionals were meeting to connect and support each other's work. In 1984, the Women's Center Caucus was officially represented "within NWSA's governance structure" (15) and has been meeting, in various iterations, annually ever since.

Our stories

Juli

In 1991, I was one of the first students hired at the newly established Women's Resource Center at the University of Maine. The director met with us to talk about what issues each of us might be interested in working on. Two of us chose reproductive rights, and the director set us up with an activist from the National Abortion Rights Action League (NARAL) Maine, who helped us start a campus chapter. We organized a bus trip to Washington, DC, for the March for Women's Lives and a silent boycott of our commencement keynote speaker, Senator George Mitchell, for refusing to sign the Freedom of Choice Act. All of this activism was encouraged and supported by our director. Inspired by this work, I applied to the master's program in women's studies and got a graduate assistantship at the University of Alabama, the first such program in the country. After graduating (and a brief stint at a conservative nonprofit), I was hired into the part-time WC director position at the University of Massachusetts–Dartmouth in 1995. I was a 24-year-old running a glorified student organization (although I didn't realize it at the time), yet it was the second oldest campus-based WC in the country, and I knew it had potential to be something bigger than it was.

Kathleen

In 1988, as a senior at the University of Connecticut (UConn), I volunteered as a peer educator for the Women's Center's Rape Education Program (REP). I was trained to provide workshops on acquaintance rape, dating violence, and pornography. I also assisted with marketing for the annual Sexual Assault Awareness Month activities. I graduated with a bachelor's degree in English, with some coursework in women's studies, as there was no women's studies major or minor at the time. I worked in community-based organizations after college, which included various staff positions at two domestic violence programs, as well as crisis intervention work at a municipal police department and providing women's services at a methadone maintenance clinic. In 1994, I was hired at UConn as the coordinator of the Violence Against Women Prevention Program (VAWPP), which was the newly named version of REP, for which I had volunteered as an undergraduate student.

Juli

I immediately sought out professional colleagues. Running a small WC is lonely work. Our institution had no other identity center at that point. I stumbled upon NAWC, the National Association of Women's Centers. This was a national professional organization of campus *and* community WCs. They worked under a feminist model of consensus. I found it fascinating and frustrating. I took on a leadership role as a regional representative. This is where I met Kathleen.

Kathleen

After two years, I became the associate director, and in 1999, was hired as the director of the center. The senior staff (Myra Hindus and Elizabeth Mejia, both of whom were contributors to Davie's book) were influential in my exposure to the network of other WC professionals through their participation in formal and informal associations.

Juli

I knew little about ACPA (American College Personnel Association) and NASPA (National Association of Student Personnel), as I had come directly out of an academic master's program. I began a lifelong education about the field of student affairs as that was (and still is) the division where my department was housed. I went to NWSA's annual conference in 1997 in St. Louis, as one of my colleagues in NAWC knew they had a women's center caucus that held a pre-conference every year. I knew this was the place I could meet more folks doing similar work. NAWC was too expansive in its mission, by including both community and campus WCs. The work being done by community WCs, who often served as rape crisis and domestic violence shelters, was much more focused than the broad mission of campus WCs who were working to eliminate sexism and promote a broader social justice mission to eliminate racism and explore gender.

Kathleen

I went to NWSA in the late 1990s and can recall being in rooms with 10 to 15 WC staff where the agenda was sharing stories of what was working and not working on our home campuses and building networks with folks who understood the often-misunderstood work of WCs. Many of the women who contributed to Davie's book were individuals I had the privilege to either work with at UConn or met through NWSA.

Juli

While I felt strongly that NWSA was a good professional place, for me, as I had gotten a master's in women's studies and felt I could speak the "language," I had colleagues with student affairs degrees who didn't always feel it was a good match for them professionally. I tried out ACPA and NASPA once. They didn't have a WC group, per se, but a women's group, which was basically folks who were identified as women administrators in student affairs. Neither of those organizations was explicitly feminist like NWSA.

Kathleen

Based on the recommendation of colleagues at NWSA, I also attended a NAWE (National Association for Women in Education) and NASPA regional conference, but NWSA and the women's center caucus/committee were the consistent professional development conferences I have attended since. For the first decade of my tenure at UConn, the WC was organizationally housed in academic affairs, along with the other cultural centers and the corresponding academic institutes. Since then the center has transitioned into and out of the Office of Multicultural and International Affairs, the Office of Diversity and Equity, and the Division of Student Affairs. We are currently housed in the Office for Diversity and Inclusion and report to the university's Chief Diversity Officer.

We both have held leadership positions in the NWSA Women's Center Committee, Kathleen with the Anti-White Supremacy/Anti-Racism and Title IX Task Forces, and Juli being an elected member to the NWSA Governing Council and chairing the Women's Center Committee.

These narratives serve as context for the use of consciousness-raising as a professional development tool, the trajectory of credentialing and developing competencies for WC work, and some of the intended and unintended outcomes of these two themes that lead to successes and challenges in the field.

Consciousness-raising

In 1989, consciousness-raising (CR) was defined by Catherine A. MacKinnon as "the process through which the contemporary radical feminist analysis of the situation of women has been shaped and shared" (143). According to Janet Freedman, in *Reclaiming the Feminist Vision: Consciousness-raising and Small Group Practice*, CR brought women together "not only to share experiences and offer support but also to analyze the ways in which personal conditions, roles and attitudes have been influenced by political and social structures" (1).

WC networks were built, no matter the overall association affiliation (i.e., NAWC, NAWE, NWSA), by sitting in small rooms and having conversations. Building off of Davie's use of "narratives both about how to build a center and how to respond to challenging issues that have an impact on institutions of higher education" (2), in those small group discussions we were also exploring how to build a field, i.e., the professionalization of gender equity work on university and college campuses, and how to develop and support WC professionals to respond to challenging issues in the field. We understood the goal of the field and our individual roles was to transform our institutions through dismantling the systems of oppression embedded in the academy. Without an explicit agreement, we were using CR as a strategy to build our individual and collective competencies to perform this institutional transformation work. CR as a professional development tool remained a consistent strategy, even as organizations folded and more WCs were established, particularly in the 2000s. hooks notes that:

> Revolutionary feminist consciousness-raising emphasized the importance of learning about patriarchy as a system of domination, how it became institutionalized and how it is perpetuated and maintained . . . Early on in contemporary feminist movement, consciousness-raising groups often became settings where women simply unleashed pent-up hostility and rage about being victimized, with little or no focus on strategies of intervention and transformation.
>
> (7)

Just as consciousness-raising in the 1960s and 1970s provided a space for women to speak their stories, find language for common experiences, and learn from each other about how their experiences differed, WC staff created these spaces of CR as a way to "unleash" our frustration that there were few, if any, colleagues back on our own campuses who truly understood the work we did.

This style of professional development does not come without its challenges. First, there is a tension between creating brave spaces for informal sharing and the need for traditional "academic" presentations, which is often required by our institutions to justify the financial support to attend conferences. Occasionally, staff expecting a more traditional academic conference are disconcerted by the focus on personal exploration work and are looking for more concrete skill-building, as these can be seen as mutually exclusive. "This method of creating time and space for authentic stages of learning is ideal, but can be difficult to accommodate" (Jennrich and Kowalski-Braun 207). Second, the voices and experiences of WC staff who are women of color and/or trans were often not centered in this form of professional development. While WCs maintain a commitment to intersectional and anti-racist feminist practice, a critical mass of women of color and/or trans professionals are often not present in these spaces as a result of not being hired as WC professionals, being hired into predominantly entry-level roles, opting out because of experiences of marginalization in these spaces, or some combination of the former. The WC staff who gathered under the auspices of the NWSA Women's Center Caucus/Committee (a group which changed every time we gathered and included seasoned and new professionals) believed that "the layering of identity, intersectionality, and social justice is not a linear process, but rather a necessary journey for those doing work in identity centers in higher education" (Jennrich and Kowalski-Braun 201). As a collective, we still have much work to do to ensure that all of our identities are fully represented, included, and engaged in this process.

We are dedicated to find spaces to gather and share, regionally and nationally. Our process and/or goal is to address the following:

1   Begin with our shared experiences to assess/ask *what is*;
2   Analyze *why* things are as they are;
3   Think about *what should* be, and plan a strategy;
4   Lastly, the *how* that can lead to change is the most effective process I have used (Freedman, "Friday").

This is a continual process. We can evolve as professionals if we continually assess our progress, as individuals and in community with our peers.

Credentialing

In the early 1990s, both of our jobs required a bachelor's degree with minimum years of experience. Given the increase in the number of positions at women's centers, there is a growing tendency to require a master's degree as a minimum qualification, and many job descriptions require a doctorate or list a PhD as a preferred qualification. As seasoned WC professionals, we question how the preference for an advanced degree serves the field. WCs seem to be struggling with the academic/practitioner divide that also characterizes two of the primary pipelines for WC professionals: Women's, Gender, and Sexuality Studies (WGSS) and Higher Education and Student Affairs (HESA).

In order to garner credibility for feminist pedagogy and scholarship, and even tenure, WGSS programs have intentionally drawn distinctions between the academic work taking place there and the service and co-curricular work of WCs. And yet, the assumption prevails that an advanced WGSS degree is sufficient preparation to take on the education, advocacy, and support roles of center staff.

Based on the job postings of 20+ years ago, gender equity work in the community and/or on campus served to credential WC staff. In fact, as exemplified in our descriptions of our work before becoming WC directors, the pipeline to professional staff roles was often filled by students and newer professionals getting connected to a WC, either on campus or through their community center/rape crisis work, or even the feminist club that used the center for their gathering space. Hence, acknowledging practice as an appropriate qualification was embedded in credentialing WC professionals. By undervaluing, and in some cases, removing this route to becoming "qualified," the field is moving towards privileging access to theory over exposure to practice.

More recently, a growing number of WC staff positions require a master's in higher education and student affairs as a minimum qualification. While this trend helps to recognize the value of practice as a competency for gender equity work, it does not foreground the significance of an explicitly feminist framework to inform such practice. As noted in the issue brief *Professional Staff Competencies in Women's Centers*, the student affairs literature offers two sets of competencies: those from the ACPA/NASPA Professional Competencies and Standards and those outlined in the competencies and ethics sections of the standards for Women Student Programs and Services (WSPS), which are published by the Council for the Advancement of Standards in Higher Education (CAS). The brief goes on to determine that the former is not specific to the needs of WCs and the latter does not speak to the entirety of WC work. The focus on student development as the primary function of the practitioner reinforces the notion that WC work is primarily about serving and supporting students at the individual level. The role of WC staff vis-à-vis staff and faculty is rendered invisible. Also, many WCs provide support to and advocacy for individual survivors of gender-based violence, which is not always part of the training for student affairs practitioners. Additionally, the institutional advocacy work that is largely understood within the field as inherent in WCs' missions is not included in many HESA programs. As Davie notes, "What seems to emerge as the leadership ethos in many women's centers is a belief of the efficacy of applying 'systems thinking' to our understanding of leadership" (450). According to Gail O. Mellow, "most women's centers that started in the early 1970s have a history of radical and public struggle – a conscious rejection of working through the system – that is diametrically opposed to the way in which many administrators function" (53).

If the work of WC staff is to transform institutions that are designed to maintain the status quo of hierarchy and systems founded on patriarchal notions of the academy, our challenge as a profession is to do so without relying on the established norms of what knowledge is valued and what it takes to be deemed an expert in the work of gender equity. It is worth noting that attempts by practitioners in the field to shift the trajectory of privileging theory or practice have come through their generating of scholarship about WC work. Two examples are the Contextual Statement for the CAS Standards for WGPS and the issue briefs produced by the Greater Cincinnati Consortium of Colleges and Universities (GCCCU)/Southwestern Ohio Council for Higher Education (SOCHE) Women's Centers Committee. What makes these significant is twofold. First, they reflect the hallmarks of collective process, a shared commitment to work at the individual and institutional levels, and being informed by feminist theory and practice. Second, this is labor that is done in spite of having few supports in place for this as a component of WC professional work. WC staff who are not connected to academic departments as a function of their roles often do not have the privilege of time and resources for research and scholarship that is afforded to and expected of faculty. Moving forward, the hope is that this form of knowledge production is recognized by our institutions and by the pipelines noted earlier as integral to the academic development and practical preparation of professionals committed to the work of advancing gender equity in higher education.

Why we stay?

Regardless of the pipeline that brought us to campus WC work, we stay because "women's and gender programs and services are informed by a broad range of academic disciplines and professions" and "serve as locations for exploring the connection between theory and practice" and "do so in their historical context and roots in social justice, community activism, and social change efforts, as well as in student development theory and administrative leadership practice" (CAS Contextual Statement, 2015). The opportunity to engage in consciousness-raising as a form of professional development contributes to relationships that are built from the shared struggle of understanding ourselves in relation to each other and to our individual and collective work. It requires us to take responsibility for a profession that has little scholarship behind it nor a professional organization to surround it. It encourages us to explore from our roots of the personal as political. The commitment to a feminist model of social justice is challenged by both the lack of clear "placement" within the higher education model and the nature of our individual and institutional advocacy work. Also, as calls for a more intersectional feminist approach are the norm, we acknowledge how this work has room to grow within the larger diversity/social justice lens. While the expansion of WCs in general means it is harder to have a small group share in a group of 100, at its core, we feel strongly that having a place to practice CR, as well as a space defined as feminist, is crucial to our professional development in a field where identity, power and privilege show up in our work and in our community. According to Bussey,

> The answer to this has been to create sustained and purposeful spaces where people have to communicate and connect. This is motivated by the knowledge that social justice awareness is born out of personal and professional struggles with injustices, but can also be purposefully taught.
>
> (qtd in Jennrich and Kowalski-Braun 207)

Works cited

Bussey, Marcus. "Embodied Education: Reflections on Sustainable Education." *International Journal of Environmental, Cultural, Economic and Social Sustainability*, vol. 43, no. 3, 2008, pp. 139–47.

The Combahee River Collective. *The Combahee River Collective Statement: Black Feminist Organizing in the Seventies and Eighties*. Albany, NY: Kitchen Table: Women of Color P, 1986.

Davie, Sharon L., editor. *University and College Women's Centers: A Journey toward Equity*. Westport, CT: Greenwood P, 2002.

Freedman, Janet L. *Reclaiming the Feminist Vision: Consciousness-raising and Small Group Practice*. Jefferson, NC: McFarland & Co., 2014.

Freedman, Janet L. "Re: Friday?" Received by Juli Parker, E-mail Correspondence, 28 Nov. 2017.

Goettsch, Jane, et al. "Women's and Gender Programs and Services: CAS Contextual Statement." *CAS Professional Standards for Higher Education*. 9th ed., edited by Jen Wells, Washington, DC: Council for the Advancement of Standards in Higher Education, 2015, pp. 489–92.

hooks, bell. *Feminism Is for Everybody: Passionate Politics*. Cambridge, MA: South End P, 2000.

Jennrich, Jessica, and Marlene Kowalski-Braun. "'My Head Is Spinning': Doing Authentic Intersectional Work in Identity Centers." *Journal of Progressive Policy and Practice*, vol. 2, no. 3, Fall 2014, pp. 199–212.

MacKinnon, Catherine A. *Toward a Feminist Theory of the State*. Cambridge, MA: Harvard UP, 1989.

Marine, Susan. "Reflections from 'Professional Feminists' in Higher Education: Women's and Gender Centers at the Start of the Twenty-first Century." *Empowering Women in Higher Education and Student Affairs: Theory, Research, Narratives, and Practice from Feminist Perspectives*, edited by Penny A. Pasque and Shelley Errington Nicholson, Sterling, VA: Stylus Publishing, 2011, pp. 15–31.

Mello, Gail O. "Women's Centers and Women Administrators: Breaking the Glass Slipper Together." *Initiatives*, vol. 51, no. 2/3, 1988, pp. 53–8.

Vlasnik, Amber L., and Melissa D. DeButz. "Professional Competencies of Women's Center Staff." Issue Brief No. 04, Greater Cincinnati Consortium of Colleges and Universities and Southwestern Ohio Council for Higher Education, Cincinnati, OH, 2013, pp. 199–212, 19 Nov. 2017, www.soche.org/formembers/councils-and-committees/womens-centers-committee/

Wetzel, Jodi. "Women's Centers: The Frameworks." *Initiatives*, vol. 51, no. 2/3, 1988, pp. 11–16.

7 Experiences of women's center directors in student affairs

Colleen Riggle and Melanie DeMaeyer

Introduction

Despite the over half-century history of campus-based women's centers, little research has investigated the work experiences of center directors. Barbara Kasper's "Campus-Based Women's Centers: A Review of Problems and Practices," and the Council for the Advancement of Standards (CAS) in Higher Education offer guidance on the structure and resources necessary for effectively administering campus-based women's centers (189, 510). However, there is a lack of scholarly exploration into the experiences of women's center directors. Achieving deeper understanding of the experiences of this group of professionals is vital for preventing burnout and increasing their longevity in the field, strengthening the services they provide, and creating crucial knowledge for new professionals entering the field of campus-based women's center work. This chapter highlights the findings of a qualitative study using narrative analysis to investigate the work experiences of women's center directors in a student affairs division.

Participants in this study were campus-based women's center directors currently working in a student affairs division, with varying personal demographics including age, sexuality, race, and years of experience (see Table 7.1). An initial questionnaire was emailed through a women's center listserv to identify potential participants and members of the listserv nominated themselves or others to participate.

Bolman and Deal's Four Framework Approach to leadership provided the theoretical foundation for investigating the question, "What are the work experiences of campus-based women's center professionals in a director role?" Bolman and Deal identified four intersecting institutional frameworks: structural, human resource, political, and symbolic (6391). Leaders operating within a structural frame focus on the roles, goals, and policies of an institution. Those utilizing a political frame focus on power, conflict, and competition. Individuals using a human resource frame focus on the skills, relationships, and needs of members of an institution (Bolman and Deal 2591). Finally, reliance on a symbolic frame yields a focus on the culture and meaning of an institution (Bolman and Deal 5683). This model gives voice to some of the salient work experiences of women's center directors in student affairs and provides a starting point for understanding those experiences.

Table 7.1 Participants' demographic profiles

Participant (Pseudonyms)	Age	Marital Status	Years as a Women's Center Director	Race	Sexual Orientation
Olivia*	65	Married	16+	White	Heterosexual
Tonia**	29	Married	5	White	Heterosexual
Fiona**	32	Single	2	White	Heterosexual
Nina*	49	Married	15	White	Heterosexual
Tina*	31	Married	11 months	Black	Heterosexual
Eliza*	45	Single	8.5	White	Heterosexual
Sophia*	32	Married	6	White	Polysexual
Sonia**	45	Divorced	20	White	Heterosexual

All participants self-identified as female.

* Four-year public institution
** Four-year private institution

Study findings

Three themes that impacted the participants' professional experiences emerged from the interviews: an emphasis on program development, student interaction, and staff size.

Program development

In Kelli Byrne's "The Role of Campus Based Women's Centers" she asserts that a key role of women's center professionals is to offer educational programs and provide support for women students (48). In alignment with Byrne's assertion, this study found that program development emerged as a prominent theme among participants' narratives and that institution type, geographic location of the university, and reporting structure impacted how centers program and serve certain student populations.

Programming was broadly defined by the participants, and ranged from creating a new women's center to initiatives seeking to increase outreach or provide safe space for community and identity exploration. In particular, participants noted that developing programs or expanding already existing ones led to success in their roles. For instance, Eliza observed, "Successful moments relate to developing new programs," and Tina agreed, noting, "I would definitely say some successful moments I've had, thus far, have been expanding the programs that were already done." Some participants characterized their programming experiences as challenging or frustrating; as Fiona noted, "Starting a new department from scratch on a very busy campus can be a challenge." In contrast, other participants described their programming work as empowering. When asked about the biggest success in her position, Tina shared, "Having the opportunity to be the first full-time director . . . and expand the programs . . . so we have more participants than ever." Given the growing numbers of women in higher education (Lopez and Gonzalez-Barrera 1; Parker 9), programming is a vital function of women's centers and a significant responsibility for women's center professionals.

Some participants had experienced changes in reporting structure, or moving from one division or reporting structure to another. For those transitioning from another campus division, the change in their unit and reporting line brought with it shift in the intended audience for program development (CAS 511; Davie 211; Goettsch et al. 4). For example, one women's center was formerly housed within academic affairs before it was moved to a division of student affairs. This switch created structural challenges because the mission of academic affairs is broadly defined to encompass service to students, faculty, and staff, whereas divisions of student affairs are limited to serving the needs of students.

These shifts happened for a variety of reasons. For instance, in one case a participant reported that she thought the decision to move her center to a different division was budgetary. These dynamics can be viewed through Bolman and Deal's structural frame, in which a deficit (in this case driven by budget concerns), leads to changes to the structural elements of an organization (1328). The impact of this type of change on participants varied; however, most identified a more circumscribed mission with a focus primarily on students, rather than incorporating faculty and staff concerns. One participant shared, "At the same time [as the change in reporting structure], we lost a position and half, so basically half of our staffing we lost . . . I did feel like at least the perception was that our mission was becoming smaller." Another consequence of this type of change was the impact on the women's center budget, as serving a smaller campus constituency led to budget reductions. This outcome aligns with the findings of Kasper and Spikes and Stillabower that women's center professionals identified a lack of funding for programs and events as a key problem they faced (188, 12).

Lastly, in some instances the shift from one division to another created unintended structural barriers that prevented the women's center director from participating in meetings she had attended in the past and reduced her opportunities to interact with other administrators. For example, Olivia had previously participated in the provost's breakfast meetings but is now no longer invited to that event, and thus has lost a valuable opportunity to connect directly with department chairs. Additionally, Olivia articulated that being able to network and collaborate with staff, faculty, and units outside of student affairs is important. For women's center professionals seeking to create successful programs and elevate the visibility and status of the women's center on campus, regardless of the structural division in which they are housed, access to both sufficient resources and campus-wide connections is essential to carrying out the center's mission and achieving its goals.

The theme of program development emerged prominently through the stories shared by the study participants. In particular, the participants discussed the impact of program development on students and the challenges of offering programming for LGBTQ students at a religiously affiliated institution or in a conservative state. This relates to the symbolic frame as the culture of the institution impacts the programmatic offerings for this identity group. Lastly, participants reflected on the advantages and drawbacks that ensue when a women's center transitions from one university division to another.

Student interaction

Student affairs professionals serve students in innumerable ways and in a wide variety of settings (Palmer et al. 36). Overwhelmingly, participants identified student interaction as vital to their work as women's center professionals. When asked to describe challenges, successes, and salient moments in their professional lives, all participants referenced some type of student impact or interaction as important. In this study, the value of student interaction was a prominent theme that emerged from the participants' narratives, and within this theme, three sub-themes were also identified: (1) interactions with feminist students, (2) LGBTQ students, and (3) student organizations. In addition, a focus on student development, individual conversations, and campus inclusion characterized the participants' comments related to student interaction.

Most often, when participants were asked to share an example of a successful or salient moment in their work, students were at the center of those stories. For example, Sophia discussed the rewards of "watching [students] evolve and being able to confidently use their voices, that you can tell that they have not felt comfortable using in a very long time, and when [students] challenge things in very wonderful and complicated ways." Tonia shared that her successful moments occurred "one-on-one with students."

Feminist students

Interaction with feminist-identified students contributed to the successful and salient experiences of women's center professionals. Such experiences can have intrinsic benefits for women's center professionals while also contributing to the student's sense of belonging, which has been found to positively influence college student development (Hurtado et al. 302; Strayhorn 8).

Sophia identified a successful moment as witnessing students awakening to an understanding of feminism and recognizing its significance for their lives. She noted, "my successful moment is seeing young students become feminists and understand what that means for them." Other participants also valued the knowledge that they were influential in encouraging students' transformative experiences through one-on-one interaction. Tonia noted that while her office plans an annual Take Back the Night event, which is an evening to raise awareness of sexual violence, she finds the rewards of her one-on-one interactions with students to be as significant as, if not greater than, the satisfaction she feels as the result of coordinating a successful campus event.

LGBTQ students

On several of the participants' campuses there had been either no women's center at all or no full-time professional in the women's center prior to their arrival, which is reflective of a staffing structure discussed by Sharon Davie in her book, *University and College Women's Centers: A Journey Toward Equity* (40–1). These participants shared that, on their campuses, this also left LGBTQ students with little institutional support. Through the creation of an LGBTQ student lounge on one campus and the integration of a drag show into the Homecoming week events on another, women's center professionals demonstrated their commitment to engaging and supporting students of all sexual identities (Broido 78). Eliza shared, "My successful moments are related to developing new programs, [like] developing LGBTQ programs for our university," while Tonia discussed surreptitiously providing advocacy and support for LGBTQ students because they don't have any other place on campus. Such work aligns with the findings of Broido that the growing number of college students who identify as LGBTQ have a need for identity-based support and services (82), and on campuses where there are not established centers to meet the needs of these students, women's center professionals often fill in the gap.

Bolman and Deal's political frame was apparent when some participants discussed struggling with working for a religiously affiliated university or for an institution located in a conservative state. Although student affairs professionals are responsible for supporting the development of all students (Evans and Reason 6; McClellan and Stringer 65), it was clear that for participants working at religiously affiliated institutions or in politically conservative states, that a student's sexual identity affected the level of support they could receive and the resources these professionals could provide. For example, Tonia reported having to "secretly" support LGBTQ students who had no other source of support on her religiously affiliated campus. A commitment to meeting the needs of all students (Broido 81), regardless of sexual or gender identity, lies at the heart of being a women's center professional and contributes to the participants' work experience in positive way.

Student organizations

Eliza, Fiona, and Olivia identified their interaction with campus student organizations as significant to their work as women's center professionals. Eliza reported that as a result of the center's engagement with student organizations, as well as Greek life and residence life, that she has 40 student volunteers who staff their crisis line. Greek life also provided support on Sophia's campus by partnering with her at Homecoming. Often, interaction with student organizations provided a way to extend women's center resources to address capacity issues (Clevenger, 5; Goettsch et al. 4). Where small staff size was an obstacle, student organizations were able to assist many women's center professionals with program development, peer education, or violence prevention initiatives. This represents a significant contribution and a means of ameliorating the problems resulting from understaffing, as reported by many of the women's center professionals in this study.

Staff size

Previous research has found that most campus-based women's centers employ at least one full-time professional staff member, typically a director or coordinator, with the rest of the staff often comprised of part-time employees, volunteers, or students (Clevenger, 6; Goettsch et al. 3). Six of the eight participants (75%) identified the challenges of having a small staff, while one participant (12.5%) was able to increase the size of her staff from one to three full-time professionals through the success of two different proposals. Eliza shared, "It required lots of proposals, conversations, and data showing the growth of our programs and services but I have [increased staff] two different times." The remaining participant, who had been in her position for less than a year, did not discuss staffing issues.

As discussed earlier, the human resource frame highlights the skills, relationships, and needs of the people who comprise an institution (Bolman and Deal 2591). Inadequate staffing, in this frame, neglects the needs of women's center directors, creating unnecessary stress and exacerbating work/life imbalances (Keener 48; Palmer et al. 37). More specifically, women's center directors with inadequate staffing are denied the benefits that are derived from developing relationships with fellow staff members, including the ability to be supported by a colleague in the same office regarding personal and professional goals, challenges, and accomplishments. A women's center director may also feel alone with no one else in the office to strategize or goal-plan with regularly.

From the perspective of the structural frame, inadequate staff size hinders the ability of women's center directors to achieve their units' goals. The structural view seeks organizational designs that promote maximum efficiency in organizing work and delegating it to staff (Bolman and Deal 7375). However, as the participants' stories vividly convey, the staff shortages that plague many women's centers undermine such efficiency in an office tasked with numerous responsibilities.

For example, multiple participants spoke of wanting to do more, but being limited in their capacity due to their small (or nonexistent) staff. Sonia shared, "Even if I had a little extra time, I'm sure that I could mentor more students or take on more interns or do other things that would both benefit the Women's Center and also the student experience, as well." This lack of personnel clearly impedes these professionals' ability to meet the goals of the unit, the division, and the larger organization.

Nevertheless, it was evident from the participants' stories that despite the lack of personnel, they were resourceful in their efforts to fulfill both the specific mission of the women's center and the broader missions of the division and the institution (Goettsch et al. 4). Tina shared, "We've gotten a lot of student volunteers who helped with our program." Many of these professionals relied on assistance from members of the campus community – women's studies faculty, an advisory board, supportive colleagues in other offices or departments, and other volunteers – to manage this ongoing challenge.

Reliance on collaboration with allies from the campus and local community relates to both the human resource and structural frameworks. While distinct, these two frameworks influence and intersect with one another through the staff size theme. The human resource and structural frameworks provide a means for assessing whether the mission and vision of each women's center should be adapted based on its staff size. If the staff size is unlikely to grow, directors may need to consider decreasing the breadth of their mission to correspond more closely to the number of personnel available to carry it out. Additionally, under-staffing also contributed to the challenges these directors faced in engaging in self-care, as it often impeded their ability to take part in activities promoting their physical and emotional well-being (Wasco et al. 734).

Implications

A number of implications emerge from the study's findings. Women's center professionals unquestionably play a significant role in program development on college campuses (Davie 211). However, the understaffing of such centers presents an ongoing challenge in accomplishing unit goals and providing the resources and services essential to supporting all students. Future research investigating the specific staffing configurations of women's centers and their impact on the centers' ability to carry out their responsibilities would support the call to increase resource allocations to these vital campus units while illuminating their unmet staffing needs.

Caroline Heldman and Baillee Brown, writers for the long-standing Ms. magazine, reported that the roles of many women's center professionals focus on leading sexual violence initiatives, however, in this sample only three of the eight participants had job descriptions in which sexual violence prevention was a primary focus (1). Thus, it is important to recognize the diverse and varied responsibilities of women's center directors and the multiple groups of students whose needs they may serve, including feminist and LGBTQ students. Fulfilling the structural mission of the women's center requires accounting for students' multiple and intersecting identities and the ways in which students with differing identities may experience college differently, and thus require various means of support (CAS, 2015).

Women's center directors need a professional home in which they are able to connect with one another and discuss the challenges, successes, and salient moments that characterize their work (CAS, 2015). For some of the participants in a one-person office, this study provided their first opportunity to engage in conversations of this kind. This finding highlights the vital importance of establishing an infrastructure at the regional and national levels, through professional organizations, to counter the isolation often experienced by women's center directors and to provide the acknowledgment, validation, and support for their work that is often lacking on individual campuses (Flaherty 1). Further, it is essential to create mechanisms that support new women's center professionals and those in one-person offices by providing opportunities to connect with others outside the walls of the campus-based women's center. While the study seeks to contribute in a meaningful way to understanding the work experiences of women's center professionals, it represents only a first step in fully understanding the experiences of this diverse group. Future research that incorporates the perspectives of women representing additional forms of diversity – for example, women of other races, ethnicities, and sexual orientations – would contribute to a fuller picture of the experiences of women's center directors. The participant pool for this study was not as diverse as it could have been, and thus presented only a limited view of the multitude of experiences and narratives of the broader spectrum of women's center professionals.

Conclusion

In the context of campus climate changes that have occurred in recent years – in relation to gender equity, racial inequality, and religious freedom, among other topics – understanding the role of these higher education professionals is more crucial than ever before. These campus changes make the work of women's centers, which have historically been associated with social justice advocacy and student activism, even more vital, urgent, and timely.

The findings of this chapter indicate that despite confronting a rapidly changing campus climate, problems of inadequate staffing, and resulting overwork and isolation, women's center directors continue to find their work not only challenging but also fulfilling. The participants cited the opportunity to support students in significant ways and to develop meaningful programming with demonstrated student impact as two of the primary rewards of their work. Not only did the women's center professionals interact with and support students on an individual level, but many were also able to create safe spaces and programming on campus for underrepresented and underserved populations, such as LGBTQ and feminist students.

Finally, and most urgently, this work issues a call to action to universities and professional organizations to address the material and human resource needs – in terms of staffing, funding, and other resources, as well as professional support, validation, and acknowledgment – to ensure the continuation of the critical work of women's centers and the vital contributions of women's center professionals.

Works cited

Bolman, Lee G., and Terrence E. Deal. *Reframing Organizations: Artistry, Choice, and Leadership.* Jossey-Bass, 2013.

Broido, Ellen M. "Understanding Diversity in Millennial Students." *Serving the Millennial Generation: New Directions for Student Services,* edited by Michael D. Coomes and Robert DeBard, San Francisco, CA: Jossey-Bass, 2004, pp. 73–85. Print.

Byrne, Kelli Z. "The Role of Campus-based Women's Centers." *Feminist Teacher,* vol. 13, 2000, pp. 48–61.

Clevenger, Bonnie M. "Women's Centers on Campus: A Profile." *Initiatives*, vol. 51, no. 2/3, Summer 1988, pp. 3–9.

Council for the Advancement of Standards in Higher Education. *CAS Professional Standards for Higher Education*. Washington, DC: Author, 2015.

Davie, Sharon L. *University and College Women's Centers: A Journey toward Equity*. Greenwood P, 2002.

Evans, Nancy J., and Robert D. Reason. "Guiding Principles: A Review and Analysis of Student Affairs Philosophical Statements." *Journal of College Student Development*, vol. 42, no. 4, 2001, pp. 359–77.

Flaherty, Colleen. "Shutting Out Women's Centers." *Inside Higher Education*, 20 Nov. 2015, www.insidehighered.com/news/2015/11/20/womens-studies-scholars-object-associations-new-stance-representation-womens-centers. Accessed 1 Mar. 2016.

Goettsch, Jane, et al. *Campus Women's Centers for the Twenty-first Century: Structural Issues and Trends*, June 2012, corescholar.libraries.wright.edu/womensctr_bib/84. Accessed 12 Mar. 2016.

Heldman, Caroline, and Bailee Brown. "A Brief History of Sexual Violence Activism in the U.S." 8 Aug. 2014, msmagazine.com/blog/2014/08/08/a-brief-history-of-sexual-violence-activism-in-the-u-s. Accessed 1 Mar. 2016.

Hurtado, Sylvia, et al. "Enhancing Campus Climates for Racial/Ethnic Diversity: Educational Policy and Practice." *Organization and Governance in Higher Education*, ASHE Reader Series, edited by M. Christopher Brown II, Pearson Learning Solutions, 2010, pp. 295–309.

Kasper, Barbara. "Campus-based Women's Centers: A Review of Problems and Practices." *Affilia*, vol. 19, no. 2, 2004, pp. 185–98.

Keener, Roger. "Burnout: Treatment and Prevention Strategies for College Student Affairs Professionals." *College Student Affairs Journal*, vol. 10, no. 2, 1990, pp. 48–53.

Lopez, Mark H., and Ana Gonzalez-Barrera. "Women's College Enrollment Gains Leave Men Behind." Pew Research Center, 6 Mar. 2014, www.pewresearch.org/fact-tank/2014/03/06/womens-college-enrollment-gains-leave-men-behind/. Accessed 29 Nov. 2017.

McClellan, George S., and Jeremy Stringer. *The Handbook of Student Affairs Administration*. Jossey-Bass, 2009.

Palmer, Carolyn, et al. "An International Study of Burnout Among Residence Hall Directors." *The Journal of College and University Student Housing*, vol. 29, no. 2, 2001, pp. 36–44.

Parker, Patsy. "The Historical Role of Women in Higher Education." *Administrative Issues Journal: Connecting Education, Practice, and Research*, vol. 5, no. 1, 2015, pp. 3–12.

Spikes, Frank, and Jane Stillabower. "Women's Centers and Postsecondary Education: A Selective Review of Recent Literature." *Education Research Quarterly*, vol. 3, no. 3, 1978, pp. 8–19.

Strayhorn, Terrell L. *College Students' Sense of Belonging: A Key to Educational Success for All Students*. Routledge, 2012.

Wasco, Sharon M., et al. "A Multiple Case Study of Rape Victim Advocates' Self-care Routines: The Influence of Organizational Context." *American Journal of Community Psychology*, vol. 30, no. 5, 2002, pp. 731–60.

8 On trauma, ambivalence, and trying too hard

Susannah Bartlow

My first day at the Women's Center was hot. It was also my first day at *any* full-time job in seven years – I'd been a server, classified ad customer service rep, grant writer, editor, faculty member, program planner/graduate assistant, and student loan recipient working my way through school. Now I had a job, with a salary and benefits, and a first day. I'd driven from Buffalo to Pennsylvania again, hung kitchen towels, and dressed with femme pride for my first hot day at work.

However, inside the Dean of Students' cool, remodeled suite, my boss wasn't there. I wanted to educate, mobilize and prepare, not idle in the air conditioning. The young man at the welcome desk, a recent graduate, invited me to lunch. He was friends with people in the Feminist Collective house; he came out as gay immediately, so we bonded over shared queerness, and he shared freely over tuna salad about student politics. Many campus feminists saw the Women's Center as institutionalized, a false gesture.

This new friend also made clear the true intensity of a stated part of the job description – how desperately the college needed to work on ending sexual assault and changing its response systems.

When I first started looking for higher ed jobs, as a survivor of child and adolescent sexual trauma, I specifically didn't apply for victim advocate jobs. I wanted to steer clear of direct work with what I thought I had already resolved. It felt like a clear, past, and sensitive trauma – something that had shaped me but didn't define me and that I didn't want to re-enter professionally.

I think now of the subconscious drive to find places that deepen the wounds we don't claim. The places that say they want a women's center but really need a sexual assault program. The settings that show us who they are – and where we show ourselves.

Trying too hard

In my first year, I worked out of an office just inside that office suite. I labored with a grandiose perfectionism: given the right layout and kitchen space, *my* center could be the first to fix the founding fathers' patriarchy. As the only full-time staff person, I joked that the brand-new center inhabited a 10-foot radius around my body. This joke became serious as I navigated projections and hopes for the new Women's Center onto my physical body, my presence, and my ideas.

When I arrived, the absence of a dedicated physical space was presented as an opportunity for development, creativity, and leadership. The committee that had advocated for creating the center, and other campus stakeholders, wanted fresh perspectives on its physical layout (while reserving their own opinions, of course). The intensity of these condensed hopes and expectations was a good fit for me, an energetic feminist in my early thirties with no direct family responsibilities and education to burn.

As an English PhD candidate, I had studied postcolonial literature, cultural studies, feminist theory, art as activism, poetics, and black diaspora literature before choosing a dissertation on healing narratives in black feminist and womanist literature. I didn't really know that student affairs was a separate, established field with its own practices; about the depth of established relationship between sexual assault services work and women's center work; or about the lived experiences of undergraduate co-education. I did know how to engage younger feminists, how to mobilize students to learn and develop empathy for one another, how to run a fabulous event, and how to navigate the many unwritten codes of elite private education.

To my mind, this work was my shot at embodying the phrase "the personal is political." When I first began graduate work, I traced the notion back to the original essay by Carol Hanisch as republished in a collection called *The Radical Therapist*. This led me through feminist theory, a black women writers course, affect studies, and social movement history to a single moment in a conversation between Lorde and Rich in Lorde's *Sister Outsider*. The two icons share their experiences of direct conflict and challenge inside their relationship as writers, lesbians, and feminists.[1] I was amazed. I had never seen (more likely: been alert to) their level of honesty in a conversation about race and gender between a black woman and a white woman. Lorde and Rich stayed *in* the conversation, actively disputing one another's point of view while remaining dedicated to the powerful connection between them as poets, activists, and friends. It just *felt* more honest. How could I have that kind of real and rigorous conversation and stay in it – for the rest of my life?

This question led me deep into black feminist and womanist literature and theory, feminist movement histories, work on whiteness in and outside of feminism, and trauma studies. I now realize that I was clawing for work that would repair the hollow core inside the promise of white liberal feminism. The rage and betrayal I felt learning the painful truths about feminist racism did not erase my need to find intersectional or anti-racist role models, and the womanist writers I read and learned from illuminated the wound at the core of my white feminist training, as well as its possible remedies.

I had already decided to stay in the PhD program but not pursue the tenure track, so a friend and colleague suggested I explore working at women's centers. Once I learned what they were, this felt like a way to get more honest – to take my skills and knowledge and start using them to make an impact greater than I could by teaching or researching. I could return to the kind of elite schools I had been socialized into and re-educate, unlearn with other white women what our true histories and opportunities were. In my eyes, we were made for something bigger than just us and better than lip service to feminism.

On ambivalence, white womanhood, and women's centers

So I started passing out condoms and lollipops and teaching women's studies. I had had a white feminist epiphany and craved nothing more than to be what Sara Ahmed calls, in the context of diversity work, "a counterhegemonic worker." Motivated equally by intersectional commitment, white guilt, privileged naivete, and genuine enthusiasm, I tumbled into the heady idea that these centers could be the answer to patriarchal wounds.

This approach felt affirmed by the professional women's center community. In 2008, when I opened the center, several hundred centers existed at universities across the country. These centers were evenly divided between student affairs and academic affairs divisions. Whatever institutional home they held, the centers all grew from feminist resistance to institutional discrimination, especially campus sexual harassment and assault; and feminist labor struggles (like equal pay and advancement/leadership brick walls). Here was an active, knowledgeable, engaged community of feminists who strategized, struggled, and celebrated together. I joined the Anti-Racism/Anti-White Supremacy Working Group of the Women's Centers Committee of NWSA. At the time I was skeptical of the institutionalization I observed, both on my campus and among women's center colleagues, but I calculated it as the cost of having chosen an institutional role.

Back on campus, the inevitable reports of sexist, racist, and homophobic microaggressions and of physical violence and sexual assault immediately poured in. I naturalized or took ownership of things that were outrageous and strange – a live date auction conducted in the main cafeteria; a fraternity whose commonly uttered letters are synonymous with the expectation of sexual assault. I felt these to be, not external symptoms of patriarchal white supremacy, but integral to my job description. To absorb the heat and shock of community and self-expectation, I adopted a wry narcissism: for a period of time, I kept "end patriarchy" on my actual to-do list as a reminder of my true responsibilities. I joined – and then left – an advocacy training program out of a need to take care of my own reawakening trauma. Before long, I was answering the phone in the middle of the night, providing support at the center of a campus sexual assault crisis. I was also working to complete my dissertation. In multiple professional communities, I found mirrors of this martyred, beloved, often codependent persona, as well as its healthier reverse archetype: a learned big sister feminist with experience to offer, professional development to attend, and sheltering community to build. The righteous reproductive labor of both models was enticing.

In its second year, the center established a physical location shared with the student affairs diversity office, and a community partner brought active support to apply for an Office of Violence Against Women grant. A colleague invited me to attend a workshop for white anti-racists, a companion experience for a people of color workshop. I realized that, by reacting to my own triggers and enacting the obligation to address campus assault, I had both supported the growth of an intersectional student movement (one that would re-emerge more powerfully a few years later) and reinforced a racist trope of white feminine victimhood. I recommitted to building the former and limiting the latter in campus anti-violence work. The following year, a great class grew into a student-led group; we got the violence prevention grant; my teaching was getting better and better – it felt like progress and success.

But I was still behind on my email, I was still oversleeping, I was still financially insecure (despite privilege, social capital, and a decent salary). I missed deadlines. It felt like the center was simultaneously over- and under-performing. What was the disconnect? Out of a valuable but misdirected desire to take responsibility for the symptoms of white supremacy, I had speedily internalized the institution's terms and conditions as my responsibility to resolve. And that internalization was slowly chiseling away the soft, powerful, flexible muscles I'd been working on: I had turned into a taut professional ready to snap.

Terese Jonsson argues that there is a narrative reproduction of white feminist racism in women's studies texts and feminist stories. Similarly, women's centers often participate in the unwitting reproduction of white feminist racism. My pragmatic and idealistic hope to re-enter and interrupt that process brought a constant uneasiness and ambivalence. I thought I could reproduce something looking enough like expected feminism so that real radical work could take place. I worked to be a director "at the level of appearance" so that I could be a counterhegemonic worker from within this performance (again, referencing Ahmed with respect to work on race).

It's telling that the way I learned to do this job was through reproductive labor among other white women directors, and that the biggest setbacks and traumas of my career in higher education were at the hands of white women in positions of authority. In my professional life, white women have provided immeasurable coaching, advocacy, and challenges; white women have also blocked community-supported efforts for sexuality education, equitable sexual assault policy change, and actively divested from intersectional work. White women mentors brought and kept me in the NWSA professional community, deepened my anti-racism work, offered grant opportunities, and collaborated on research and student projects. White women or supervisors have provided neutral or misleading feedback when I was cutting too close to the curb – and, ultimately, white women fired me or pushed me out. Many other smaller experiences reinforced the intergenerational tensions of white feminism, especially around intersectionality and the press of conservative forces on higher education.

In *On Being Included*, Ahmed makes a critical distinction between equality and diversity, the latter of which "does not have a necessary relation to changing organizational values." At many institutions, there is an even further (dys)functional divide between gender and sexuality work and diversity *or* equality work. Just as white women are provisionally included in white supremacy, women's centers are provisionally included in institutions to the degree they consent to white supremacist operations (such as Department of Justice-based violence prevention grants[2]). The war to end sexual assault on college campuses, and women's centers' internal struggles to operate intersectionally, are two active spaces where this provisional inclusion is tested.

Women's centers are positioned in the tension between diversity and equity work, because of their privileged relationship to what Lorde calls the "different pitfalls surrounding us because of our experiences, our color" (103). Whatever their actual historical origins or present-day leadership, at least on historically white campuses, women's centers often are coded as white – because "woman" is often coded as white and because of institutional racism limiting access to people of color for leadership and involvement at women's centers.

Intellectually I knew this, but emotionally, psychologically, somatically, I was not prepared or conditioned to take responsibility for what it meant: because I identified with the power structure of white supremacy, albeit counter-hegemonically, I demanded to be both a successful director and a subversive worker. I perceived this tension as an essential job function, and received complex, often positive feedback about it, but I didn't realize until much later the subconscious drive to be rewarded by the institution. I also missed the cost to others of this stiff performance – and the cost to myself.

The education you need

Fast-forward seven years, to an early May Monday in Milwaukee. My routine was to get in as soon as I could drag myself out of bed – whether exhaustion, depression or ambivalence, a good waking routine has always been a challenge. But this morning I had woken up early and turned off the alarm, the phone call from the night before replaying in my mind. On my five-minute car ride, I felt determined, clear, and terrified. I parked as usual on a side street a few blocks from campus. Often I would feel myself armoring with every step of the walk. I now know that I was in a near-constant, low-level freeze state during my academic career – in crisis moments, that constant nervous system spike became even more elevated. I crossed the block closest to the office and noticed the program assistant who had supervised and supported the creation of the mural walking across the street rapidly, her head bowed. Her experience, expertise, and open-heartedness were a major reason for the mural's success and power. I knew she had walked in to the office to face a sheer white wall where, for the past six weeks, there had been a community-painted mural of black woman freedom fighter Assata Shakur.

It's a fundamental contradiction of academia, of white supremacy, that this work was whitewashed – a literal erasure of a mural that celebrated black power and resisted the erasure of black knowledge by quoting Assata: "No one is going to give you the education you need to overthrow them. No one is going to teach you your true history, teach you your true heroes, if you know that knowledge will help set you free" (Lewis). I still marvel that I lost my livelihood as an educator by supporting learning. On the other hand, the experience was predictable.

On my own blog and in *Feminist Studies*, I've offered my perspective both on the events that led to the whitewashing of the mural and on the implications for feminism and women's centers. In all my other public tellings, I have only made a sidebar out of a central fact: how actively I was trying to leave both my current employer and academia as an industry. I had consulted with therapists, partners, friends, coaches and astrologers about my career. Before I moved to Milwaukee, I turned down a job as a labor organizer because I was holding too much consumer debt to make the finances work. I believed that the new role with its salary bump would empower me and, from that place of stability, I could choose a career more consistent with my temperament and values. Instead, I got deeper in debt. I applied for other jobs, went to therapy, budgeted, talked to my friends, practiced meditation, and started shuffling the parts of my divided life toward what I thought was a necessary acceptance: a job I both loved and hated, a contented and slightly checked-out existence. I had already begun to dissolve this passive acceptance with a renewed job search when I got the phone call in May 2015 asking me whose idea it was to do a mural of Assata Shakur.

After I got fired, several close people pushed me to promote myself or share the story. A media strategist advised me to hold a press conference using her contacts. "It would be really good if you can cry on TV," she told me. I paid her for her press release and we didn't talk again. A friend urged me to figure out how to get on national news. But I wasn't connected with local prison abolition organizing and I knew how quickly the story would get spun into my victimization (or my leftist stupidity). I was so shattered by years of testifying against myself and didn't want to break down on TV – didn't want to feed my white lady tears to the curated pit. I chose instead to tell the story in ways that others asked for, like a speaking event; in consultation as a team with the students and program assistant; and in a feminist publication – all places in which I could truly testify.

To this day, I worry that I didn't capitalize enough on that moment, not for me but for movement opportunities. But those opportunities don't happen because they are forced – they happen because they are called for, because people are called up when they are needed. I have seen so many media stories, before and since, about academics (many faculty of color) whose work has been questioned or careers destroyed because of academia's unwillingness to change. The mechanism of this experience was similar: local right-wing media gets picked up by national right-wing media, universities react without informed perspective, and the false equivalence of right-tending opinions and left-leaning facts drives the conversation. At the time of writing this essay, a call for papers on academic pushout, betrayal and re-rerouting has been issued by the journal *Feminist Formations* – a call that focused primarily on faculty experiences but that was explicit about tracking the patterns of these events.

Conclusion

In grad school, I participated in early iterations of leaving-academia/alt-ac platforms – but I didn't quit, because I found this space of praxis in women's centers and women's and gender studies. In that practice, I saw the potential for liberation, and for applying my own skills and privilege iteratively. There are so many meaningful, effective, long- and short-term contributions of that career that I haven't described here. There are hundreds of students, staff, and faculty with whom I learned and supported and grew. There's the backbone and professional community of the National Women's Studies Association and Women's Centers Committee of NWSA. There are dozens of collaborative efforts I still think of with pride – projects to share and redistribute institutional resources, to support local artists and organizers, bridge community and academia, teach outside conventional classroom practices, introduce students to radical speakers, and cultivate meaningful intersectional spaces. Many effective meetings, coalitions, and heartfelt support conversations established lasting community. Those are the things that matter and they are worth always trying for.

In all of this effort, though, at some other level, I was simply trying too hard to do something I couldn't bear. My goal has always been to do racial justice work that accounts for white feminism and white feminists. As an administrator, I navigated a triangulation of liberation, collusion, and complicity – because I brought into that triangulation a white feminist craving for a kind of escape. From SlutWalk and the Women's March to Hillary Clinton and carceral feminism, white feminism continues to claw for a safe space, one that can protect us from the self-betrayal patriarchy requires. To be clear, the desire to wrench free of patriarchy is required and beautiful. But the investment in white feminism, institutional practice, or neoliberal education is less likely to provide that liberation than will our committed divestment.

What I've done here is describe the underside, the complexities, the tricky motivations that can show up when our work engages individuals and institutions in the friendly, vicious marriage of transformation. The hope is that this narrative reflects truths that help other women's, gender, and sexuality fighters resist white supremacy and work honestly for a future we create together.

Notes

1 *Audre*: Adrienne, in my journals I have a lot of pieces of conversations that I'm having with you in my head. I'll be having a conversation with you and I'll put it in my journal because stereotypically or symbolically these conversations occur in the space of black woman/white woman where it's beyond Adrienne and Audre, almost as if we're two voices.

 Adrienne: You mean the conversations you have in your head and your journal, or the conversations we're having on this earth?

 Audre: The conversations that exist in my head that I put in the journal. This piece, I think, is one of them – about the different pitfalls [black and white women face]. I've never forgotten the impatience in your voice that time on the telephone, when you said, "It's not enough to say to me that you intuit it." Do you remember? I will never forget that. Even at the same time that I understood what you meant, I felt a total wipeout of my modus, my way of perceiving and formulating.

Adrienne: Yes, but it's not a wipeout of your modus . . . I was trying to say to you, don't let's let this evolve into "You don't understand me" or "I can't understand you" or "Yes, of course we understand each other because we love each other." That's bullshit. So if I ask for documentation, it's because I take seriously the spaces between us that difference has created, that racism has created. There are times when I simply cannot assume that I know what you know, unless you show me what you mean.

Audre: But I'm used to associating a request for documentation as a questioning of my perceptions, an attempt to devalue what I'm in the process of discovering.

Adrienne: It's not. Help me to perceive what you perceive. That's what I'm trying to say to you.

Audre: But documentation does not help one perceive. At best it only analyzes the perception. At worst, it provides a screen by which to avoid concentrating on the core revelation, following it down to how it feels. Again, knowledge and understanding. They can function in concert, but they don't replace each other. But I'm not rejecting your need for documentation.

(103–4)

2 To be clear, I am not advocating that women's centers should not accept DOJ funding or work strategically with campus resources. This is a point of observation to reconsider where or how women's centers' mutual interests are truly aligned.

Works cited

Ahmed, Sara. *On Being Included: Racism and Diversity in Institutional Life.* Duke UP, 2012.

Hanisch, Carol. "The Personal Is Political." *Carol Hanisch*, 2009, www.carolhanisch.org/CHwritings/PIP.html.

Jonsson, Terese. "The Narrative Reproduction of White Feminist Racism." *Feminist Review*, vol. 113, no. 1, 2016, pp. 50–67, doi:10.1057/fr.2016.2.

Lewis, Heidi R. "Feminists We Love: Assata Shakur (Love Note)." http://www.thefeministwire.com/2013/05/feminists-we-love-assata-shakur-love-note/. Accessed 29 July 2018.

Lorde, Audre. *Sister Outsider: Essays and Speeches.* Crossing P, 2015.

Lorde, Audre, and Adrienne Rich. "An Interview with Audre Lorde." *Signs: Journal of Women in Culture and Society*, vol. 6, no. 4, 1981, pp. 713–36, doi:10.1086/493842.

Shakur, Assata. *Assata: An Autobiography.* Belford, NJ: Lawrence Hill Books, 2001.

9 Putting our oxygen masks on first

Women's and gender center staff and self-care

Brenda Bethman and Anitra Cottledge

Historically, women's and gender centers and women's and gender studies programs have been viewed as sites of caring within bureaucratic institutions, with women's center staff often taking pride in the ways in which they create what Bettez calls "critical community" (10). In keeping with the feminist and justice-based frameworks that inform their work, many centers are adept at offering programs and initiatives that attend to the holistic selves of their constituents. In contemporary women's and gender equity centers, this attention to the holistic self can take the form of intentional programming for students, staff, and faculty about self-care. Despite placing importance on creating an environment of care for others, women's and gender center staff have not been as effective at performing self-care for themselves, often leading to staff burnout and attrition. These complexities raise two critical questions about women's centers as communities of care: (1) What is the importance of intersectionality in reframing self and community care in the context of women's and gender equity centers? and (2) What are some practical strategies for women's center staff to prevent burnout, particularly in environments that do not prioritize self and community care and institutions that value productivity over sustainability?

Intersectionality as a critical element in communities of care

When Flavia Dzodan used the words, "My feminism will be intersectional or it will be bullshit!" to express her anger at a racial slur being used as a means of feminist protest (Ms. magazine), the mantra became a rallying cry for many who had long critiqued mainstream feminist movements' lack of attention to the many other systems of oppression that intersect with gender-based oppression. Women's centers, along with many other organizations in various sectors, also focused on intersectionality, a term coined by legal scholar and critical race theorist Kimberlé Crenshaw.

This attention to interlocking oppressions in the context of gender equity work is in line with the ways in which women's centers have, over time, worked to evolve and expand their missions beyond their early focus on helping white, cisgender women gain access to higher education. However, centers still have work to do when it comes to more completely integrating intersectionality into their practices and programming. Some of this work has to do with the understanding of intersectionality itself. Intersectionality is not simply about "naming and recognizing different, multiple social identities," nor is it the same as "intersections of identity" (Lange). It is, instead, a means of identifying the "intersecting patterns of racism and sexism, and how these experiences tend not to be represented within the discourses of either feminism or antiracism" (Crenshaw 1243–4). Intersectionality as a theory invites individuals, organizations, and institutions to examine and interrogate "the interaction between race, gender and other categories of difference in individual lives, social practices, institutional arrangements, and cultural ideologies and the outcomes of these interactions in terms of power" (Davis 68).

Clarity about the nature of intersectionality has implications for the ways in which women's and gender equity centers conceptualize and enact practices and communities of care. Many people, including women's center staff, point to a quote by black lesbian feminist activist and author Audre Lorde, as a foundation of their emphasis on self-care: "Caring for myself is not self-indulgence, it is self-preservation, and that is an act of political warfare" (131). Center staff can and should do the necessary work to appropriately locate themselves in relation to Lorde's famous saying, and be mindful not to decontextualize it and remove Lorde's emphasis on "the importance of staying cognizant of racial difference in feminist movements" (Aftab).

In other words, self-care priorities and practices do not manifest themselves universally across all people, including women's center staff. Historically, women's centers have been staffed by white, cisgender women, a condition that, while slowly shifting, still holds true in contemporary centers. As women's and gender center staff experience varied intersections of oppressions based upon their multiple identities, the ways in which they care for themselves as individuals and others is complex. Self-care itself can mean many different things in the context of women's center staff facing various interlocking oppressions. Sara Ahmed notes about the aforementioned Lorde quote, "Lorde says self-care is *not* self-indulgence but self-preservation. Some have to look after themselves because . . . their being is not cared for, supported, protected."

Self-care doesn't mean the same thing for all people, because survival doesn't mean the same thing for all people. In women's centers, employing an intersectional view of self-care can affect practices within staff, e.g., views about taking vacation time, opportunities for staff professional development, distribution of labor, etc. For example, what kinds of unseen and emotional labor are staff with multiple oppressed identities asked to do? How does the precarity experienced by those staff members affect their job satisfaction, retention, and overall well-being? Explicitly asking and implicitly expecting staff of color, indigenous staff, nonbinary staff, and staff with disabilities to consistently educate other staff with more dominant identities, or to perform certain outreach duties with underrepresented communities may, for instance, erode that staff member's ability to persist in the job, much less to conceptualize and implement self-care programming for people *outside* of the center.

Women's and gender equity centers are not alone in grappling with the issue of self-care and sustainability. College students and community activists alike are seeking balance in meeting their responsibilities, addressing issues of inequity and injustice, and maintaining a sense of wholeness and health within demanding and rapidly changing sociopolitical environments (Eligon; Reilly). Given their historical foundations in feminist care ethics, women's and gender center staff are uniquely positioned to imagine fresh models of care. Their challenge is to ensure that the self-care practices that they promote externally match efforts within the women's and gender center space. Educator and activist adrienne maree brown, in *Emergent Strategy: Shaping Change, Changing Worlds*, discusses the need for organizations to be "fractal" in their approaches to change and transformation, i.e., ensure that the small scale aligns with the large scale. A failure to do this results in real and serious consequences for the organization: "Burn out. Overwork, underpay, unrealistic expectations. Organizational and movement splitting. Personal drama disrupting movements. Mission drift, specifically in the direction of money. Stagnation – an inability to make decisions" (53). Exploring and adopting intersectional ways of self and community care position women's center staff to not only sustain themselves, and more fully meet the needs of the diverse constituents they serve, but also provides centers with the opportunity to model innovative approaches to colleagues in education and other sectors.

Practical strategies for self and community care[1]

Very few women's and gender professionals would disagree with the above-mentioned rationale on the need for feminist self-care. Nonetheless, while gender equity workers *talk* a lot about the importance of self-care, they tend to be less adept at putting the ideas into practice. Taking care of oneself is not only beneficial on individual and personal levels; it also helps women's center staff to be better leaders and allows them to serve as role models for students and other staff.

The key question here, of course, is *how* – when staff are all juggling multiple roles (professional, student, partner, parent, etc.), how do they make time to take care of themselves? Below are some practical tips for practicing self-care.[2]

Schedule breaks

Working nonstop on projects, while thought to be a surefire way of getting things done, tends to actually decrease productivity. Facilitate taking short, regular breaks by using a Pomodoro timer or a break-scheduling app.

Use vacation/sick/personal leave

Many women's and gender center professionals do not use their vacation/personal leave or come to work sick. Staff should instead use their paid leave time, if their institution provides it. Paid leave time is part of a salary package, and not using it is akin to leaving money on the table. Vacations are key, whether they are longer vacations of a week or more or long weekends here and there. Getting away for a while can be especially rejuvenating, especially if staff remember to turn their email off while on vacation.

Create rituals

Women's center staff members are often invested personally and professionally in the issues they address at work, and can easily bring their work home with them. Creating a ritual to separate the work part of the day from the non-work part is important, and different types of rituals resonate with different people. For professionals who value justice and equity in multiple areas of their lives, the key is finding something that works and sticking with it.

A word to supervisors

All of the preceding are individual actions aimed at workers, but practicing self-care is very challenging in a higher education culture that values overwork and sees self-care as an act of weakness or indulgence. Supervisors should think about the conditions they are creating in their centers and the models they are setting: Do they subtly or overtly communicate dissatisfaction when employees take time off? Do they themselves take time off? When they take time off, do they really take time off or do they check in constantly? Do they send emails at all hours of the day and night (Morton and Curzan)? Supervisors should critically examine their own actions and think about ways they can support themselves and their employees in committing to self-care. Overall, staff members advocating with their supervisors and other leaders at their institutions on the importance of self-care is the most effective way to make change for everyone within the campus context.

Incorporating healing and self-care into center programming

All of the aforementioned tips are important and necessary; however, self- and community care are not all about bubbles and relaxation. Rather, as Brianna Wiest points out:

> Self-care is often a very unbeautiful thing.
>
> It is making a spreadsheet of your debt and enforcing a morning routine and cooking yourself healthy meals and no longer just running from your problems and calling the distraction a solution.
>
> It is often doing the ugliest thing that you have to do, like sweat through another workout or tell a toxic friend you don't want to see them anymore or get a second job so you can have a savings account or figure out a way to accept yourself so that you're not constantly exhausted from trying to be *everything, all the time* and then needing to take deliberate, mandated breaks

from living to do basic things like drop some oil into a bath and read Marie Claire and turn your phone off for the day.

Wiest's article makes clear that for many people, self-care is not just about working too hard, but is often also tied to what she calls "relentless internal pressure," and for many women's center constituents, is directly related to previous trauma. Many centers have incorporated a focus on addressing trauma into their programming. An example of this is found at the University of Missouri–Kansas City, where the UMKC Women's Center sponsors a Healing Arts Program, which offers workshops across campus as well as a regular part of its programmatic offerings. Promoting self-care is one of the major goals of the initiative:

> Healing Arts Workshops create a moment in time for individuals to focus on their own needs, their own emotional health, and their own well-being. Workshops are offered in a safe, relaxed environment that promotes personal transformation where art becomes a path to self-esteem, self-expression, and self-empowerment.
>
> ("Healing Arts Workshops")

Since starting the program in 2013, the UMKC Women's Center has held 270 workshops with 5,766 participants, the majority of whom express deep satisfaction with the workshops and the healing they receive through participating. Women's Center staff have also experienced an unexpected benefit; because they also participate in the workshops when hosting them, staff members have been able to foster healing and care for themselves, as well as for the students, faculty, and staff they serve. Integrating self-care into the center's programming has thus resulted in a healthier climate for staff in the UMKC Women's Center.

Conclusion

Women's and gender equity centers, while varied in their specific foci and programs, all generally share a mission of advocacy for those facing gender-based oppression. Due in part to the counseling role held by some women's centers, and the long history of women's centers providing sexual violence and trauma intervention and response, centers are seen as sites of healing and care. Further, women's center staff members are sometimes seen as helping professionals, regardless of their actual educational background and training. As professionals who help to care for and advocate for others, it is imperative that women's center staff are equipped to also care for themselves. Being able to implement self-care practices in ways that are individually authentic is critical to ensuring that staff don't experience conditions like compassion fatigue, which is defined as "an extreme state of tension and preoccupation with the suffering of those being helped to the degree that it can create a secondary traumatic stress for the helper" ("Compassion Fatigue Awareness Project"). As mentioned earlier, this compassion fatigue can lead to burnout for women's center staff and potential departures from individual women's centers or the field itself. The toll of caring for others, if not properly balanced with care for self, is often exacerbated in women's centers by the fact that many center staff themselves also have lived experiences with gender-based oppression, which can compound the fatigue.

Along with the call for individual self-care practices is a call for women's centers to focus on what Grise-Owens calls "organizational wellness."

> Because self-care and other aspects of organizational wellness have reciprocal effects, we can use self-care to mitigate organizational dysfunction. A change in one part of the system affects other parts of the system. With integrated and activated self-care, we can change the way we respond and interact with the organization and other stressors. We can modulate negative impacts and maximize positive strategies.
>
> ("Self-Care, A-to-Z")

The relationship between self and community care is interdependent, and women's and gender equity centers should also be intersectional in their approach to care. Care is not separate from systems of oppressions and privilege, which are often major factors in people's capacities to care for themselves and others.

As women's and gender equity centers continue to incorporate issues of self-care into their programming, they also have the opportunity to look at the ways in which the models of self-care they share externally with their campus communities align with their own internal practices. A focus on intersectional staff and organizational wellness can result in greater and more robust partnerships, healing for women's center staff and their constituents, and an increased ability to advocate for more sustainable systems and policies throughout institutions.

Notes

1 Part of the following is adapted from a blog post previously published by Bethman.
2 Note the above caveats on self-care practices manifesting differently for different individuals holds true for this list, which is not intended to be exhaustive, but rather as a starting off point.

Works cited

Aftab, Aqdas. "Appropriating Audre: On the Need to Locate the Oppressor within Us." *Bitch Media*, 22 Feb. 2017, www.bitchmedia.org/article/appropriating-audre/need-locate-oppressor-within-us. Accessed 8 Apr. 2018.

Ahmed, Sara. "Selfcare as Warfare." *Feminist Killjoys*, 25 Aug. 2014, feministkilljoys.com/2014/08/25/selfcare-as-warfare. Accessed 8 Apr. 2018.

Bethman, Brenda. "Commit to Self Care." *Gross, Point Blank: Tips & Tricks for Communicators, Innovators, and Leaders*, 3 Jan. 2015, lizgross.net/commit-self-care/. Accessed 8 Apr. 2018.

Bettez, Silvia Cristina. "Critical Community Building: Beyond Belonging." *Educational Foundations*, vol. 25, no. 3–4, 2011, pp. 3–19.

brown, adrienne maree. *Emergent Strategy: Shaping Change, Changing Worlds.* Chico, CA: AK P, 2017.

"Compassion Fatigue Awareness Project." *Compassion Fatigue Awareness Project*, www.compassionfatigue.org/index.html. Accessed 16 Apr. 2018.

Crenshaw, Kimberlé Williams. "Mapping the Margins: Intersectionality, Identity Politics, and Violence against Women of Color." *Stanford Law Review*, vol. 43, no. 6, 1993, pp. 1241–99.

Davis, Kathy. "Intersectionality as Buzzword: A Sociology of Science Perspective on What Makes a Feminist Theory Successful." *Feminist Theory*, vol. 9, no. 1, 2008, pp. 67–85.

Dzodan, Flavia. "My Feminism Will Be Intersectional or It Will Be Bullshit!" *Tiger Beatdown*, 10 Oct. 2011, tigerbeatdown.com/2011/10/10/my-feminism-will-be-intersectional-or-it-will-be-bullshit/. Accessed 8 Apr. 2018.

Eligon, John. "They Push. They Protest. And Many Activists, Privately, Suffer as a Result." *New York Times*, 26 Mar. 2018, www.nytimes.com/2018/03/26/us/they-push-they-protest-and-many-activists-privately-suffer-as-a-result.html. Accessed 8 Apr. 2018.

Grise-Owens, Erlene. "Self-care, A-to-Z: Organizational Accountability and Practitioner Self-care – NOT an Either/Or Option." *The New Social Worker*, www.socialworker.com/feature-articles/self-care/organizational-accountability-and-practitioner-self-care-not-either-or/. Accessed 16 Apr. 2018.

"Healing Arts Workshops." *UMKC Women's Center*, info.umkc.edu/womenc/programs/healing-arts-workshops/. Accessed 12 Apr. 2018.

Lange, Alex C. "The (Mis)use of Intersectionality in Student Affairs: A Call to Practitioners & Researchers." *Alex C. Lange*, 15 Oct. 2017, www.itsalexcl.com/blog/2017/10/15/the-misuse-of-intersectionality-a-call-to-student-affairs-researchers-practitioners. Accessed 8 Apr. 2018.

Lorde, Audre. *A Burst of Light*. Ithaca, NY: Firebrand Books, 1988.

Morton, Andrew D., and Anne Curzan. "What Happened When the Dean's Office Stopped Sending Emails After Hours." *ChronicleVitae*, 12 Apr. 2018, chroniclevitae.com/news/2035-what-happened-when-the-dean-s-office-stopped-sending-emails-after-hours. Accessed 14 Apr. 2018.

Reilly, Kathy. "Record Numbers of College Students Are Seeking Treatment for Depression and Anxiety – But Schools Can't Keep Up." *Time*, 19 Mar. 2018, time.com/5190291/anxiety-depression-college-university-students/. Accessed 8 Apr. 2018.

Wiest, Brianna. "This Is What 'Self-care' Really Means, Because It's Not All Salt Bath and Chocolate Cake." *Thought Catalog*, 16 Nov. 2017, thoughtcatalog.com/brianna-wiest/2017/11/this-is-what-self-care-really-means-because-its-not-all-salt-baths-and-chocolate-cake/. Accessed 8 Apr. 2018.

"Woman Is the 'N' of the World?" *Ms. Magazine Blog*, 6 Oct. 2011, msmagazine.com/blog/2011/10/06/woman-is-the-n-of-the-world/. Accessed 8 Apr. 2018.

10 Seeking relevance in an age of inequity

A case study of the identity struggle of one women's center

Susan V. Iverson and Cassie Pegg-Kirby

Introduction

On college and university campuses, women's centers are grappling with their role, relevance, and identity. These centers emerged in the 1960s and 1970s to institutionalize support for women on campus. Yet, 50 years later, women's centers are experiencing a midlife crisis of identity, as what initially defined them, most notably what it means to be a woman, is being contested. While women's centers, as sites of empowerment and liberation, continue to support the needs of students, faculty, and staff, they have also become "lightning rods for accusations of self-segregation or campus balkanization" (Renn 244).

In a world where culture is changing at a record pace and the media are having a field day with feminism, it is imperative that college administrators find a way to unite across differences without sacrificing the values upon which women's centers were founded. The messy terrain of identity politics that these centers must navigate is not new, but in an era where women comprise the majority in so many categories – particularly in their attendance rates at US institutions of higher education – many question the utility and relevance of women's centers. Many centers have changed their names to be inclusive of gender and sexuality, but such decisions are fraught with debate surrounding the need to retain women-identified programs and services.

We concur with Lori Patton Davis who argues (in Nicolazzo and Harris) that Women's Centers (in particular, and identity centers more broadly) "remain vital to the fabric of institutions of higher education, specifically in their ability to confront and redress the inequity that is always already present on college and university campuses" (2). Yet, Patton also raises many questions that we seek to engage in this chapter: How can women's centers unite, rather than divide, through their (historical) mission to support women on campus? How might women's centers be positioned to disrupt institutional "practices and policies that separate students and reproduce inequitable structures" (Patton 256)? Coupled with that objective, how might women's centers provide leadership for engaging "majority students in ways that make them recognize and understand the unearned privileges they solely possess" (Patton 256)? Further, in exercising their mission, how do Women's Centers acknowledge and respond to the "insidious ways that privilege operates to marginalize some in a movement that proposes to be liberatory" (Nicolazzo and Harris 5)?

Drawing upon critical, feminist, and intersectional theories, this chapter delves into these questions, using one public university's women's center as a case of feminist praxis to examine the institutional contexts surrounding women's centers. The authors (a faculty member and women's center administrator, respectively) advance four ideals for women's centers grappling with role, relevance, and identity in an age of inequity: (1) seeking unlikely alliances for disrupting our work, (2) being responsive to the complexities and intersectionality of identity, (3) embracing activism, and (4) increasing dialogue. First, however, we provide some descriptive context for the women's center that serves as the point of analysis and example in this chapter.

The Women's Center is fairly young, compared with women's centers nationally that were founded in large numbers in the 1970s and 1980s. The center was originally founded in 1996 as the Women's Resource Center, following a recommendation from a university stakeholder committee to the (now former) university president. It reported to Human Resources and its purpose – to contribute to a climate at the university that is responsive to and supportive of women's needs – largely served the needs of staff women on campus. Fifteen years later, as the scope of the center expanded and its work focused more on the needs of students, the center moved into the Division of Student Affairs and changed its name to the Women's Center. A few years later, following the hiring of a vice president for diversity, equity, and inclusion, and a reorganization of all identity-based centers under this new division, the Women's Center again changed its reporting structure. The scope of the work continues to expand, serving students, faculty, and staff. The center operates at a public university in a socio-politically conservative state – realities that can further constrain the already politically charged work of gender inequities.

Unlikely alliances disrupting our work

Nicolazzo and Harris ask, "how does a women's center go about enacting feminist values in its space as well as across campus?" (2). Women's centers often accomplish their work by building alliances and coalitions. Due to turf issues and scarce resources, these alliances can be challenging to develop and sustain even when the allies are "sister centers" such as women's studies, LGBTQ centers, multicultural programs, and advocacy centers for sexual and relationship violence. Exponentially harder is when unlikely alliances are sought – or stumbled upon. In these moments, our assumptions, vulnerabilities, and blind spots are revealed.

Recently, a request for collaboration brought to the surface implicit (or explicit) beliefs held by staff in the center about what constitutes, and who does, "our work." Two students, who serve as campus representatives for Victoria's Secret PINK, asked the Women's Center to collaborate. Seasoned Women's Center staff were paralyzingly perplexed about, and initially balked at, a possible partnership between the center and Victoria's Secret. Their reluctance was fueled by their awareness of Victoria's Secret, a powerful corporation selling the ideal of body autonomy and sexuality by capitalizing on the sexualization and objectification of young women. Yet, the eager, self-proclaimed (third wave) feminists were motivated and persisted in disrupting the (second wave) assumptions undergirding the Women's Center staff's beliefs about "our work."

At risk of missing an opportunity for collaboration, we needed to find a way to bridge the generational and ideological gap. Through the struggle to understand each other's perspectives and, in particular, for the Women's Center staff to gain insight into what brought these students to us with this idea, an important dialogue unfolded around sexuality and agency over women's bodies. As Zeilinger noted, third wave feminists

> envision a world in which we can make informed and healthy choices about our sex lives; a world where different attitudes about sex are as natural as the desire to have it. But more than anything else, third-wave feminists envision a world where we can accept and embrace our own sexual desires, needs and attitudes – and don't question or judge anybody else's.
>
> (74)

To return to Nicolazzo and Harris' question, we must wrestle with not only how to enact our core values but also question what our core values *are*. This can lead to other questions, including "what does the term 'feminism' really mean?" (Nicolazzo and Harris 2). We shouldn't sacrifice our core values for an opportunity to collaborate, but we should be prepared to question our assumptions about our work, and even what it means to be a feminist in the current moment.

The Women's Center was experiencing – on a micro scale – the same debates and controversies encountered at a macro level with the Women's March in January 2017. The organizers of the march boasted partnerships with over 100 organizations, from Planned Parenthood to AFL-CIO, from the League of Women Voters to Human Rights Watch. Yet, when the New Wave Feminists, an anti-abortion group, was given partnership status, controversy ensued, resulting in its removal from the partners' page (Green). We are not prescribing who should or should not be included in the work of women's centers; rather, we experienced and are acknowledging the need to anticipate and potentially partner with unlikely alliances in doing feminist work.

We offer a provocative example to illustrate this ideal: C.P. Ellis. He was a white American segregationist and active Klansman. Ellis, in a story memorialized by Studs Terkel (1980), was paired with Ann Atwater, a poor African American civil rights activist, to co-chair a committee charged with ensuring peaceful (court-ordered) school desegregation. As they delved into the issues of race and poverty, the two became the unlikeliest of friends, seeing in each other how, as poor people, they were both oppressed. Building such unlikely alliances is messy, challenging work, and such outcomes are perhaps rare, but we argue that is imperative to find and focus on what we have in common instead of succumbing to the rhetoric of difference which continues to divide. To do this, it is necessary to respect and value each other even in the face of difference. Otherwise, the dialogues (our fourth ideal) will end before they even begin.

Being responsive to the complexities and intersectionality of identity

In 1851, in Akron, Ohio, Sojourner Truth gave an extemporaneously delivered speech that came to be known as "Ain't I a Woman?" More than 150 years later, Laverne Cox, transgender advocate and actress, gave a speech on campus, also titled "Ain't I a Woman?" Ms. Cox used her platform to rebuke anti-trans* policies, practices, and behaviors, and to advocate for being recognized and appreciated for who you are even when your identities do not fit into or align with socially normative or culturally dominant traits or stereotypes. She also described the necessity of valuing the intersectionality of identities and experiences (Crenshaw 1242).

Laverne Cox's remarks were situated at the nexus of feminist debate regarding whether trans* persons uphold and reinforce gender binary, or challenge repressive gender norms (Goldberg). Her speech challenged all who attended – including the staff of the Women's Center – to wrestle with what we mean by "women"; with race, gender, sexuality; to further explore social class, national origin, and ability; and interrogate the challenges and possibilities in advocating for equity in higher education. For a women's center on a college campus to remain relevant it must understand that "supporting the success of women-identified students involves working with individuals of all gender identities to raise awareness about and contribute to cultural change related to gender issues more broadly" (Boyd et al. 390). Assuming a mono-dimensional conception of a particular dimension of identity (i.e., being a woman) is limited and limiting (Iverson, "Interlocking Oppressions"). Instead, women's centers must understand and work to combat the interrelated forces of oppression acting on intersecting dimensions of identity (Crenshaw 1244).

In this way, our work is far more than collaborating on programs or events with likely – or unlikely – allies; it is far more necessary – and complicated – to do work that reflects an understanding of the interaction of different forms of oppression and disadvantage. We offer two examples of ways we have attempted to do this work, but we also acknowledge that it is very challenging to do work that recognizes relational and structural dimensions of inequality (Iverson, "Interlocking Oppressions").

- In late February or early March, as Black History Month concludes and Women's History Month begins, the Women's Center in collaboration with the student multicultural center and the Department of Pan African Studies, delivers a program titled, "This is what a black feminist looks like!" This event showcases black, female-identified students, faculty, and staff who share their unique experiences and discuss how it is difficult to find space in the traditional celebrations of Black and Women's History months. They further contest "additive" notions of identity, instead illuminating in their stories the interlocking oppression and hierarchies individuals experience as members of multiple groups (Bowleg).

- As women's centers grapple with the complexity and intersectionality of identities, they too must consider how we are assessing our work. We, like many service providers and researchers (Garvey), are adding sexual identity as a demographic question, in addition to expanding beyond gender binary (e.g., male, female). Thus, it is critical that we consider how we request demographic information, and to enable students, faculty, and staff the opportunity to self-identify instead of trying to fit into the narrow framework generally provided. Best practices continue to evolve and women's centers must contribute to this evolution in their own practices.

- At a university where the international student population, especially from China and Saudi Arabia, has increased steadily in recent years, it was imperative that we consider what we are doing for the women who come from many countries and represent diverse cultural backgrounds (and are sometimes on campus as students, but also in the US as family members of students). In particular, the Women's Center, in collaboration with other offices on campus, hosted a "Women's Only Tea" with invitations in both Arabic and English; those invited were encouraged to bring two to three friends with them. Muslim women, in particular, found this was a "safe" place to remove their hijabs and open up in conversation. With the encouragement and support of campus colleagues working with visiting scholars and with a deeper understanding of the international student community, we have connected more than 30 women with us and with each other; and engaged conversations on topics ranging from current political climate to how to juggle motherhood in graduate school.

Embracing activism

Not all women's centers would necessarily identify as feminist organizations, and depending upon institutional context (i.e., being a public university), a center may encounter challenges in doing feminist activist work. Yet, in keeping with Baumgardner and Richards's call, we view activism as central to our work – "not as a choice between self and community, but as a link between them that creates a balance" (280).

Forms of activism vary. While dominant images are often of someone marching on Washington, chanting slogans, and holding picket signs high, courageous and empowering acts can range from the seemingly frivolous to the obviously political (Solomon).

> Once you embrace the idea that you can change your world, you begin looking for the tools with which to do so. Although activism can take forms ranging from picking up your phone and calling your congressperson to picketing

your phone company for paying women less, some work better than others. Clear intention, a realistic plan and an identifiable constituency distinguish political activism from random acts.

(Baumgardner and Richards 295)

From its origins 20 years ago as a resource center, the Women's Center has evolved into a site for organizing and taking action for social change. This goal, to be social justice oriented, can be fraught with challenges. This has been most evident in our efforts related to reproductive justice. Simply using that term – reproductive justice (versus health) – has at times been a form of activism, especially on a public university campus. One initiative (among many, including supporting students in forming a reproductive justice group) has been to provide menstruation products for free on campus. The Women's Center convened a collective of faculty, staff, students, and community members representing various perspectives; we researched other institutions, explored funding opportunities, and implemented awareness-raising programming and education. The center sought to recognize and address the global impact of menstruation on girls' access to education, consider the added stigma of menstruation based on religious or spiritual beliefs, attend to access to products for homeless and incarcerated women, and use neutral language (menstruation products vs feminine care products) to be inclusive of all identities who menstruate, with particular awareness of the unique challenges with access and safety for transgender individuals. Guided by the other ideals we discuss in this chapter, the Women's Center adopted multiple perspectives in the service of its goal:

- *Global*: A "Days for Girls" Team sought reusable menstruation products and educated on the impact this can have on girls' access to education.
- *Religious*: Staff brought together persons representing a variety of religions and spiritual identities to engage in conversation and tackle stigmas around menstruation.
- *Socio-economic status and access*: Staff sought to address the unique challenges and solutions for those who are homeless or incarcerated.
- *Inclusion of all genders*: The Women's Center ensured its language and the outcome would be inclusive of all who menstruate whether or not they identify as women.

Increasing dialogue

Achieving the preceding three ideals will not be possible without consistent *and difficult* dialogues. In an era when one can easily block (or "unfriend") those with views that are disagreeable, the need is even greater for courageous conversations in brave spaces (Arao and Clemens 135). The aim is not for us to achieve consensus; rather "We're open to . . . promoting a possibility of us all looking very very different from one another while we fight together in a new world" (Spade 15).

Resonating with the consciousness-raising (CR) groups, which blossomed in the late 1960s and early 1970s, such dialogues are an essential part of feminism: they are a mechanism by which to gain awareness and a means through which to organize, strategize, and act (Keating). We will not be able to impact real and lasting change until we bring all voices and identities to the table around the inequity of experiences, resources and representation for women.

To illustrate this ideal, we recall the realization by the Women's Center staff of the need to involve and mobilize men in its work on sexual assault. During a workshop around the topic of "consent" the importance of including men in the work presented itself – not just for the benefit of women but for the benefit of men as well. Jennifer Seibel's (2015) film, *The Mask You Live In*, highlights the narrow, shallow messages that men are receiving about "acting like a man" and being masculine. Although the importance of including men may be clear, the Women's Center was cautious about how to approach such dialogues. The center did not want to unwittingly re-inscribe "existing gender and sexual inequalities" and reify "the normative assumption that sexual violence means male violence against women" (Kamis and Iverson 86). Staff at the Women's Center initially sought male allies among the faculty and staff who understood their male privilege. As Gay (17) observes, it is essential to

> understand the extent of your privilege, the consequences of your privilege, and remain aware that people who are different from you move through and experience the world in ways you might never know anything about and use the opportunity to speak to issues and advocate for equity and inclusion for all.

These allies could model difficult dialogues as they ventured out of the "man box" (Kivel) and provide entry points for male students to engage in a class, as an active bystander, or by engaging in a discussion about masculinity after screening the film *The Mask You Live In*.

In dialogues, we must explore what identities and perspectives are missing. Intersecting with our previous ideals, this can mean unlikely alliances will form around complex identities and diversity of thought. Consider recent political realities as an example: in the 2016 presidential election, 94% of African American women voted for Hillary Clinton, 48% of white women voted for Clinton, while 52% voted for Donald Trump (CNN). More recently, in the controversial senate race in Alabama, 96% of African American voters supported Doug Jones, with nearly two-thirds of white women voting for Roy Moore (Bolton). To impact change, it is imperative that we figure out how to engage in messy and difficult dialogues across difference. For instance, we are now pondering how we will engage white women – in particular those who are *not* college educated – to raise consciousness in ways that not only increases awareness but also leads to action (Bickford and Reynolds). Campus–community partnerships, such as the Women's Center Food Pantry, already blur the artificial boundaries that define the spaces in which we do our work. The work of women's centers tends to be dominated by a focus on students (who are pursuing college degrees) and faculty (who hold advanced degrees), and perhaps staff (typically administrators who are also college educated); yet, other women on campus, who may not be college educated (e.g., housekeeping and dining staff), can also benefit from the services of women's centers. Thus, it is essential for women's centers to wrestle with how to reach and initiate dialogue with *all* campus constituents, and deepen our relationships and dialogues with off-campus partners. In this way, such dialogues may contribute to the internalization of a sense of responsibility to dismantle causes of inequality (Rosenberger) – or as @FrontRowMama asserted, "actions speak louder than your words."

Leila McCloud @FrontRowMama

Stop thanking Black women SHOW
US THE CHANGE WE VOTE FOR.
Your actions speak louder than your
words.
10:38 PM – 12 Dec 17

Baumgardner and Richards observe, "although feminists may have disparate values, we share the same goal of equality, and of supporting one another in our efforts to gain the power to make our own choices" (280).

Concluding thoughts and considerations

We believe women's centers continue to have relevance in these challenging times; however, it is essential that these centers understand and are responsive to the needs and concerns of their constituents. Broadly defining and even reconceptualizing those needs and concerns is critical to the evolving work. This work, however, is not without many challenges. In conclusion, we offer some considerations and closing thoughts for leading women's centers in an age of inequity.

Managing risk

The personnel who lead and manage women's centers are typically "at will" employees, meaning they occupy tenuous and unprotected positions. Thus, doing the political, activist-oriented, feminist work we describe comes with much risk, as the administrators (and legislators) to whom they report are not likely to support revolutionary change (Helms 307). Women's center personnel may be viewed as "being too controversial" and may face "possible negative repercussions" from supervisors (Zalaquett et al. 328). Solidarity-building and "cultivating an armor of allies" with those who may have protections (e.g., tenured faculty, off-campus community partners, and students) is a strategy to compensate for this risk (Iverson, "Multicultural Competence" 79).

Inviting disruption

If we believe, as Nicolazzo and Harris argue, that feminism is "a way of being in the world that seeks to address, dismantle, and rebuild spaces in a way that promotes increased life chances for marginalized communities" (6), then unlikely alliances should be sought as potential partners in the work of women's centers. Having our work and purpose disrupted and "troubled" is not an interruption or diversion to our purpose, but rather a welcome invitation for us to engage in "metadialogues" as a tool by which to reflect upon and reveal defenses and resistances, with the goal of thinking differently about our work (Case and Hemmings).

In sum, the current climate can be challenging and exhausting; however, we are in a space and time of incredible opportunity with a renewed sense of passion and purpose. The four ideals delineated earlier serve as a guide for women's centers as they grapple with their purpose and priorities, and in forging strategic (and unlikely) alliances. They guide us as "a way of being in the world that seeks to address, dismantle, and rebuild spaces in a way that promotes increases life chances for marginalized communities" (Nicolazzo and Harris 2). Through "togetherness" that consists of "honest and authentic communication, compassion and mutuality, celebration and a genuine desire to understand and work through the conditions of those within our community," women's centers can look to a bright future (Nicolazzo and Harris 2).

Given the current political environment, faculty and student on campus finding and raising their voices and demanding to be heard, along with a renewed sense of purpose, the Women's Center has an incredible opportunity to have impact change, make a difference and to create a legacy of inclusion and activism for those here and now and those to come.

Works cited

Arao, Brian, and Kristi Clemens. "From Safe Spaces to Brave Spaces." *The Art of Effective Facilitation: Reflections from Social Justice Educators*, edited by Lisa Landreman, Stylus Publishing, 2013, pp. 135–50.

Baumgardner, Jennifer, and Amy Richards. *Manifesta: Young Women, Feminism, and the Future*. Macmillan, 2010.

Bickford, Donna M., and Nedra Reynolds. "Activism and Service-learning: Reframing Volunteerism as Acts of Dissent." *Pedagogy*, vol. 2, no. 2, 2002, pp. 229–52.

Bolton, Kerra. "How Black Women Saved Alabama – and Democracy." CNN, 14 Dec. 2017, www.cnn.com/2017/12/13/opinions/black-women-voters-white-feminism-bolton-opinion/index.html.

Bowleg, Lisa. "When Black+ Lesbian+ Woman≠ Black Lesbian Woman: The Methodological Challenges of Qualitative and Quantitative Intersectionality Research." *Sex Roles*, vol. 59, nos. 5–6, 2008, pp. 312–25.

Boyd, C., et al. (2009). "The role of women student programs and services: CAS standards contextual statement." CAS professional standards for higher education (7th ed.), edited by L. A. Dean, Council for the Advancement of Standards in Higher Education, pp. 390–392.

Case, Kim A., and Annette Hemmings. "Distancing Strategies: White Women Preservice Teachers and Antiracist Curriculum." *Urban Education*, vol. 40, no. 6, 2005, pp. 606–26.

CNN. "Exit Polls: National President." *CNN*, 23 Nov. 2016, www.cnn.com/election/results/exit-polls.

Crenshaw, Kimberlé. "Mapping the Margins: Intersectionality, Identity Politics, and Violence against Women of Color." *Stanford Law Review*, 1991, pp. 1241–99.

Garvey, Jason C. "Considerations for Queer as a Sexual Identity Classification in Education Survey Research." *Journal of College Student Development*, vol. 58, no. 7, 2017, pp. 1113–18.

Gay, Roxane. *Bad Feminist Essays*. Harper Perennial, 2014.

Goldberg, Michelle. "What Is a Woman? The Dispute Between Radical Feminism and Transgenderism." *The New Yorker*, 4 Aug. 2014, www.newyorker.com/magazine/2014/08/04/woman-2.

Green, Emma. "The Pro-lifers Are Headed to the Women's March on Washington: Is There Room in the Movement for People Who Morally Object to Abortion?" *The Atlantic*, 16 Jan. 2017, www.theatlantic.com/politics/archive/2017/01/pro-lifers-womens-march/513104/

Helms, Janet E. "A Pragmatic View of Social Justice." *The Counseling Psychologist*, vol. 31, no. 3, 2003, pp. 305–13.

Iverson, Susan V. "Multicultural Competence for Doing Social Justice: Expanding Our Awareness, Knowledge, and Skills." *Journal of Critical Thought and Praxis*, vol. 1, no. 1, 2012, pp. 63–87.

Iverson, Susan V. "Interlocking Oppressions: An Intersectional Analysis of Diversity." *Intersectionality in Educational Research*, edited by. Dannielle J. Davis, Rachelle J. Brunn-Bevel, and James L. Olive, Stylus Publishing, 2015, pp. 211–30.

Kamis, Kristi, and Susan V. Iverson. "Powerful or Playful? A Critical Case Study of Walk a Mile in Her Shoes." *Preventing Sexual Violence on Campus: Challenging Traditional Approaches through Program Innovation*, edited by Sara C. Wooten and Roland W. Mitchell, Routledge, 2016, pp. 86–104.

Keating, Cricket. "Building Coalitional Consciousness." *NWSA Journal*, vol. 17, no. 2, 2005, pp. 86–103.

Kivel, Paul. *Boys Will Be Men: Raising Our Sons for Courage, Caring and Community*. New Society Publishers, 1999.

Nicolazzo, Z., and Crystal Harris. "This Is What a Feminist (Space) Looks Like: (Re) Conceptualizing Women's Centers as Feminist Spaces in Higher Education." *About Campus*, vol. 18, no. 6, 2014, pp. 2–9.

Patton, L.D. "Promoting Critical Conversations about Identity Centers." *Contested Issues in Student Affairs: Diverse Perspectives and Respectful Dialogue*, edited by Peter M. Magolda and Marcia Baxter Magolda, Stylus Publishing, 2011, pp. 255–60.

Renn, Kristen A. "Identity Centers: An Idea Whose Time Has Come . . . and Gone?" *Contested Issues in Student Affairs: Diverse Perspectives and Respectful Dialogue*, edited by Peter M. Magolda and Marcia Baxter Magolda, Stylus Publishing, 2011, pp. 244–54.

Rosenberger, Cynthia. "Beyond Empathy: Developing Critical Consciousness through Service Learning." *Integrating Service Learning and Multicultural Education in Colleges and Universities*, edited by Carolyn R. O'Grady, Lawrence Erlbaum Associates, 2000, pp. 23–43.

Solomon, Rivka (Ed.). *That Takes Ovaries: Bold Females and Their Brazen Acts*. Three Rivers Press, 2002.

Spade, Dean. "Dress to Kill, Fight to Win." *LTTR*, vol. 1, 2002, p. 15.

Terkel, S., and C.P. Ellis. "Why I Quit the Klan." *American Dreams: Lost and Found*. New P, 1980.

Zalaquett, Carlos P., et al. "Multicultural and Social Justice Training for Counselor Education Programs and Colleges of Education: Rewards and Challenges." *Journal of Counseling & Development*, vol. 86, no. 3, 2008, pp. 323–9.

Zeilinger, Julie. *A Little F'd Up: Why Feminism Is Not a Dirty Word*. Seal P, 2012.

11 "Blue" language in a red state

Inclusive sexuality education in a conservative climate

Lysa Salsbury, Julia Keleher, and Erin Chapman

Background

Newly minted high school graduates, at the twilight of adolescence and dawn of young adulthood, often set off for college and university campuses to enter worlds for which they are ill-prepared. Older adults – their parents, university administrators, faculty, staff – might assume these young people are equipped with the knowledge, skills, and confidence to lead healthy sexual and relational lives. Unfortunately, due to the insufficient and potentially detrimental nature of K-12 sexuality education in parts of the country, many young people arrive on campus with vast gaps in their understanding of sexuality and sexual health. Traditional sexuality education on US college campuses often focuses on issues of personal safety and is largely remedial in nature; due to federally funded abstinence-only curricula in elementary and secondary schools based largely in a heterosexist paradigm (Kennedy and Covell 151), institutions of higher education find it necessary to make up for education that should have occurred prior to students' arrival (Bruess and Schroeder 209). This programming often inadequately addresses the broad sexuality and relationship-oriented questions, curiosities, and concerns of today's college students. Without standardized guidelines for sexual health programming, colleges and universities take a variety of different avenues to provide education, services, and outreach.

Sexuality education in K-12 systems varies tremendously from state to state and classroom to classroom – the federal government does not provide specific curriculum guidelines nor have a direct role in local decisions about sexuality education (SIECUS, *Sexuality*). States and communities have the final say regarding any formal sexuality education that may or may not happen in individual communities, and local school districts cannot go against state mandates. Any sexuality education program that occurs in Idaho's public schools must keep the following in mind: programs should give youth "the scientific, psychological information for understanding sex and its relation to the miracle of life." They must also include "knowledge of the power of the sex drive and the necessity of controlling that drive by self-discipline" ("Section 33-1608-Idaho State Legislature"). If their experience with sex ed as a youth was limited or nonexistent, college students may feel caught in a double bind: feeling as though they *should* know, coupled with the sense of embarrassment that they *don't* know.

In addition to being predominately white (73.8%), approximately two-thirds of University of Idaho students report in-state residency (University of Idaho Institutional Effectiveness & Accreditation). This suggests that a large number of students attending the University of Idaho have matriculated through a public K-12 school system in which abstinence-only or abstinence-based sexuality education was taught, if at all. According to the *State Profiles 2017* compiled by the Sexuality Information and Educator Council of the United States (SIECUS), approximately 97% of Idaho secondary schools teach adolescents "about the benefits of being sexually abstinent in any of grades 9, 10, 11, or 12" (5). Additionally, less than one-quarter (24.6%) of Idaho secondary schools provide students with "curricula or supplementary materials that included HIV, STD, or pregnancy prevention relevant to LGBTQ youth" (6). The intent behind creating an inclusive, sex-positive sexuality education and sexual health awareness program was to "fill in the gaps" for University of Idaho students, and also to encourage an atmosphere of openness, with the goal of facilitating changes in both perceived and actual campus climate for all identities; promoting acceptance of diverse experiences of sex and sexuality, specifically, inclusion of LGBTQ+ issues; and encouraging students to cultivate their own knowledge base.

Program origins

Since 2006, Trojan condoms has released its Sexual Health Report Card, an annual ranking of sexual health resources available to students at US colleges and universities. The data is collected via a survey of student health center representatives, with follow-up research on services provided across campus. Institutions are graded on services across various categories, which include: the quality of sexual health information and resources on their website; availability of contraceptives; availability of (free) condoms; HIV/STI testing; outreach programs and peer sexual health education; sexual assault prevention programs, resources, and services; website usability and quality; hours of operation; and ease of appointment scheduling. In 2010, the University of Idaho ranked 140th out of 140 institutions surveyed. This was concerning to university health educators who work tirelessly to ensure access to comprehensive services, education, and health care options for students. Campus efforts, while multiple and varied, were somewhat siloed and underpromoted.

Following the widely publicized results of the survey, the university convened a Sexual Health Education Task Force to build a collaborative institutional effort to streamline sexual health initiatives. The task force was composed of campus and community constituents engaged in education around sex and sexuality, violence prevention, gender advocacy, and health care, including staff representing the Student Health Center, the Women's Center, the Violence Prevention Programs office, a faculty member in biological sciences, a professor of human development and family studies, Planned Parenthood of Greater Washington and North Idaho, and Alternatives to Violence of the Palouse (ATVP), the local victim services agency.

The task force determined several courses of action, one of which was to hire a student health education coordinator to centralize and facilitate all aspects of health education on campus. The university's website was quickly updated to include comprehensive information on sexual health. In discussing opportunities for maximum educational impact, the task force prioritized the development of a broad, inclusive, discussion-based program to provide education on sexuality and relationship issues. A monthly conversation series was created, where topics of interest could be explored by students. Thus emerged *The Vagina Dialogues: Talking about Reproductive Health and Wellbeing.* The original title of the program was suggested by an influential male faculty member in biological sciences who had offered to present the first discussion in the series, and whose area of research expertise is vaginal microorganisms. His vision for the program was to focus on women's biological health. Other task force members had strong misgivings about the narrow focus that this title implied; it was not consistent with the intended audience, but other ideas were lacking, and the team was under a tight timeline for launching the program. In an effort to be more inclusive than the title implied, the program was billed as "a new campus forum to promote open discussion around issues of sexuality, reproductive health, birth control, social pressures, and sexual practices and behaviors." The series was intended "to create and support honest, respectful interpersonal dialogue on touchy topics in a space where everyone can feel safe to ask questions and speak their mind." The forum was initially held in the middle of the day in a conference meeting space in a central area of campus. Snacks were provided to incentivize attendance. The first program on vaginal health was not well attended, and it was immediately apparent that an academic approach was not in line with the program's goals. The next three programs featured introductory presentations on (1) demystifying annual exams, (2) social pressures and sexual behaviors, and (3) human sexuality and perceptions of self. The programming team developed learning outcomes for *The Dialogues* based on position statements issued by SIECUS, the Future of Sex Education Initiative (FoSE), and the 2001 Surgeon General's Call to Action to Promote Sexual Health and Responsible Sexual Behavior. The learning outcomes for *The Dialogues* were:

1   Demonstrate an understanding and appreciation of the diversity of sexual health "norms," both physiological and social; understand that "normal" is unique to each person.
2   Develop the personal security, courage, and skills needed to challenge social taboos about sexuality-related issues for personal health and well-being.

The programming team also developed facilitation guidelines for presenters, intended to create an optimal environment to ensure maximum comfort and candid sharing of experiences.

The Vagina Dialogues ran for a year, and was sparsely attended. Evaluation feedback indicated that attendees benefited from the discussions, and many returned every month, but there was a lack of appeal to the general student population. After reviewing evaluation forms, small but important changes were made to the promotion and format of the program:

1   The program was moved to a smaller, more intimate setting on the edge of campus and switched to evenings.
2   In an effort to "de-medicalize" the program and increase appeal, the name was changed to *Got Sex?* and the promotional material was redesigned with less text and more enticing imagery.
3   Curiosity-inviting topic titles were developed, for example:

   a   *Fairy Dust and Unicorns: Contraception as Magical Thinking* (a program on birth control methods)
   b   *Sex for the First Time Ever/Again* (exploring the concept of virginity)
   c   *Do Your _____ Hang Low, Do They Wobble To and Fro?* (about genital aesthetics)

4   A partnership was fostered with the LGBTQA Office to ensure that topics were inclusive of multiple identities, sexualities, and orientations.
5   Program topics proposed by students were offered, such as masturbation, pornography, BDSM (Bondage and Discipline, Dominance and Submission, Sadism and Masochism), non-monogamy, sexual fantasies, and foreplay.
6   Question cards were provided (later replaced by the online polling tool, Poll Everywhere) so attendees could ask questions anonymously.
7   ATVP had a trained advocate present at each program to address questions related to assault, and provide resources to survivors.

These changes in the format and structure of the program eventually resulted in at-capacity crowds almost every month. Sample comments from students on evaluation forms included:

> Demystifying female sexuality and normalizing women's sexual needs is so important. That just was a really positive aspect of the whole discussion. De-shaming sex while providing clear ideas about how to honestly engage in happy sexual relationships was excellent.
>
> Establishing the norms and expectations for the discussion is part of what makes it so successful. It is done in such a sincere way that people seem to trust that it really is a safe place to talk openly.
>
> I'M NOT AFRAID TO ASK QUESTIONS!! I think the most important thing was that it was personally, validation for me, in that I AM at the age where it's ok to talk about this. I AM at the age where I can talk about it like an adult, can correspond with other adults about it. I was treated like an adult while I was there, it was a certain level of respect that I really appreciated.

Evaluations clearly showed that changes made to the program from its inception were significant in creating a more student-centered environment. As the program evolved, the planning team was intentional in adjusting the format and content in response to students' needs.

Feminist pedagogy

In her article on the role of campus-based women's centers, Zaytoun Byrne emphasizes the importance of applying principles of feminist pedagogy to learning experiences that take place outside of a traditional classroom setting (48). The programming team did not consciously set out to use feminist pedagogy as a way to develop and deliver the program; however, it was a natural fit. In keeping with the characteristics of feminist pedagogy, the goals of *Got Sex?* were to facilitate student empowerment, create community, give voice to different perspectives and identities, and challenge traditional learning ideals.

Student empowerment

Honoring the concept that students and teachers are partners in the learning experience and in the construction of knowledge (Barkley et al. 9), *Got Sex?* was structured as a discussion-based program, while acknowledging the power dynamics inherent within traditional classroom structures (Sarroub and Quadros 252). *Got Sex?* intentionally sought to decenter the presenter as the source of knowledge: facilitators invited to introduce topics were not presented as "experts," but as conversation guides. Speakers were selected for their ability to ensure open and inclusive coverage of content, and were given detailed guidelines on inclusive facilitation techniques. Formal presentations with complex academic jargon were discouraged. Students were invited to ask questions and engage in open discussion throughout the duration of the program, and efforts were made to create a safe and comfortable space where students felt empowered to share their personal narratives.

Creating community

Following instances of disruption and disrespect during the first few programs, it became apparent how critical it was to create community among participants. Thus, community agreements were developed to ensure the safety and inclusion of all attendees. Feminist value systems emphasize the importance of living and working in solidarity with one another (hooks 43), and the significance of establishing common goals and holding space for the intentional building of community by ensuring that everyone has a chance to express their views, share their stories, and listen patiently and respectfully to others (Valle-Ruiz et al.).

Giving voice to different perspectives and identities

One of the greatest challenges to running a program with a broad audience and diverse perspectives, values, and beliefs was encouraging participants to speak their truth while acknowledging and validating the differences between people's lived experiences. Clearly stating at the outset and providing periodic reminders of the community agreements was key to providing participants the opportunity to express their thoughts and feelings without fear of being ridiculed, talked over, or dismissed. It also allowed for facilitators to explicitly acknowledge and honor the voices of those who are typically silenced, marginalized, or absent (Valle-Ruiz et al.).

Challenging traditional learning ideals

A warm, intimate space and "off the beaten path" location creates a level of comfort for students that is difficult to achieve in traditional classroom settings, and is integral in encouraging students to share authentically of themselves within the learning space. Feminist pedagogy recognizes that personal experiences, values, and beliefs and their corresponding emotions play an important role in the creation of knowledge (Valle-Ruiz et al.) and as such, the creation of a mindful space conducive to frankness of conversation is critical to achieve intended program outcomes.

Legal repercussions in a rural, conservative state

For institutions located in socially conservative states, educational statutes and policies provide little opportunity for K-12 educators to provide instruction on sexual health, and many high school students subsequently enter higher education with limited knowledge of these topics. While public universities are not subject to the same content limitations, restrictive state educational policies create increased scrutiny of sexual health education provided on campus.

Some state laws and statutes also contribute to a socially conservative and sexphobic climate. For example, in Idaho, fornication between adult heterosexual individuals and adultery are still punishable by imprisonment and fines (Section 18-6601 and Section 18-6603-Idaho State Legislature). While these statutes are rarely enforced, they are historical testaments to the conservative influence of state social politics, and the fear and mistrust of open and inclusive sexuality.

Pushback

Attitudes towards sex education in conservative states are often anti-inclusive, creating potential pushback from campus and community constituents regarding the provision of comprehensive and inclusive sex and relationship education. Due to the increased risk of negative reactions, the development of more "risqué" program topics should proceed with caution. With *Got Sex?*, topics related to polyamory, BDSM sexuality, and anal sex were sometimes misinterpreted by external audiences as influential propaganda, rather than educational topics. Prior to the *Got Sex?* program on BDSM, the office of the president received a complaint alleging that the university was encouraging students to engage in "deviant" sexual practices. Proactive measures to handle potential objections to program content and marketing might include intentionality around drafting the program title and description to reflect its educational mission, and being mindful to omit any language that might be perceived as "instructional."

"Hot button" topics like abstinence, queer sexuality, and other potentially polarizing issues have increased potential to create a disruptive and hostile space for participants who already feel uncomfortable talking about sex and sexuality. Purposeful development of a learning environment that maximizes opportunities for students to express multiple points of view is critical to ensuring a safe and diverse learning experience.

Physical space

Locations for programs can be very unique and specific to individual institutions and programming efforts. There are many variables to consider when trying to create a safe and inclusive space for discussion of these issues. *Got Sex?* was held in the University of Idaho's Women's Center's lounge. While this type of space is warm and welcoming for many students, choosing a small, intimate location can have both positive and negative repercussions. At the University of Idaho, the location and the layout of the lounge created difficulties for accessibility and access to seating. Participation varied from program to program, based on the popularity of the topic and accessibility of the subject matter. The Women's Center's lounge often had beyond-capacity crowds for the space, which created a cramped environment that generated challenges for temperature control and means of egress.

Holding programs in public meeting spaces or classrooms can often feel stark and sterile, discouraging attendance and open discussion. Casual "living room" style spaces allow participants to relax and ask questions more freely. The University of Idaho Women's Center is located in a remote area of campus with limited foot traffic, which allowed for an atmosphere of privacy that helped participants feel safe.

The program's location in the Women's Center did create one notable complication – organizers were concerned that transmasculine and male-identified students would be discouraged from attending a program in a gendered space. In thinking about how to convey the space as open to all gender identities, the *Got Sex?* planning team chose to list only the building and room number on promotional material, which helped to market the space as open to individuals of all gender identities.

Varying levels of knowledge and experience

Selecting a variety of topics that appeal to a broad audience can be challenging. Taking into consideration that audience members will have vast ranges of experience in sexuality and sexual health, it can be difficult to plan topics that provide a sufficiently wide variety of information to reach the greatest number of students. The *Got Sex?* planning team addressed this challenge by offering introductory-level topics at the beginning of the semester, providing basic information on anatomy, reproduction, relationships, and STI protection. As the semester progresses, topics may become more complex and esoteric, including discussions on fetishes, and kink or other communities. Attendance will likely fluctuate, depending on the topic. For example, *Got Sex?* conversations about anal sex, BDSM, or sex toys drew near-capacity crowds. Programs focused on more specialized topics, such as sex for survivors of interpersonal violence, or polyamory, generally drew smaller crowds. While a smaller audience can lead to intimate discussions, program attendance may decline due to specialized content alienating students seeking more introductory material.

Getting the information to students

Another ongoing challenge in the planning and implementation of this type of program is providing a learning environment that is conversational in nature, while ensuring fidelity to the program's mission, goals, and learning outcomes. The *Got Sex?* planning team asked facilitators to refrain from giving formal presentations, limiting use of classroom technology in an attempt to establish an atmosphere of conversation. Students may not connect with the material if the delivery of content is excessively formal, or if they feel "put on the spot" to answer questions. This can result in tension and discomfort, which may hinder students' learning, decreasing the program's effectiveness. Feedback from students via post-program evaluations allows for continual adjustment of presenter guidelines.

Reaching vulnerable populations

An important goal for a successful college sexual health program is to be inclusive of as many identities as possible. Sexual health education by default frequently only includes topics that are presented within a heteronormative framework and focused primarily on Western, white identities (McNeill 839). Programs on birth control and contraceptives often provide a heteronormative view of sexual health education, and may alienate LGBTQA+ participants. Facilitators should be discouraged from using language that promotes the gender binary, and avoid assumptions that students are in or are seeking monogamous relationships. Providing presenters with guidelines for using inclusive language can help to reduce heterosexist and cissexist attitudes. For example, the use of language like, "people with a vagina or penis" to describe physical bodies, rather than "man" or "woman," should be encouraged. Discussion of romantic or sexual partners should not be limited to monogamous experiences, and program content should make every effort to acknowledge the complexities of gender identity and sexuality.

Programs should strive to recognize the intersections of race, ethnicity, and culture in participants' comprehension and acceptance of sexual health information. In order to provide inclusive learning environments for multicultural student communities, efforts should be made to avoid cultural and racial bias. Focusing on the needs of the racial majority student population at the University of Idaho often made students of color who attended the programs feel uncomfortable or disconnected from the material, and negatively impacted the number of multicultural students who attended subsequent programs.

Conclusion

Got Sex? was successful in meeting the needs of some students for basic sexual health education and more complex sexuality-related topics; however, a number of student populations required more relevant and responsive programming, challenging heterocentric norms and addressing cultural barriers to open and inclusive discussion of sexuality and relationships. In response, the planning team developed a number of sexual health education forums for specific populations. Recently, the planning team piloted *Lo Que Tú Mamá No Te Dijo* (What Your Mother Never Told You) in partnership with the Office of Multicultural Affairs, aimed at providing culturally relevant information around sex and sexuality for Latinx students. Another program, *Queering Sex Ed*, focusing on queer sexuality, was revived in partnership with the LGBTQA Office. Finally, a program for Native American students, *What Your Aunties Never Told You*, was launched. These programs, presented by members of each community, have been well received and well attended. Meanwhile, in order to broaden its appeal and increase attendance, *Got Sex?* has been renamed *Sex in the Dark*, and now incorporates quizzes, games, prizes – and glow sticks. The program is run by the university's health education office, in a further effort to de-stigmatize sex education and promote it as another area of overall health and well-being, along with stress, nutrition, drug and alcohol awareness, and sleep hygiene. It is held in a more neutral location, the basement common room of the main residence hall on campus.

The most important lesson learned by the *Got Sex?* planning team is that programming must continually evolve to meet the needs of students. As topics around sex and sexuality become less taboo and students feel more comfortable seeking information, university educators must be prepared to address the broad range of sexual experiences and identities that students present.

Works cited

Barkley, Elizabeth F., et al. *Collaborative Learning Techniques: A Handbook for College Faculty*. Hoboken, NJ: Jossey-Bass, 2004.

Bruess, Clint E., and Elizabeth Schroeder. *Sexuality Education: Theory and Practice*. 6th ed. Burlington, MA: Jones and Bartlett, 2014.

Fall 2016 University Population by Race/Ethnicity. U Idaho Institutional Effectiveness & Accreditation, Fall 2016.

hooks, bell. *Feminist Theory: From Margin to Center.* 1984. New York: Routledge, 2015.

Kennedy, Charlene, and Katherine Covell. "Violating the Rights of the Child through Inadequate Sexual Health Education." *The International Journal of Children's Rights,* vol. 17, no. 1, 2009, pp. 143–54.

McNeill, Tanya. "Sex Education and the Promotion of Heteronormativity." *Sexualities,* vol. 16, no. 7, 2013, pp. 826–46.

Sarroub, Loukia K., and Sabrina Quadros. "Critical Pedagogy in Classroom Discourse." *The Routledge Handbook of Educational Linguistics,* Routledge, 2015, pp. 252–60. Digital Commons @ University of Nebraska – Lincoln. Accessed 6 June 2017.

"Section 18-6601- Idaho State Legislature." *Idaho Statutes,* https://legislature.idaho.gov/statutesrules/idstat/Title18/T18CH66/SECT18-6601/. Accessed 17 Oct. 2017.

"Section 18-6603- Idaho State Legislature." *Idaho Statutes,* https://legislature.idaho.gov/statutesrules/idstat/title18/t18ch66/sect18-6603/. Accessed 17 Oct. 2017.

"Section 33-1608-Idaho State Legislature." *Idaho Statutes,* https://legislature.idaho.gov/statutesrules/idstat/Title33/T33CH16/SECT33-1608/. Accessed 17 Oct. 2017.

"Sexuality Information and Education Council of the United States (SIECUS)." *Sexuality Education Q & A,* http://siecus.org/index.cfm?fuseaction=page.viewpage&pageid=521&grandparentID=477&parentID=514. Accessed 15 Nov. 2017.

"Sexuality Information and Education Council of the United States (SIECUS)." *State Profiles Fiscal Year 2017: Idaho,* http://siecus.org/index.cfm?fuseaction=page.viewPage&pageID=1681&nodeID=1. Accessed 20 Nov. 2017.

Valle-Ruiz, Lis, et al. *A Guide to Feminist Pedagogy.* Vanderbilt U Center for Teaching, Mar. 2015, https://my.vanderbilt.edu/femped/. Accessed 6 June 2017.

Zaytoun Byrne, Kelli. "The Roles of Campus-Based Women's Centers." *Feminist Teacher,* vol. 13, no. 1, 2000, pp. 48–60.

12 Ohio women's centers' reflections on evaluation and assessment: revisited

Nicole Carter, Lisa Rismiller, Amy J. Howton, Susanne B. Dietzel, and Kimberly A. Fulbright

Introduction

In March 2010, the Ohio Women's Centers Committee published its first issue brief (Ohio Women's Centers: Statement of Philosophy) describing the process of drafting our first collective statement of philosophy and the statement itself (Vlasnik 2–4). In 2011, at our annual retreat in July, the committee identified other topics of interest to address in subsequent issue briefs (Howton et al. 1). After some discussion, it was determined that the next logical topic to consider, following the statement of philosophy, would be evaluation: its role in our work and issues related to its accomplishment. In 2016, the committee discussed the possibility of updating our issue briefs through this publication opportunity with the permission of some of the earlier authors of the original publication. Therefore, this piece continues the conversation concerning evaluation and assessment.

In 2011, three themes emerged among Ohio women's centers that are still relevant today: (1) women's centers increasingly appreciate the need and value of doing meaningful evaluation, (2) women's centers experience a discrepancy between the institutional expectations of what constitutes evaluation and our own "best practice" of what feminist evaluation might mean, and (3) women's centers struggle to develop and implement evaluation that accurately captures the nature of our work. While these issues are shared among many Ohio women's centers, they are certainly not unique to our state. In a 2004 study of 75 United States, campus-based women's centers, many directors expressed concerns about a climate of budget cuts and the resulting scarcity of resources and growing sentiments that women's centers are no longer needed or relevant to students' lives (Kasper 189). Despite these concerns, it has been noted that women's centers continue to provide spaces for feminist leadership, femtorship, hands on experience, and alternative opportunities for knowledge production and dissemination. Evaluation and assessment can aid in maintaining the existence of women's centers in a climate bombarded by budgetary limitations and cuts and compliance-heavy environments.

While many women's centers share common issues related to evaluation, these issues are often experienced and responded to differently due to the diversity among us. The very process of co-authoring this brief underscored where these commonalities and differences intersect. Together, we questioned the terms evaluation and assessment, deliberated on our audience, and contemplated "our" message. In doing so, we experienced evaluation as deeply political and hope we effectively complicate the issue of evaluation and begin a sustained dialogue on how to make meaning of women's centers' work.

Traditional forms of evaluation

The resulting analysis can assist us in doing various things. First, it will help to quantify our centers' impact on our varying institutions. Specifically, we can see a numerical representation of what our institutions have gained. Second, it can potentially assist in understanding and providing information to various institutional administrators about the cost versus benefits of our centers. This, therefore, provides justification for continuing certain programs and initiatives. Third, through assessment we can learn about and pinpoint the structural and resource-based issues. Fourth, it ensures that the centers' missions are relevant to their intended constituents and in alignment with the larger institutional goals. Fifth, it can help in establishing a strategic direction for our centers' future. This can be done through highlighting critical issues that need to be addressed and resolved by creating or maintaining initiatives that meet the needs of the campus community. Finally, evaluation can assist in engaging other students, faculty, and staff in the centers' work by discovering new and innovative ways that will invite them to our centers. Traditional evaluations are said to specifically be connected to the need for accountability and costs due to increased scrutiny (Prince et al. 2).

If the evaluation is truly comprehensive, meaning it not only captures the centers' work but also the impact they have on constituents and the institution as a whole, we can use the results to develop future plans aligned with both the centers' missions and the missions and strategic plans of the institutions within which they are situated. These could include objectives such as advocacy for additional staff and/or resources, identification of specific goals for fundraising and grant writing, or illustration of where the bulk of our centers' impact is focused. Having both short- and long-term foci can result in strategic plans that include specific goals, objectives, and outcome measures that will ensure that our centers "stay the course" and continue to have a positive impact on their communities.

The politics of evaluation

Tensions continue to exist regarding evaluation in the interdisciplinary field of women's studies and beyond (Haylock and Miller 65). While evaluation is necessary due to internal usefulness and external mandates, the evaluation of student learning in women's studies classrooms also present unique challenges connected to conflicting institutional and organizational needs and ideologies. According to Levin, typical institutional-driven methods of evaluation are generally not aligned with feminist values, nor capable of fully capturing the scope and impact of our work. In feminist evaluation practices, other factors are at play such as the specific need to create change through evaluation and the recognition that evaluation is not objective – instead it is a political act (Haylock and Miller 65). Campus-based women's centers experience the same tensions.

Other concerns are that most evaluation tools and assessment methods are, by design gendered or biased, as are the ways in which assessment results are used. In the field of women's studies, as well as in other fields of study, it is widely documented that women instructors are evaluated differently from instructors who are men; evaluative tools and the results they produce are gendered; and women's studies courses, because of their challenging content and feminist pedagogy, are evaluated more negatively than many other courses (Levin 1). A similar dynamic applies to programs that are sponsored by women's centers. Some of our programs are designed to challenge the status quo and therefore not always appreciated or valued by students, which can be seen by the small number of attendees at women's center programs at times. Immediate feedback from programs can often be negative because these programs are designed to challenge the thinking and actions that exist on many of our campuses and in the larger society (Davis). In addition, the meaning of our programs is difficult to assess longitudinally for various reasons, such as programs taking place only one time or students graduating.

Consider the larger context in which these increasing institutional demands for evaluation are instituted – namely, the increasing corporatization of higher education. Assessment and evaluation trends are part of a larger transformation of higher education that has been going on since the 1970s and coincides with when women began to enroll in numbers than larger than men. (Many of the members in the southwest Ohio consortium that contributed to this piece have student bodies where women outnumber men in significant numbers.) As a result, some argue that trends toward assessment reflect a re-masculinization of higher education as fears over the feminization of higher education are expressed by pundits and state legislators (Laube et al. 92; Leathwood and Read 13). Therefore, assessments that are primarily numerically based and that minimize initiatives, programs, and practices to a numerical value are prevalent in institutions of higher education. In addition, as it relates to women's centers, there are budgetary pressures that many of our centers are facing as well as political questioning of the value of women's centers (Nicolazzo and Harris 2).

Development and implementation of feminist evaluation

Understanding the politics of evaluation is critical for us to develop and employ strategic evaluation methods that are meaningful – to us, to our institutions, and to our constituents. Many questions remain for women's centers in terms of evaluation: How exactly, in the short term, do we measure the institutional transformation and climate change with which many of our centers are charged? How do we assess the increased awareness and understanding of women's issues among the student body? How do we measure the success, for example, of a poster campaign on sexual assault prevention or a Women's History Month program? We can count the number of posters printed or program attendees, but these outputs do not reflect the cumulative impact of our work. Moreover, the personal nature of much of what we do such as advocacy or providing resources is difficult to translate into numbers. Furthermore, and perhaps most importantly, how do we prioritize evaluation with steadfastly dwindling resources and increasing constituent demand for our services? The challenges to the existence of women's centers and the increased focus on evaluation as a mechanism to justify their continuation makes feminist evaluation necessary.

Despite the challenges in evaluating our work, Ohio women's centers continue to consider ways in which we might do this. Traditionally, for an evaluation to accurately capture both the scope and impact of a women's center it should include both quantitative (e.g., usage data, numbers of and reactions to programmatic efforts, budget histories, etc.) and qualitative (e.g., constituent surveys, results of focus groups or interviews, input from any advisory bodies, etc.) data. Benchmarking the center's efforts and achievements against other campus-based women's centers can also be very useful and is made possible by an active communication network and strong sense of shared mission and collaborative spirit among women's center staff at hundreds of US colleges and universities. Assessment using other "external" measures, including the Council for the Advancement of Standards in Higher Education (CAS) standards, can also enrich a formal evaluation (Council for the Advancement of Standards in Higher Education).

Most Ohio women's centers employ some or all the above-mentioned evaluative measures. The challenge is going beyond – employing evaluation as a feminist strategy to gauge how well we are doing what we say we do. Do we really develop students as leaders? Do we increase students' critical thinking? Do we support students in ways we hope to support them? To think about evaluation in this way calls for a centering of evaluation in our work. Rather than thinking about evaluation as an add-on, something to be done at the completion of a project, reframing evaluation as process-oriented can be transformative and feminist by design.

In 1992, Shapiro wrote about feminist evaluation, proposing its practice in classrooms and beyond. Others have built upon this since then as well (Haylock and Miller 65; Podems 3). Feminist evaluation values advocacy for marginalized peoples as opposed to centering the needs of those in power. Feminist evaluation is participatory, meaning that those who are the subject of the research are also part of the research process and design. Feminist evaluation is subjective as it is shaped by institutional culture as well as the evaluator's subjective self (Podems 3). Therefore, any assessment or evaluation must attend to the context and the possible positionalities of the evaluator. Feminist evaluation is connected to feminist activist theories and pedagogies that focus on collaboration and collectivity; therefore, welcoming the voices of the "whole learner, the whole community, the whole program" (Shapiro 4). Likewise, it is shaped by engaged relationships that foster learning. Feminist evaluation also considers women's ways of knowing or women's ways of naming and attaching meaning to experiences that are different that patriarchal notions of knowledge construction. Therefore, feminist evaluation is written with these frameworks in mind. Feminist assessment also allows for the qualitative definitions and explanations from those creating the assessment as well as those being assessed.

In 2011, our collective provided the example of University of Cincinnati Women's Center as an exemplar of feminist evaluation. It was discovered that the center shifted its focus to year-long student developmental programs rather than one-time programs, and new opportunities for different evaluative methodologies emerged. The focus of their evaluations shifted from a product-centered approach to a process-focused, student-centered, subjective, valued-laden, and engaged process. As an example, approximately ten students a year committed to the Women's Center's Reclaim Peer Advocate Program to respond to the 24-hour helpline and provide support services to students victimized by sexual and gender-based violence. Rather than having an evaluative outcome of the program be a certain number of direct service experiences for each advocate, the focus of the program evaluation evolved as developmental assessments of the advocates themselves: how they develop as leaders and activists loosely based on selected Council for the Advancement of Standards in Higher Education (CAS) standards. Various evaluative tools such as journal writing, art projects, and Photovoice8 have been integrated throughout the year-long experience to explore the advocates' understanding of the role their program involvement plays in their own self-development. The evaluation culminates at the end of the year as the advocates present to their peers and the incoming advocates for the following year a creative representation of what the program has meant to them. It is an important opportunity to hear what the program has meant to students through a creative project. The process of participants sharing their final project with their peers can be an important aspect of feminist evaluation, with emphasis on constructing knowledge through relationships and through participatory evaluation. By exploring and claiming various methodologies, custom evaluation can be applied to programs in women's centers.

From 2014 to 2015, the University of Cincinnati Women's Center did another comprehensive program evaluation to assess programming, services, strengths, and weaknesses. The evaluation process was led by two external reviewers but featured a committee of Women's Center personnel from the University of Cincinnati as well as other constituents from the campus community. Listening sessions and interviews were completed with faculty, administrators, student leaders, and center staff. The information from the evaluation was shared at regional and national conferences by those who took part in the project.

Conclusion

As noted before, many questions remain for women's centers regarding evaluation. One fact is clear: finding meaningful ways to evaluate our work is critical for our survival. Because we are each unique, evaluation will likely (and should) look differently on each of our campuses. Promising evaluation practices include ways to integrate the evaluation into our current work rather than "adding on" assessment tools. Centering evaluation in our work will help us reframe how we make meaning of our work and how we enact our feminist missions. Evaluation in a women's center should reflect feminist values and help to promote the goals and mission of the center. Creating these opportunities for ourselves not only promises transformation for our organizations but for our institutions as we lead the way to new ways of thinking and practicing evaluation.

Works cited

Council for the Advancement of Standards in Higher Education. "Women Student Programs and Services: CAS Standards and Guidelines." *CAS Professional Standards for Higher Education.* 8th ed., edited by D.I. Mitsifer. Washington, DC: Author, 2012, pp. 513–21.

Davis, B. G. "Demystifying Assessment: Learning from the Field of Evaluation." In *Achieving Assessment Goals Using Evaluation Techniques, New Directions for Higher Education,* no. 67, edited by P. Gray. San Francisco: Jossey-Bass, 1989.

Haylock, Laura, and Carol Miller. "Merging Developmental and Feminist Evaluation to Monitor and Evaluate Transformative Social Change." *American Journal of Evaluation,* vol. 37, no. 1, 2016, pp. 63–7.

Howton, Amy Johnson, et al. "Ohio Women's Centers' Reflections on Evaluation and Assessment." Issue Brief 02, 2011.

Kasper, Barbara. "Campus-based Women's Centers: Administration, Structure, and Resources." *NASPA Journal,* vol. 41, no. 3, 2004, pp. 337–499.

Laube, Heather, et al. "The Impact of Gender on the Evaluation of Teaching: What We Know and What We Can Do." *NWSA Journal,* vol. 19, no. 3, 2007, pp. 87–104.

Leathwood, Carole, and Barbara Read. *Gender and the Changing Face of Higher Education: A Feminized Future?* McGraw-Hill Education, 2008.

Levin, Amy K. *Questions for a New Century: Women's Studies and Integrative Learning.* College Park, MD: National Women's Studies Association, 2007.

Nicolazzo, Z., and Crystal Harris. "This Is What a Feminist (Space) Looks Like: (Re) Conceptualizing Women's Centers as Feminist Spaces in Higher Education." *About Campus,* vol. 18, no. 6, 2014, pp. 2–9.

Podems, Donna R. "Feminist Evaluation and Gender Approaches: There's a Difference?" *Journal of Multidisciplinary Evaluation,* vol. 6, no. 14, 2010, pp. 1–17.

Prince, Ciji A., et al. "Examining Critical Theory as a Framework to Advance Equity through Student Affairs Assessment." *The Journal of Student Affairs Inquiry,* vol. 2, no. 1, 2017.

Shapiro, Joan. *What Is Feminist Assessment?* In Musil. C. *Students at the Center: Feminist Assessment.* Washington, DC: Association of American Colleges and U, 1992. Print.

Vlasnik, Amber L. "Ohio Women's Centers: Statement of Philosophy." Issue Brief 01, 2010.

13 Paying homage to college and university women's centers

Gender justice work in the center for diversity and inclusion

Emelyn dela Peña, Purvi Patel, and Brittany Harris

What parallels exist between the roots of cultural center and women's center work? What parts of women and gender centers' histories must we honor and preserve; what elements must be examined and critiqued through a more critical lens? And why have women's centers been historically seen as spaces primarily for white women? Three women of color describe our early careers in women-centered work and our evolution into our current roles at a center for diversity and inclusion at a university without a women's center. In discussing our professional histories and experiences, we hope to shed light on these important questions. Reflecting on the personal impact of working in gender-based spaces on predominantly white campuses, we discuss the limitations we faced as women of color and the circumstances that led to our eventual decisions to seek spaces that addressed broader issues of diversity, inclusion, and social justice.

Three professional histories in women-centered work

Emelyn dela Peña

In my 1995 graduate school application, I stated I wanted to be director of a multicultural center. My bachelor's degree in ethnic studies, my undergraduate student activism centered around issues affecting students of color, and the 1992 Rodney King verdict motivated my desire to serve students like me at the university level. Yet, after earning a master's degree and working for five years in residence life, I joined the University of California (UC), San Diego Women's Center in 2000 and called it my professional home for over 11 years, including nine as its director. At the time, there were few women of color directors of women's centers across the country, as evidenced by a simple scan of the room during the Women's Center Caucus at the National Women's Studies Association conference.

Despite my determination to manage the Women's Center from an intersectional lens and my commitment to hire staff and interns from diverse backgrounds, our staff struggled to make it a place that was not steeped in whiteness (a common criticism from the women of color who frequented the space) and where women of color felt at home. Given my commitment to intersectionality, I sometimes wondered if it was the very nature of women's center work itself that alienated women of color.

For example, lectures and workshops about the advancement of women, often gave advice such as "hire a nanny" or "hire someone to clean your house" as a means to free up time to pursue tenure or promotion. In other words, mainstream feminist practice advocated for women's participation in the public sphere through a delegation of work in the private sphere. As a woman with a full-time job, doctoral work, and an already busy schedule, I understood why these became viable solutions for many. As a woman of color, however, the underlying message was of white middle class women's achievements on the backs of poor and working-class women of color. I struggled against what I eventually termed the "feminism of advancement" in a blog post for a transnational, anti-imperialist women's organization, arguing "independence achieved by the privileged few women under capitalism is not true liberation, because women's oppression itself is entrenched in the class struggle" (dela Peña, AF3IRM.org).

Despite these challenges, the women's center was the place I developed my feminist activism after many years of involvement in male-dominated movements where I experienced sexism. As a young activist, I felt pulled between fighting for women's voices in anti-racist movements and speaking up for men of color criticized by white feminists. I often felt myself translating between women's spaces in which I did not feel completely at home and anti-racist spaces in which I felt marginalized as a woman. This notion of bridging borderlands is a familiar one within queer feminist literature. In *Borderlands/La Frontera*, for example, Anzaldúa discusses the creation of a cultura mestiza, a new culture of border consciousness, as a necessary prelude to political change. As such, the work of queer women of color have been the most influential in shaping my anti-racist feminist praxis.

Additionally, it was through my Women's Center work that I found other women (albeit outside the space) to explore a radical feminism grounded in anti-capitalist class analysis and for whom the idea that women's liberation as secondary to the liberation of "the people" was unacceptable. I owe my current commitment to gender justice to my 11 years of leadership at the UC San Diego Women's Center.

Purvi Patel

My identities as a first generation South Asian-American woman are central to my perspective and analysis of how inequality manifests within higher education. Much of my involvement in student affairs began after being involved with student activism concerning racial profiling and anti-racism on campus. My own exposure to an identity-based unit was a multicultural affairs office that took an intersectional approach to their programming and student development initiatives. The Department of Women and Gender Studies, which mainly advocated for gender narratives steeped in whiteness, designated itself as the education unit around gender justice. This unit alienated me because I could not see my own lived experience visible in the curriculum, advocacy, or personnel.

The cornerstone of my involvement in women-centered spaces was as an organizer of a woman of color affinity group housed in the campus Multicultural Center. This space was central to my identity formation, learning, and community organizing on campus. It provided me a space to create and nurture kinship around a shared intersectional experience with other people who identified as women of color. This work, illuminated by bell hook's reflections in *Sisters of the Yam*, allowed me to find a healing counterspace to reflect on both the trauma of misogyny and racism. I went on to create more of those spaces as a graduate student and early career professional. The spaces took multiple shapes – a class, a retreat, and a conference. My commitment to nurturing the shared communal space for women across racial backgrounds to reflect and learn about their experiences as simultaneously racialized and gendered is everlasting.

Although I wasn't engaged in a women's center, I was exposed to and interacted with spaces whose mission was gender advocacy. These experiences include participating in a women's retreat at my undergraduate institution, and directing a residential women and trans* collective as a graduate staff member. All of these experiences with women-centered spaces included interacting with mainly cis-gender white women. While each of these experiences was valuable, they didn't share the same transformative power as the initiatives which prioritized intersectional approaches.

Brittany Harris

Whenever I'm asked to share which of my identities I first gained consciousness of, I remember growing up in St. Louis, Missouri. At age 6, I was harassed by some white children in my neighborhood, who, up until that time, I'd considered great playmates. It was the first time (though not the last) I was called a racial slur and marked the heartbreaking, unforgettable moment when my mother had to have "the talk" with me. It's the same heartbreaking talk that most black parents have with their children about what it means to be born into a world that hates you for the color of your skin and how we must navigate certain spaces and situations to make it home to our parents alive. I've always been committed to racial justice and even at the earliest stages of my academic pursuits could speak to the many movements and people who have contributed to creating equity and access for my people. My commitment to intersectional gender justice work, however, started long before I knew much about feminism, intersectionality, and the erasure of women of color from these conversations.

My first undergraduate job was to support the intake process for women entering a domestic violence shelter. Seeing women in vulnerable and dangerous situations impacted me in ways that still guide me today. I soon realized that these much-needed services were underfunded and under-resourced. Additionally, I didn't see any black women like me being supported by this organization. It made me angry that services, classes, and support groups were not accessible to women of color – especially black, Latinx, and indigenous women.

Similarly, during graduate school, I served as an intake support specialist for a women's shelter. Having more responsibility and access to bureaucratic processes, I began to understand that the violence against women's movement, in many ways, had excluded women of color, trans* women, poor women, and immigrant women because these systems were not designed or equipped to support them. As such, the private lives of women of color struggled against the structural inequalities within a racist and sexist society.

My post-graduate journey led me to one of the oldest university-based women's centers in the country. I quickly realized that the work still felt too white, too cis, and too wealthy. The macro- and microaggressions did not stop and women of color, trans* women, undocumented women, and first generation/low-income women still were not using the resources. The lack of intentionality from leadership in creating access to resources for students who are disproportionately affected by interpersonal violence infuriated me as one of very few people "in the work" who saw how oppressive our resources were. My black feminist self needed to be doing intersectional work, where intersectionality wasn't an afterthought but a paradigm that guided praxis.

As I continue to reflect on my journey thus far, I know that without my experiences engaging in women's and gender equity work, I would not be the scholar practitioner I am today. I am grateful that strong black feminist scholars like bell hooks taught me that rage is a necessary and natural part of our journeys to liberation. Audre Lorde's writings showed me self-care and commitment to myself is a revolutionary act. And Kimberlé Crenshaw created a space for black women to be honored and highlighted through her work on intersectionality. I am thankful for growth, for my experiences thus far, and for the opportunities to connect my experiences to a larger conversation that is long overdue.

Our shared experiences struggling with whiteness

Our collective experience included feeling marginalized in organizational and structural spaces that designed themselves around women's advocacy. Many of these spaces were rooted in whiteness and left each of us feeling frustrated, alienated, and angry. Although each of us have contributed to women's center spaces, the experiences of emotional trauma from assumptions and structures that were not intersectional from their inception ultimately led each of us to struggle against the paradigms and practices in these spaces. These practices and paradigms were evident in our day-to-day interactions with the individuals who frequented women-centered spaces. As such, women's centered spaces were not able to retain the talent, perspective, and leadership of each of the authors. The racism we experienced through erasure and microaggressions illustrates the limitations and nuances of how women of color can navigate and lead in women-centered spaces.

In the following sections, we explore root causes of the alienation that we experienced.

Literature review

In response to increased enrollments of students of color on predominantly white college campuses in the 1960s, cultural centers emerged as a response to the lack of capacity within traditional student affairs offices to meet the needs of diverse groups of students (Jones et al. 21). Much like campus-based women's centers, cultural centers promoted both awareness activities, nurturing for students, and campus activism (Hefner 27).

Both types of centers emerged from efforts of campus activists to meet the needs of specific constituent groups to find places on campus for belonging, safety, and advocacy.

Although the first campus-based women's center was established at the University of Minnesota in 1948, the majority were established in the 1970s at the height of the early women's movement, as a response to issues of gender equity raised by students, staff, and faculty (Koikari and Hippensteele 1269). Given the challenges to intersectional work and the inclusion of women of color in the early women's movement (hooks 1), however, the foundations of campus-based women's centers are grounded in a particularly white, middle-class feminist praxis. Additionally, an examination of the literature regarding campus-based women's centers, feminist leadership, and feminist community organizing reveals a related theme: the tension between the public and private sphere. This tension, we argue, is important to why women of color struggle to find belonging in university women and gender centers.

Caring labor and the private sphere

In the middle nineteenth century, women's activities were confined to the domestic private sphere to protect them from what was considered a corrupted public sphere (Cameron and Gibson-Graham 145). Consequently, these two dimensions have often been used to describe not only differences in work locations but to mark gender differences with the public sphere of competitive markets and paid labor positioned as the realm of men, and the private sphere of family and social relationships as the realm of women (Folbre and Nelson 123). Feminist economists, however, have pointed out the limitations of mainstream capitalist economics, with its emphasis on competition and production, in incorporating the complexities of the economy as it relates to women's caring labor and domestic activities. In many societies, including the United States, women's work is undervalued, and women in particular are penalized, by close association to work that involves care, comforting, and nurturing (Folbre 75).

It is important to note, however, that women of color and poor women have often been excluded from the protected private domain (Naples 4). Rather, women of color and low-income women have been considered laborers, often permeating the boundaries of public and private spheres through extended networks of family and community. But in the realm of the "feminism of advancement" (dela Peña), we find that privileged women themselves are able to draw clear lines between their public and private spheres particularly because they do so through the labor of poor women and, in particular, women of color. This is but one example of the ways much of the discourse we experienced within mainstream feminism seemed to exclude our experiences as women of color who occupied the liminal space between our public and private sphere lives.

Caring labor in a capitalist framework

Similarly, within mainstream liberal feminism we, as women of color in women-centered spaces, were challenged by a focus to advance women to leadership and its efforts for women's rights absent an intersectional analysis that included race and class. People like Sheryl Sandberg and Melissa Mayer are held up as successes of the women's movement, excluding the working-class women of color upon whom their liberation depended – namely, their domestic workers who performed the household caring labor. The "feminism of advancement" has failed working-class women by focusing obsessively on equality within a capitalist system (with its rhetoric of equality with men) and the race to break the glass ceiling. As Shultz states,

> Sandberg and Mayer live in a reality different from most women. They are not single divorced moms living on a shoestring. They did not grow up poor, Black, or Hispanic. . . . The feminism of Sandberg and Mayer is that of rich white women. It is a view of the world that forgets the experiences of most women, but it is mostly a view that is cloaked in class biases.
>
> ("Class and the New Anti-Feminism")

It was the failure to consider this intersectional approach and the tension we felt within the public/private sphere divide that ultimately led to our search to find spaces where our work could be grounded in anti-racist and anti-classist paradigms.

Intersectionality

In an opinion piece for *The Washington Post*, Kimberlé Crenshaw laments, "today, nearly three decades after I first put a name to the concept, the term [intersectionality] seems to be everywhere. But if women and girls of color continue to be left in the shadows, something vital to the understanding of intersectionality has been lost."

Intersectionality was introduced into feminist theory by Crenshaw in her 1989 essay "Demarginalizing the Intersection of Race and Sex: A Black Feminist Critique of Antidiscrimination Doctrine, Feminist Theory and Antiracist Politics."

Although the understanding of intersectionality has expanded since its inception, it is important to note that the term was originally intended to highlight the plight of American black women. Intersectionality also acknowledges social injustices as overlapping and simultaneous, while examining how intersecting marginalized identities can create susceptibility to multiple layers of social injustice.

The tragic deaths of Sandra Bland, Aiyanna Stanley Jones, and so many other marginalized and minoritized women, coupled with the disproportionately high rates of violence against trans* communities of color, have created a new platform to discuss intersectionality. Intersectionality gives us a powerful feminist tool to create more inclusive spaces for historically oppressed women, while shedding light on traditional western feminist praxis rooted in white supremacist ideology. Intersectionality and its analysis of how race interacts with other salient identities critiques spaces that are not inclusive of women of color, trans* women, women from low-income communities, immigrant women, and women with disabilities. It is important to note that this specific focus on race and racism at the intersections of other identities and systems of oppression sets intersectionality apart from theories focusing on multiple dimensions of identity without a critical race analysis.

Beyond multidimensionality, intersectionality directs our attention to the struggles of people with multiple marginalized identities and the multiplied effects of those overlapping identities (African American Policy Forum 4). An intersectional approach to feminism, therefore, would consider not only the multiple dimensions of women's identities but also recognize the problematic pursuit of "equality with men" as a goal. After all, in a system of white supremacy, and more specifically in an era of overt anti-blackness, all men are not created equal.

An intersectional praxis

Davie (7) describes women's center work as the delicate balance between "binding wounds" and "changing the world." We argue that it is at the intersection of this delicate balance where experiences of women of color can be made marginal or affirming. Although social norms, traditions, and economic models that associate being female with care of others contributes to women's economic disadvantage and oppression, women of color and low-income women have been considered laborers within the public economy, often permeating the boundaries of public and private spheres. In these ways, women of color and poor women have provided examples of ways to bridge these two seemingly distinct spheres. Perhaps in adopting a primarily private sphere framework of safe space and community, many women and gender centers have alienated those women who have traditionally been excluded from the protected private sphere – women of color. In what ways, then, can campus-based women's centers create a borderland "Third Country" for women of color, as Anzaldúa (22) describes? Specifically, how can women-centered spaces incorporate an intentional race and class analysis within an intersectional feminist practice?

Gender justice work in a center for diversity and inclusion

As women of color who have experienced feeling invisible in women-centered spaces, we intentionally practice an intersectional social justice praxis within our broader diversity and inclusion work, as we have also seen how anti-racist movements render women, particularly women of color, invisible. "When feminism focuses exclusively on gender, or antiracism on race, or LGBT on sexual identity, they often fail to comprehend that countless numbers of their constituents confront circumstances and challenges that reflect more than one barrier or obstacle" (African American Policy Forum 4). One need only examine the current #MeToo movement to see that even within progressive spaces women continue to be marginalized. #MeToo is a hashtag created by activist Tarana Burke as a way to empower women of color (Ohlheiser). The hashtag went viral in 2017 following public allegations of sexual assault against Harvey Weinstein and other Hollywood celebrities, to highlight the prevalence of sexual assault and harassment. Additionally, the near election of Roy Moore in December 2017, when nearly two-thirds of white women in Alabama voted for an accused child molester, gives us a visible reminder of the vastly different experiences and priorities between white and black women (Mohdin).

The mission of the Center for Diversity & Inclusion (CDI) at Washington University in St. Louis is to support and advocate for students from underrepresented and traditionally marginalized backgrounds. Our work within the center encompasses race, ethnic, gender, sexuality, class, disability, and spirituality. As such, our orientation to social justice work is necessarily intersectional in its approach. Additionally, however, our experiences within women-centered spaces have provided us a feminist foundation from which to approach our work within and between the communities we serve. More specifically, our commitment to intersectionality in this work centers the experiences of queer women of color.

The literature on campus-based women's centers underscores the tension of women's center work between "binding wounds" and "changing the world" (Davie 7), and provides valuable lessons for our broader social justice work. The building of community and creation of safe space is our caring labor while the social justice and activism endeavors can be viewed as our public sphere work. Rather than experience these two seemingly opposing sides as tension, however, our women-centered work helped us see them both as integral to our mission at the CDI. As such, three years after the establishment of the CDI as a response to campus needs and community crises, the CDI introduced a new paradigm of work grounded in equity, inclusion, and social justice under the pillars of education, capacity-building, response, and healing. In this way, we expand upon Davie's concept of a delicate balance, creating a space in which the act of healing wounds facilitates the work of changing the world.

Works cited

Anzaldúa, Gloria. *Borderlands/La Frontera: The New Mestiza.* Aunt Lute Books, 2007.

Cameron, Jenny, and J.K. Gibson-Graham. "Feminising the Economy: Metaphors, Strategies, Politics." *Gender, Place & Culture*, vol. 10, no. 2, 2003, pp. 145–57, doi:10.1080/0966369032000079569.

Crenshaw, Kimberlé. *Demarginalizing the Intersection of Race and Sex: A Black Feminist Critique of Antidiscrimination Doctrine, Feminist Theory, and Antiracist Politics.* U Chicago Legal Forum, 1989.

Crenshaw, Kimberlé. "Opinion | Why Intersectionality Can't Wait." *The Washington Post*, WP Company, 24 Sept. 2015, www.washingtonpost.com/news/in-theory/wp/2015/09/24/why-intersectionality-cant-wait/.

Davie, Sharon L. *University and College Women's Centers: A Journey toward Equity.* Greenwood P, 2002.

Dela Pena, Emelyn A. "Myth of the Modern Woman." *AF3IRM: A Transnational Feminist Organization*, AF3IRM, 9 Dec. 2011, www.af3irm.org.

Folbre, Nancy. "'Holding Hands at Midnight': The Paradox of Caring Labor." *Feminist Economics*, Taylor & Francis Journals, 1 Jan. 1995, econpapers.repec.org/RePEc:taf:femeco:v:1:y:1995:i:1:p:73–92.

Folbre, Nancy, and Julie A. Nelson. "For Love or Money – or Both?" *The Journal of Economic Perspectives*, vol. 14, no. 4, 2000, p. 123.

Hefner, David. "Black Cultural Centers: Standing on Shaky Ground? As College Campuses Become More Diverse, Many Find the Future of Black Cultural Centers in Question." *Black Issues in Higher Education*, vol. 18, no. 26, 2002, pp. 22, Ethnic NewsWatch; ProQuest Social Sciences Premium Collection; Social Science Premium Collection.

hooks, bell. *Sisters of the Yam: Black Women and Self-recovery.* Routledge/Taylor & Francis Group, 2015.

Jones, Lee, et al. "Examining the Ethnic Student Experience at Predominantly White Institutions: A Case Study." *Journal of Hispanic Higher Education*, vol. 1, no. 1, Jan. 2002, pp. 19–39, doi:10.1177/1538192702001001003.

Koikari, Mire, and Susan K. Hippensteele. "Negotiating Feminist Survival: Gender, Race, and Power in Academe." *Violence against Women*, vol. 6, no. 11, 1 Nov. 2000, pp. 1269–96, doi:10.1177/10778010022183631.

Mohdin, Aamna. "A Majority of White Women in Alabama Backed Accused Child Molester Roy Moore." *Quartz, Quartz*, 13 Dec. 2017, qz.com/1155156/alabama-senate-race-result-and-poll-majority-of-white-women-backed-defeated-republican-candidate-roy-moore/.

Naples, Nancy A. *Community Activism and Feminist Politics: Organizing across Race, Class, and Gender.* Routledge, 1998.

Ohlheiser, Abby. "The Woman Behind 'Me Too; Knew the Power of the Phrase When She Created It – 10 Years Ago." *The Washington Post*, www.washingtonpost.com/news/the-intersect/wp/2017/10/19/the-woman-behind-me-too-knew-the-power-of-the-phrase-when-she-created-it-10-years-ago/?utm_term=.4952ce933231. Accessed 19 Oct. 2017.

"A Primer on Intersectionality." *African American Policy Forum*, www.aapf.org/publications/.

Shultz, David. "Sheryl Sandberg and Marissa Mayer: Class and the New Anti-feminism." *Twin Cities Daily Planet*, 29 Apr. 2013, www.tcdailyplanet.net/sheryl-sandberg-and-marissa-mayer-class-and-new-anti-feminism.

14 Beyond the label

Leveraging the iconography of "feminist" from moments to movements

Uyenthi Tran Myhre

Certain moments in history tap into a collective consciousness, linking generations. For many of us, during the 2014–2015 academic year, the word "feminist" immediately brought to mind a moment during a performance at the MTV Video Music Awards, which aired in late August 2014: Beyoncé, in a power stance with her high heels planted firmly, coming into focus as a silhouette. Behind her, "feminist" is projected in larger-than-life, glowing white letters, all-caps, sans serif, and Chimamanda Ngozi Adichie's voice fills the air. The words, sampled from Adichie's 2012 "We Should All Be Feminists" TED Talk, flashes across the screen on stage: "We teach girls to shrink themselves, to make themselves smaller. We say to girls, 'You can have ambition, but not too much. You should aim to be successful, but not too successful. Otherwise, you will threaten the man.'"

The morning after the 2014 MTV VMAs, HuffPost columnist Amanda Duberman wrote of Beyoncé's "***Flawless" performance: "The moment represents a culmination of feminism's trickling from the edges into the pop culture mainstream – a process Beyoncé, whether one agrees with her approach or not – shot into overdrive." Duberman went on to note that while "Beyoncé's VMAs proclamation of feminism doesn't alleviate women's inequality, sexual assault, reproductive injustice or economic disparity . . . it's a ringing endorsement for gender equality on a massive scale – and at the very least, it got us talking."

This moment quickly became a cultural touchstone, and it was what the University of Minnesota Women's Center staff had in mind as we began to think about ideas for a new giveaway item for the campus community. Women's centers (and other campus departments across the country) have long used "swag" as a way to entice students to stop by, learn more about the center, and then return in the future for involvement opportunities, programs, or events.

It was the spring of 2015, and the semester had just wrapped up. It was blissfully quiet on campus, and the weather was that fleeting perfection between Minnesota's snowy, endless winter and hot, sticky summer. We were done with major programming for a couple months, and had time to stretch, dream, and be creative about our plans for the upcoming academic year. As we brainstormed potential swag items, we eventually landed on the idea of putting "feminist" on a knit winter hat, one of those retro styles with the pom-pom on top, in maroon and gold, our school colors. Knowing that winter was coming in a few short months, it was easy to imagine our hats as a direct complement to the similarly styled "Minnesota" hats stocked by the university bookstore.

Even before pricing out the hats, we knew that offering them as a free swag item wouldn't be feasible. For the past several years, the Women's Center, a unit in the Office for Equity and Diversity (OED), had a modest but steady budget, which included funding for our programming; several student, faculty, and staff awards and grants; as well as salaries for two or three undergraduate student staff. While we discussed the possible "feminist" hats and our upcoming programming, we had to keep in mind that due to overall budget cuts at the university and in OED, our budget would be decreased by 20% for the upcoming 2015–2016 academic year.

Although our budget doesn't include our student scholarships, we also needed to be creative in fundraising for our Dr. Nancy "Rusty" Barceló Scholarship. The scholarship, formerly the Alumnae Society Scholarship, had languished for a number of years before being revived by Women's Center Director Peg Lonnquist. In 2011, the Women's Center renamed the scholarship in honor of our then-Vice President for Equity and Diversity, Dr. Barceló. The scholarship had always assisted University of Minnesota women-identified students with financial need in completing their education at the university, but now it included a special focus on supporting women of color, new immigrants, and first-generation college students. By the spring of 2015, with the scholarship fund dwindling, we were preparing to review scholarship applicants for perhaps the last time – unless we were able to raise funds going forward.

Deciding to sell "feminist" hats was not a decision the Women's Center made lightly, as a later section of this chapter will explain. Selling the hats just for profit or for our general Women's Center budget felt suspect, but selling them as a fundraiser for the Barceló Scholarship seemed like a perfect fit. And, because of the inspiration provided by Queen Bey's song, we decided to offer two kinds of maroon and gold hats – one hat that read "feminist" and another that read "flawless." Although we had much to work through first (from securing permission to sell hats as a scholarship fundraiser, to the logistics of turning our Women's Center into a mini retail store), we decided the possibility of growing the Barceló Scholarship for future scholars would be worth the various challenges.

Launching the #UMNfeminist fundraiser

As we coordinated our first order of hats from a family-owned, Minnesota-based vendor, Bronwyn Miller, our program coordinator, continued making numerous phone calls and emails to various university offices attempting to determine whether we needed any specific approval for this fundraiser. After checking with our central OED office, the Controller's Office, and the University of Minnesota Foundation, the fundraising arm of the campus, we received the go-ahead for our scholarship fundraiser.

Our first order was for exactly 144 hats, which was the lowest quantity we could order that made sense for our budget. As a way to provide a bit of education for our buyers on what the hats represented, and to let them know where their money was going, we created and printed tags to attach to the hats. In a moment of ultimate nerdery, the font for the tags matched the font of the "feminist" that was projected behind Beyoncé at the 2014 MTV VMAs (which was also the font in her eponymous album that included the song "***Flawless"). On one side of the tag, we provided our definitions of the words on the hats:

FEMINIST: the person who believes in the social, political, and economic equality of all genders

FLAWLESS: a statement of radical self-confidence

The feminist definition is similar to the dictionary definition that Chimamanda Ngozi Adichie provides in her TED Talk, which was then sampled in Beyoncé's "***Flawless" recording. We edited the original wording of "equality of the sexes" to "equality of all genders," in an effort to move away from the gender binary, and also as a nod to the belief that feminism should benefit everybody. The flawless definition, meanwhile, was inspired by a March 2015 *New York Times Magazine* article by Parul Sehgal, "How 'Flawless' Became a Feminist Declaration," which included a subhead that read: "To be beautiful is to be pleasing to others, but to be 'flawless' is a statement of radical confidence: It means pleasing yourself." The other side of the tag thanked the buyer for supporting the Barceló Scholarship, explained the scholarship's special focus on women of color, new immigrants, and first-generation college students, and included the Women's Center logo along with a link to give directly, plus the hashtags #UMNfeminist and #UMNflawless.

Over the next several weeks, whenever one of us needed a break from sitting at a computer, we would tag a few of the hats. Boxes of hats and the tags were brought to staff meetings, where we would set up an assembly line as we went through the meeting agenda. We had the hats ready to go for Welcome Week, the week before fall semester begins, and debuted them at various resource fairs where we were tabling.

Although it was the first week of September, the days were still sunny and temperatures were topping 90 degrees, so we were thrilled to see how quickly students (and staff and faculty) snapped up the hats. News of the hats spread quickly through word of mouth and through the personal social media networks of our buyers. Nearly everyone who dropped by our offices to purchase one said, "I saw my friend post about this and I had to come get one!" or "A student worker in our office came by with their hat the other day!" Many people bought hats in multiples, to give as presents, or because they wanted one of each. To keep the hats as financially accessible as possible while still raising funds for the scholarship, we priced the hats at $15 each, or two for $25, and accepted cash only.

By mid-September 2015, two weeks into the fall semester, we had sold out of the 144 hats from our first order. Over the next two years, we continued to sell the original winter hats, and over time, we added baseball hats and pashmina scarves, as well as some online products such as sweatshirts and t-shirts. As of this writing, minus the cost of stocking the hats and scarves, we have raised over $20,000 for the Dr. Nancy "Rusty" Barceló Scholarship.

#UMNfeminist hats as guerilla marketing

We didn't realize, at the beginning, the extent to which the hats would drive marketing for and engagement with the Women's Center. While most of our supporters were from campus, we also got many off-campus visitors to the center, who either had a U of M connection or maybe just saw a stranger on the light-rail train wearing a hat, and tracked us down by searching online for "U of M feminist hat." When people stopped by in-person to buy a hat, nearly every supporter signed up for our monthly e-news. Even when we sold out and kept waiting lists in-between new shipments, supporters would still grab one of our informational postcards or a poster with our semester calendar of events. Most visitors would also receive an elevator speech about the Women's Center, and receive an impromptu tour of our space, including the study/lounge, which debuted at the same time as the hats.

In general, we found that the hats and all of the #UMNfeminist gear marketed themselves. There were a few instances in which we boosted Facebook posts for a small cost, to promote our gear. We also had success using the online platform Rafflecopter, which was a very useful way to run a giveaway for a couple of the hats. As users entered the online giveaway, they could enter for more chances to win by promoting the giveaway (and therefore, the hats) on their social media networks. Most of the hats were sold during posted "store hours" through our offices in the Women's Center, and our career and student staff would take turns being in charge of sales.

We also held successful pop-up hat sales, most notably at the Beyoncé concert on campus at the TCF Bank Stadium in May 2016, and at the Minnesota Women's March in January 2017. These audiences were more than happy to support the scholarship and don the hats. While we did not have as much success at the Homecoming Parade pop-up sale, we still get tagged in selfies of Gopher fans in #UMNfeminist hats at football, hockey, and volleyball games. Even Karen Kaler (whose husband, Eric Kaler, is the president of the university) has tweeted photos of herself and loved ones proudly wearing hats at various Gopher games.

Beyond #UMNfeminist as a label

Today, in the post-Women's March/pussy hat era, the idea of wearing a hat or sweatshirt emblazoned with the word "feminist" may seem passé or meaningless. A quick Google search will reveal a market that is saturated with products like this, typically made overseas and sold for a mere $5.53 at retailers known for fast and cheap fashion (and terrible labor practices). And in 2017, at a show during New York Fashion Week, a model came down the runway wearing a sweatshirt that simply said, "INTERSECTIONALITY." However, in the spring and summer of 2015, apparel declaring one's feminist allegiances was not as common; and as far as we could tell, none of them were locally made or supported anything other than capitalism. When the Women's Center began preparing to sell the original "feminist" hats, the proceeds needed to go toward a worthy cause. We knew that campus Women's Centers, like women's movements overall, have been viewed as spaces for white feminism. In "Race And Feminism: Women's March Recalls the Touchy History," an article in the Code Switch section of National Public Radio, scholars and activists speak to the troubled, exclusionary past (and present) of women's movements:

> A professor of Asian American and Gender Studies at UCLA, [Grace] Hong says for decades, white women didn't have to consider any interests beyond their own because "historically, the category 'woman' has, implicitly, meant white women." The call to put womanhood above all else, Hong says, is based on the idea that "critique and dissent undermine a unity that's based on the lowest common denominator: Find the one thing everyone has in common."
>
> The fact that the feminist movement was so white for so long, says Ashley Farmer, is the reason so many women of color steered clear of it. Farmer is a historian at Boston University, and concentrates on African-American women's history. She says women of color noticed when their interests and needs didn't get a full hearing.
>
> (Grigsby Bates)

Although we debuted the #UMNfeminist hats and other apparel long before the Women's March, the history that Grace Hong and Ashley Farmer reference in this NPR article is what we had in mind as we grappled with the ethics of commodifying "feminist." Not only did we want to choose a worthy and feminist cause that included and centered women of color, we also needed to ensure that our work as a Women's Center was impactful. While scholarship fundraising and raising awareness of the Women's Center was important in and of itself, we also needed to be intentional about creating programming and spaces that would also uplift and center the voices and experiences of women, particularly indigenous women and women of color. With the heightened awareness of our center as a resource, we had a duty to continue practicing *and* educating ourselves and others about intersectional feminism.

From #UMNfeminist hats to #UMNfeminist spaces

In the summer leading up to the launch of the #UMNfeminist hats, our staff organized several ongoing programs to engage and advance critical conversations around feminism and gender justice issues. Bronwyn Miller, Women's Center program coordinator, coordinated the Women's Center's new student volunteer program, the Feminist Ambassador Brigade (FAB), as a way to provide students of all genders a way to grow their understanding of feminism, strengthen community, support Women's Center initiatives, and lead their own projects. Students can join at the beginning of each semester, and commit to a four-hour training (co-led by student officers) that includes introductions to the center's work, privilege and oppression 101, intersectionality, and allyship.

Thanks to the work of the student volunteers, FAB is now a registered student organization on campus, which gives them greater access to various university resources such as grant funding, spaces to hold meetings or events, and more. Because it is a student-driven program, the initiatives they lead draw in a greater and more diverse student population than our three full-time staff can attract. Their networks of friends and classmates will stop by events from a Women's Center Open House to a zine-making, button-making, photo-booth-taking, awareness-raising event for International Women's Day. More recently, FAB has collaborated with other student groups on campus as well, from cross-trainings with ambassadors in our multicultural center, to holding discussions on navigating multiracial identities with the multiracial student union.

The fall of 2015 also saw the beginning of the Women's Center's Feminist Friday series, a monthly program highlighting issues from #SayHerName, to disability justice, to transformative masculinity, to the politics of femme identities. Feminist Fridays provided the perfect opportunity for the Women's Center to build connections with campus and community partners. The first step was usually to have a conversation about what issues or topics were timely or most important to our partners, whether they were community members or faculty and staff on campus. The Women's Center was able to provide a platform and logistical support, from booking space to advertising, and consult with our partners as they put together an interactive presentation, a film screening and dialogue, or a panel discussion.

Ultimately, our partners would drive the focus and content of the Feminist Friday, and because of the collaboration, attendance at these events would draw attendees who might only be familiar with one, but not both, of our offices. In that way, these partnerships not only provided connection between our staff and our colleagues, but amongst our attendees as well. Another benefit of having a regular platform like Feminist Friday means that we've also had an easy way to coordinate timely and relevant programs to respond to current events. For example, in the winter of 2016, following the presidential election, our student staff worked with a community organizer (and former Women's Center student staff herself) to coordinate a panel of women and femmes of color to speak about "intersectional feminism in this new political reality." Even though it was a 7 p.m. event on a cold February night, we packed a 200-seat lecture hall with students and community members. Panelists and community members dialogued about everything from the Women's March to the work being done to release undocumented Cambodian Minnesotans (the Minnesota 8) who had recently been detained by ICE.

Programs like the Feminist Ambassador Brigade and Feminist Fridays have provided the campus community ways to learn about gender justice issues from each other, and often, from speakers who represent communities who are most directly impacted. At the same time, we recognize that our campus members who hold marginalized identities are often asked (or tasked) with educating those with dominant identities. Within a predominantly white institution like the University of Minnesota, it is also necessary to create spaces for processing and healing within and across marginalized communities. One example of this is the Indigenous Women and Women of Color Student Summit (IWWOCSS), which was created in response to focus groups with women of color students who asked for more spaces to connect with and learn from each other. Although our university includes many vibrant and active student cultural centers, there aren't many spaces for IWWOC students to connect with each other, across identities. The summit, which has been organized bi-annually by the Women's Center since 2011, provides an essential opportunity for students to connect with each other and grow in their leadership, professional, and personal development, all in a space that prioritized their identities and experiences as indigenous women and women of color students.

Because of our small staff and modest budget, as with the #UMNfeminist scholarship fundraiser, the Women's Center has had to be creative in how to respond to the needs of our students. This summit, for instance, has been held bi-annually due to staff capacity and funding, but following the third summit in March 2016, several students and staff members (who volunteered or led workshop presentations at the summit) expressed a desire to see an ongoing, regular space for IWWOC students and staff to engage with each other. Through a collaboration with the Multicultural Center for Academic Excellence, a sister unit in the Office for Equity and Diversity, and Multicultural Student Engagement, under the Office for Student Affairs, the Women's Center launched Our Voices: Indigenous Women and Women of Color. This biweekly, drop-in dialogue group began meeting in September 2016, and has been a regular opportunity for incoming first year students, transfer students, and even graduate students to find community, decompress, and receive encouragement and support.

During the first semester of meetings, Our Voices included more direction and guidance from the staff of the three collaborating offices. Over the last year, however, it has been a pleasure to see the students take ownership of the group, whether that means dropping by to get hugs and cheers before heading to an exam, or warmly welcoming new faces at the meetings and drawing the quieter students into conversation. Like Feminist Fridays and the bi-annual summit, Our Voices has also been an opportunity to partner with our indigenous women and women of color campus colleagues, who have guest facilitated dialogues on topics ranging from generational trauma to battling imposter syndrome.

Visioning the future: feminist moments, feminist movements

When the Women's Center created the tags with definitions of "feminist" and "flawless" for the hats, we had to be concise because of space constraints. Yes, a feminist is a person who believes in the social, political, and economic equality of all genders, and/also feminism is so much more than that. Perhaps one of the best explanations of what feminism is working toward can be found in the writing of adrienne maree brown, a Detroit-based writer, organizational healer, and doula:

> we are bending the future, together, into something we have never experienced. a world where everyone experiences abundance, access, pleasure, human rights, dignity, freedom, transformative justice, peace. we long for this, we believe it is possible.
>
> ("All Organizing Is Science Fiction")

Although brown is writing about organizing work here, and not feminism, specifically, these three poetic sentences help us imagine the world we want to create, and remind us what we are working toward. The #UMNfeminist hats began as an idea inspired by Beyoncé, became a fantastically successful scholarship fundraiser, and provided a framework to build ways for the University of Minnesota community to grow in their understanding of feminism and gender justice.

Two years after the launch of the original #UMNfeminist hats, we are now taking a hiatus on hat sales due to staff capacity, but of course the work to connect the iconography of *feminist* to a critical, engaging, and intersectional practice continues. The programs highlighted in this chapter were created based on the needs of the campus community, and have primarily focused on education and creating change at the personal and interpersonal level. As we approach our 60th anniversary in 2020 (we have the distinction of being the oldest campus-based women's center in the country), we plan to continue fundraising for the Barceló Scholarship and offering engagement opportunities like the Our Voices dialogue group, Feminist Ambassador Brigade, Feminist Fridays, and more. In addition, we hope we can grow our budget and staff, so we can do more in engaging men in the work of gender justice and equity, and so we can increase our capacity to create systems-level change on our campus and beyond.

In the future, perhaps we'll bring the #UMNfeminist hats back, too. In the meantime, there might be a few hidden away in a drawer, waiting for their chance to be gifted to Blue Ivy, Sir, and Rumi Carter.

Works cited

Adichie, Chimamanda Ngozi. "We Should All Be Feminists." *TEDxEuston*, 2012, www.youtube.com/watch?v=hg3umXU_qWc.

"Beyonce – Medley Live @ VMA." *Vimeo*, uploaded by Benzzhit BTH, 4 Sept. 2015, vimeo.com/138290967.

Duberman, Amanda. "Beyoncé's Feminist VMAs Performance Got People Talking about Gender Equality." *Huffington Post*, 26 Aug. 2014, www.huffingtonpost.com/2014/08/25/Beyoncé-feminist-vmas_n_5708475.html.

Grigsby Bates, Karen. "Race and Feminism: Women's March Recalls the Touchy History." *National Public Radio*, 21 Jan. 2017, www.npr.org/sections/codeswitch/2017/01/21/510859909/race-and-feminism-womens-march-recalls-the-touchy-history.

maree brown, adrienne. "All Organizing Is Science Fiction." *Art in a Changing America*, artsinachangingamerica.org/nyc-launch-highlight-the-response/.

Sehgal, Parul. "How 'Flawless' Became a Feminist Declaration." *New York Times Magazine*, 24 Mar. 2015, www.nytimes.com/2015/03/29/magazine/how-flawless-became-a-feminist-declaration.html?smid=pin-share.

15 The personal and the professional

Intersectional experiences in gender justice work

Jessica Jennrich, Sharalle V. Arnold, and Allison C. Roman

This chapter explains how the staff of the Grand Valley State University Center for Women and Gender Equity (CWGE) was able to grow in unique ways by embracing an intersectional gender justice frame and applying it towards our work. In this chapter, we provide a history of our center and, in celebrating our 15th anniversary, reflect on our history and our intentional shift from a traditional women's center (WC) space to a radically inclusive space that equally values lived experiences and scholarship.

In preparation for this anniversary, we uprooted efforts that were no longer reflective of our new intersectional gender justice mission and set the trajectory of where we wanted to go. As a result, each author reconciled their relationship with how the WC was perceived under a different mission. This includes the tenets of feminism that assisted with the founding the center and still could be found in the expectations of the WC and could feel impossible to extricate from our work. In this chapter we share how we navigate this work; from the strategic to the fumbling, from the frantic to the futile, as we expose our intersectional identities and challenges, believing there is value in our stories that reflect intersectionality. In exploring our lived experiences and storytelling as a liberating practice in our work, we model doing gender justice work as incredibly personal and important to the work of understanding the full history of our center and other centers.

Historical context

The CWGE was founded in 2001. Originally named The Women's Center, it was staffed by just a part-time director and graduate assistant. It has since grown to encompass four full-time staff members and an office coordinator.

Like many women's centers (Davie 2002), it was the voices of many on Grand Valley State University's campus that created the center. In the late 1990s, faculty, staff, and students formed a task force, which presented a proposal for a women's center that was approved by then-President Arend D. Lubbers in 2000.

The WC built its foundation on collaboration with other units across campus and emphasized community engagement and service learning. The WC moved to its current location in 2009, but did not stop its growth; adding an independent food pantry, foster student grant program, Violence Against Women Act (VAWA) grant in 2010 and 2013, and expanding services for women and girls of color.

In addition to changes in and around the center, larger administrative changes have also occurred. In 2015 the center moved to the Division of Inclusion and Equity alongside other social justice centers: the Lesbian, Gay, Bisexual and Transgender Resource Center and the Office of Multicultural Affairs. This represented a shift in the population the center would now be tasked with serving. Being part of a division that included compliance offices changed the student-centered nature of the CWGE's divisional partners. The entire focus of our division was no longer solely on students but on meeting federal and state requirements, which took time and money away from student-centered work.

The most recent change of the center is our name. In spring of 2017, our name was changed to the Gayle R. Davis Center for Women and Gender Equity. This name change honors the retirement of our provost, Gayle R. Davis, and reflects a more inclusive title as "Women's Center" was often seen as exclusionary to Trans and gender nonconforming students as well as male-identified students. Much has changed over the past 16 years and, as result of these changes, those of us who work in the center wrestle with others' perception and understanding of our role.

Each of us experienced these changes differently. Due to working here various lengths of time, having different experiences at GVSU, and different roles at the center, we all had various positionalities (Alcoff 405). Further, in considering the theory of intersectionality, what we understood through experience was that most "importantly, the layering of identity, intersectionality, and social justice is not a linear process, but rather a necessary yet messy journey for those doing work in identity centers in higher education" (Jennrich and Kowalski-Braun 201). Thus as queer woman, as women of color, women of different faith backgrounds, different socio-economic backgrounds, and so forth, we all had different stories and experiences.

Individual experiences

Director's experience

As the director of the center, I inherited a very well run Women's Center where I suffocated under the weight of expectations to do things the way they had always been done. I approached the doors on a gleaming summer day coming from having directed another women's center at a private college in New England. Presently, only the office coordinator remains; otherwise all new staff work in the center. I realize not everyone is able to hire their own team, a task I approached with equal measure excitement and terror. After two contentious searches filled with internal candidates, I was able to hire a new associate and assistant director as well as a new victim advocate. With a new team in place, an idyllic era at the WC began.

But there were demands of an administration which wanted simplicity. Instead, I shoved our team's questions across the board table, complicating issues of policy, procedures, and programs by raising questions of gender justice. I was reminded of the reconfiguration of postmodern autonomy specifically as "feminist theories of difference and otherness allege that the notion of autonomy is a historically, social and culturally specific ideal that parades as a universal norm" (Mackenzie and Stoljar 11). In other words, autonomy is not desirable; individual needs should be subsumed into those of the groups. But was that a strategic leadership decision? My doctoral training in educational leadership and policy analysis warned me it was not, and yet my feminist education insisted it was the best way to lead.

Further, my identity as a queer woman was particularly difficult to navigate in this conservative area of the country. As I gathered privilege for my whiteness, I was kept at a distance for my queerness, or worse, assumed to be straight and then awkwardly removed from the club once discovered. The religiosity of this particular community made my lack of belief a barrier to joining those racial communities for whom faith is crucial. Additionally, because I had a wife and three children I was not welcomed into the queer community, as I was accused of being too heteronormative. I found myself adrift; dodging microaggressions, isolated from my own communities and unable or unwilling to capitulate to managerial norms.

Yet, the WC was flourishing. I chose to use the power of success to advocate for the staff I worked with to receive visibility and accolades, as well as to refuse to continue hostile partnerships, reasoning that we no longer needed to engage with those who treated us as unequal partners. As we broke off partnerships that had existed for decades, and limited the number of celebrations the WC was known for, feelings were hurt and accusations about my leadership and the qualifications of our staff were made. I also questioned my behavior: Was I engaging in a white savior complex, "saving" the women of color whom I had helped to hire so I could prove I was good? It did not feel that way but benevolent acts on the part of the powerful white woman often do not. I wondered what I was doing, as it seemed I never made anyone happy, least of all myself. My dissatisfaction grew each day despite the small successes, as it was clear large wins were beyond my grasp. The work we were doing was successful, but the administration grew, if not less supportive, then less inclined to look our way. It seemed gender justice sank lower on the rungs of the importance of the institution. If I was a leader, what was my leadership motto for the center? Some days it was a jubilant "we've got this!" and other days it was a dejected "at least I tried."

Associate director

My personal narrative begins with my tenure at the Children's Enrichment Center (CEC). The gendered nature of the former role gave me an ongoing opportunity to work collaboratively with the WC. I felt as though I had "made it" when the

WC welcomed my participation. Engaging in this work began a burgeoning of sorts, later identified by bell hooks as my personal "consciousness-raising." In *Feminism Is for Everybody: Passionate Politics*, hooks writes, "Feminist are made, not born. One does not become an advocate of feminist politics simply by the privilege of having been born female. Like all political positions one becomes a believer in feminist politics through choice and action" (*Feminism Is for Everybody*, 7). The transformation that started with an invitation to an annual tea party led to the development of identity awareness that has shaped my advocacy, in my current role as associate director of the CWGE, around issues that disproportionately impact those with multiple identities.

For years, I assigned a rather glamorous label to the WC which always appeared connected to the right people. It seemed to have influence, highlighted the struggles of women, endorsed anything reflecting racial justice, and provided students of color with plenty of employment opportunities.

With feelings of trepidation, I jumped at the opportunity to secure a position in the center, which was in the early stage of developing its second iteration of WC history. With all new staff, there would be occasion to rethink previously celebrated acts of solidarity and problematize the work in an effort to avoid replication. In looking at the prior work of the center, I soon realized that some of my assumptions of feminist efforts were based on my distant view. For example, celebrating Equal Pay Day and supporting the needs of faculty that were experiencing inconsistent tenure track treatment were important, but these concessions would not benefit janitorial staff. Further, a practice of intersectionality would have forced the realization that this inconsistent treatment of junior female faculty was exacerbated when compounded with race and ability. There were elements of second wave feminist thought that were at the roots of this organization. The WC was for rights of women but economically stable white women seemed to be the focus, leaving plenty of lesbian women, trans folks, and low wage earners asking, similar to Sojourner Truth, "Ain't I a Woman?"

Shortly after being hired, I found myself constantly questioning my ability to do the job and grappling with my version of feminism. The impostor phenomenon had begun to manifest itself in extreme self-doubt, which was confirmed when a faculty member questioned the legitimacy of my qualifications, even though I possessed the required *and* preferred qualifications for the position. The accusation came as a power-packed punch, delivered in part by a "black feminist," resulting in a familiar sting. This type of pain is often discussed in circles centered on racial inequalities. The online Crunk Feminist Collective offers alignment with my emotions: "You feel the need to constantly prove yourself worthy of your job or opportunity. You know that some people assume you got your job, promotion, award, or special recognition, not because you worked your ass off or deserve it" (Crunk Feminist Collective).

My response to this questioning of my credibility now manifested itself as anger, and attempts to prove my worth became a mainstay on my weekly calendar. Unfortunately, I would fall short; not even could a federal award *grant* me approval as I was deemed "unqualified." It was almost as if Claudia Rankine's *Citizen* had been written for me when she wrote:

> You begin to think, maybe erroneously, that this other kind of anger is really a type of knowledge: the type that both clarifies and disappoints. It responds to insult and attempted erasure simply by asserting presence, and the energy required to present, to react, to assert is accompanied by visceral disappointment in the sense that no amount of visibility will alter the ways in which on is perceived.
>
> (24)

This malignant treatment of black women has roots grown centuries ago, when we were chattel, harnessed with both sexist and racist insults across our backs as we drove the American economy (Harris 3).

In fall of 2016, a local study was designed to elevate the conversation about the absence of leadership roles occupied by women of color. As women of color seeking advancement, we are not only subject to what is above us, but we have to fight that which literally boxes us in, making it impossible to grow. The presentation powered by W.K. Kellogg Foundation fellows Shannon M. Cohen and Patricia Sosa VerDuin, *Invisible Walls, Ceilings and Floors: Championing the Voices and Inclusion of Female Leaders of Color in West Michigan*, is an unapologetic cathartic unveiling of what many women of color already know. The lack of women of color in leadership is due in part to systemic racism, the surreptitious kind and the hooded sheet kind. They note,

> Emerging quantitative data identifies clear gaps and disparities in the presence of and opportunities for women of color in executive leadership roles (Shannon Cohen and Patricia Sosa VerDuin).

This absence is strategic, fathered by racism, materialized by patriarchy and upheld by female leadership that evaluates women of color as unworthy and inexperienced. If we women of color can't get a seat at the table, we are consequently ill equipped to decolonize and respond to institutionalized bias. As we continue to expand our gender justice framework, marginalized identities will be a visible focus area, moving past the simplicity of endorsing "diversity" programs and food festivals. Instead, our work will include strategic accessibility, subject matter that centers POC and their experiences, and creating a space that is radically inclusive. Additionally I envision a more aggressive approach in K-12, highlighting racial and gender justice. The CWGE currently works with K-12 schools on bystander and consent education but would like to expand our offerings to include gender justice education.

Assistant director

Prior to joining the center, I served as the assistant director for the Office of Multicultural Affairs (OMA). While my work focused primarily on the experience of people of color, I had increasingly began focusing on the experiences of women and girls of color, as well as LGBTQ people of color. Every morning, I would pass by the WC. We were close in physical proximity, but the work was different. This siloed approach often excluded the perspectives of those with intersecting identities. One example of this was a panel that highlighted police brutality where black women were absent from the narrative. When asked why the panelists were all black cisgender men, leadership responded that "eventually" we would discuss others. As a black woman, this dismissal rendered me, and women like me, invisible. I felt as if I needed to choose my race over my gender, although both are key parts of my identity and cannot be separated.

In the WC, finding representations of women of color was also challenging. Walking past the center, I remembered not seeing myself in the space. Calling myself a feminist did not feel reflective of my experience as a woman of color. Although I didn't even have the language to describe my lived experiences, that soon changed. Our division was assigned *The Combahee River Collective* to guide us as we began discussing intersectionality. *The Combahee River Collective* states "We also often find it difficult to separate race from class from sex oppression because in our lives they are most often experienced simultaneously" (4). This was the first time I began to think of my identities as inextricably linked; addressing issues of racial injustice and gender inequities meant having to look at how they upheld and maintained one another.

As a black Latina woman, my unapologetic discussion of gender justice through an intersectional frame created tension. Lorde shares that "Black women have on one hand always been highly visible, and so, on the other hand, have been rendered invisible through the depersonalization of racism" (42). While my presence became known to some feminist colleagues, my racialized experiences were rendered invisible, or mentioning race created discomfort and hostility. I began to internalize the exclusion and hostility directed my way, however, my silence was not serving anyone, especially my students. Lorde said in *Sister Outsider*, "And it is never without fear – of visibility, of the harsh light of scrutiny and perhaps judgement, of pain of death. But we have lived through all of those already, in silence, except death" (43). She went on to state "your silence will not protect you" (41); staying silent about my reality would not make my oppression stop. Therefore, it was imperative that I spoke truth to power, because it mattered to myself and to my students. Through speaking my truth, it makes space for various experiences that may not have been reflected in the former WC.

Honoring our whole selves

While engaging in this work, our approach has been grounded in authenticity and transparency. Much of the work requires us to model praxis, not only how we live feminist theories and ideologies but also how we create our own theoretical frame grounded in our identities and lived experiences. By engaging in gender justice work from an authentic frame, we create dissonance with those who preach feminist theories but do not practice them. When there is not a synthesis of theory and practice, those with more marginalized identities (e.g., women of color, queer and trans people, gender nonconforming individuals, those with mental health issues, etc.) are often pushed to the margins. This exemplifies the performativity of those who hold privilege in feminist spaces. On the surface, they project a "model feminist" persona, readily quoting their favorite Audre Lorde or Judith Butler piece, but what happens when you do not fit neatly into their box of what it means to be a feminist? You find yourself once again in the margins. As an example, while I refuse the "unqualified" label offered by colleagues who rejected me in my new position, I wholeheartedly accept a chosen title that inadvertently supports some of their perceptions about me. I stumble, sometimes falling, as I attempt to come to terms with both the lack of voice and my personal politics, permitting me to hold space for parallel contradictions that allow me "to attempt to express the totality of [my]self" (Hill Collins 109).

Be it my constant state of visibility juxtaposed with my invisibility or my love for music that chants resistance in one verse and objectifies women in the next. This weight is not easy to bear, "resolving contradictions of this magnitude takes considerable inner strength" (Hill Collins 110). For example, I sing the chorus to *Bodak Yellow* celebrating my bossy "bloody moves," then on any given Sunday I'll shout hallelujah to Ty Tribbett's homophobic declaration to "come out" the LGBT life because I enjoy the beat. It is complicated, but I do recognize that this is one of the problems inherent in the theoretical application of feminism. There is no perfect way to be feminist because "feminism is flawed, but it offers, at its best, a way to navigate this shifting cultural climate. . . . In truth feminism is flawed because it is a movement powered by people and people are inherently flawed" (Gay x). Gay goes on, "I am not trying to be perfect. I am not trying to have all the answers. I am not trying to say I'm right" (xi). What I am trying to do is be better.

Storytelling

As a strategy to deal with this complexity, CWGE uses storytelling as both a framework, practice, and an outcome. Through utilizing an intersectional frame, the center has hosted programs that provided space for students, faculty, and staff to engage in storytelling for liberation. Storytelling as praxis serves various functions and can be seen in several key programs of the center. In marginalized communities, storytelling fosters connections in groups, serves as a way to validate and affirm their experiences, and provides space for catharsis (Banks-Wallace 20). This can be seen in spaces such as NIARA, the center's mentoring program for women of color, and in center programming. Storytelling affirms our whole selves, whether we are "bad feminists" or not.

Storytelling is an act of resistance and serves as a "a powerful tool for deconstructing and re-visioning research" (Banks-Wallace 20) and "by identifying themselves as subjects, by defining their reality, shaping their new identity, naming their history, telling their story" (hooks, *Talking Back* 43), marginalized communities can theorize their existence. We see this when women of color students and queer and trans students of color reclaim the space and use storytelling as a tool. In our programming, we have provided space for students to discuss stereotypes and narratives that are associated with their marginalized identities. They then have the opportunity to reclaim or counter the narratives that had been set for them. A woman of color student shared that she often would get referred to as "loud" and how it was associated with being "ratchet or ghetto." She then said "I am loud, so what? It's only ghetto or ratchet if I am loud, but if a man, or specifically a white man is loud, he is seen as assertive or is a boss." This quote shows that when a woman of color has the space to explore narratives, she is then able to counter those narratives in a way that is reflective of her lived experiences.

Conclusion

Through this act of telling our stories and unpacking the history of the center, we have shared our insecurity as professionals and leaders, as bad feminists, and as those who question their belonging in doing radically inclusive gender justice work. Do we think that makes us different than others engaging in gender justice work? No, it simply makes us willing to share our struggle in hopes that others will engage in similar dialogues. Knowing we are all fumbling along in this imperfect journey, might make all outsiders feel less alone and stronger in their ability to serve students. Serving students is our ultimate purpose and knowing ourselves makes that journey all the more useful.

Works cited

Alcoff, Linda. "Cultural Feminism versus Post-structuralism: The Identity Crisis in Feminist Theory." *Signs*, vol. 13, no. 3, 1988, pp. 405–36.

Banks-Wallace, Joan. "Emancipatory Potential of Storytelling in a Group." *Journal of Nursing Scholarship*, vol. 30, 1998, pp. 17–21.

Cohen, Shannon, and Ver Duin. "Invisible Walls, Ceilings and Floors Championing the Voices and Inclusion of Female Leaders of Color in West Michigan." Presentation, 13 May 2017, Grand Valley State U.

The Combahee River Collective. "A Black Feminist Statement." *Feminist Theory Reader: Local and Global Perspectives*, edited by C. McCann and K. Seung-kyung, 1977. Routledge, 2002.

Davie, Sharon. "Introduction." *University and College Women's Centers: A Journey toward Equity*, edited by Sharon Davie, Greenwood P, 2002, pp. xi–1.

"For Whites Who Consider Being Allies but Find It Much Too Tuff." *Crunk Feminist Collective*, 13 Dec. 2017, www.crunkfeministcollective.com/2012/08/06/for-whites-who-consider-being-allies-but-find-it-much-too-tuff/

Gay, Roxane. *Bad Feminist: Essays*. Harper Perennial, 2014.

Gayle R. Davis Center for Women and Gender Equity. Grand Valley State U, 20 Oct. 2017, www.gvsu.edu/cwge/.

Harris Winfrey, Tamara. *The Sisters Are Alright*. Berrett-Koehler Publishers, Inc., 2015.

Hill Collins, Patricia. *Black Feminist Thought*. Routledge, 2000.

hooks, bell. *Feminism Is for Everybody, Passionate Politics*. South End P, 2000a.

hooks, bell. *Talking Back: Thinking Feminist, Thinking Black*. Toronto: Between the Lines, 1988.

Jennrich, Jessica, and Marlene Kowalski-Braun. "My Head Is Spinning: Doing Authentic Intersectional Work in Identity Centers." *Journal of Progressive Policy Analysis*, vol. 2, no. 3, 2014, pp. 200–10.

Lorde, Audre. *Sister Outsider*. 1984. Ten Speed P, 2007.

Mackenzie, Catriona, and Natalie Stoljar. *Relational Autonomy: Feminist Perspectives on Autonomy, Agency, and the Social Self*. New York: Oxford UP, 2000.

Rankine, Claudia. *Citizen, an American Lyric*. Graywolf P, 2014.

Sojourner, Truth. *Ain't I a Woman?* Women's Convention in Akron, Ohio, 1851.

16 Addressing and dismantling cisgenderism in womxn's centers

Reframing womxn's centers work toward an intersectional critical trans politic[1]

Heather C. Lou

Womxn's centers provide critical community and vital counter-spaces for students to access educational and advocacy resources to combat and dismantle sexism. In their founding, cisgender, middle class, able bodied and minded, heterosexual white womxn were at the center of the work. As postsecondary education student, faculty, and administration demographics continue to diversify, the need for womxn's centers to provide an intersectional feminist (Crenshaw 1989) and gender equity lens is necessary to address the needs of queer and transgender womxn of color in the academy. Womxn's centers must critically interrogate the legacies of their founding, and develop politically savvy tactics to move beyond inclusion for people with multiple marginalized identities navigating the complexity of academic systems. With queer, undocumented, black and brown transgender womxn of color navigating violence, assault, and administrative violence at higher rates than other populations in the United States context, practitioners must re-evaluate internalized cissexism and transphobia. Utilizing critical trans politic (Spade 2015), this chapter provides tools and tactics for womxn's center administrators to address and dismantle cisgender privilege engrained in postsecondary education, and provide creative and tangible recommendations to re-center the most marginalized populations in daily praxis.

Examining our histories

The University of California, Davis (UCD) Womxn's Resources and Research Center (WRRC) was founded in the 1971 as a result of white womxn students navigating sexual harassment from faculty members and supervisors, and is situated on colonized lands of the Patwin people. The WRRC provided referral services and support groups for survivors of harassment and violence, later expanding to academic discipline support through libraries and research to address and eliminate gender bias, primarily in the science, technology, engineering, and mathematics (STEM) fields. In its founding, the WRRC was located in a temporary building and was later moved to the basement of a building on the periphery of campus. After having the budget essentially eliminated, students protested at the main administration building. Students engaged in a sit-in and the WRRC's budget was restored, along with the center being moved to the first floor of a building on the main quad, creating ample visibility for resources and support for students navigating sexual harassment and gender bias. The WRRC and the womxn's studies program were housed together, in an effort to institutionalize the bond between academic and support services for womxn on campus.

The WRRC career and student employees reflected the racial demographics of UCD, and was led primarily by white and cisgender womxn until the 2000s, when several staff members of color joined the team. In 2012, there was a national search for a director, which was successful in hiring a womxn of color in this vital leadership role on campus. Within two years, the WRRC career and student employees were primarily queer and trans people of color engaging in critical identity reflection; confidential support services for sexual harassment, violence, and reproductive health; intersectional feminist educational programming; institutional advocacy; counseling and referral services; and outreach to local non-profit and government organizations serving womxn, transgender, femme, gender nonconforming, agender, or gender expansive populations.

I joined the WRRC team in 2014 as the assistant director of outreach. As a queer, disabled, cisgender, survivor/surviving womxn of color administrator who utilizes critical theory and praxis, it is essential to examine our hxstories to better understand the potential of our futures. Our team's ability to recruit, retain, outreach to, learn with, and support queer and trans students of color didn't occur overnight. It took years of critical community building, collaboration, reflection, continued unlearning of internalized homo- and transphobia, and feedback with and for the communities we served before creating a safer space for people with multiple marginalized identities to exist and resist in the spaces we shared. These growing pains to create more inclusive counter-spaces (Solórzano et al. 2000) with and for students, staff, and faculty on the gendered margins at UCD were humbling and are lessons I continue to bring with me as I interrogate my own performance of gender, race, sexuality, and other intersectional identities in my every day. The following provides practical tools and tactics for womxn's centers to explore their understanding of performing gender, gender roles, internalized transphobia, cissexism, and cisgenderism.

Context

The UCD WRRC staff includes eight student community organizers, two student graphic/web designers, one graduate research coordinator, one program/budget/finance coordinator, two assistant directors, and one director. Creating a common context within the team was necessary in order to explore identities, identity politics, narratives, power, and privilege within a hierarchical and bureaucratic postsecondary education system. Within an intersectional feminist praxis, we attempted to flatten the hierarchy, and operate through a critical community and consensus-building perspective. Bettez (10) defines critical community as:

> interconnected, porously bordered shifting webs of people who through dialogue, active listening, and critical question posing, assist each other in critically thinking through issues of power, oppression, and privilege.

Critical community and consensus is emphasized to staff in all processes: interviewing, training, budgeting, educational programming, and evaluating. Practicing critical community and consensus allows for all voices in around the table to be heard, and to recognize who isn't in the space to make decisions. This opens a channel for staff members to recognize their positionality and privilege of being able to access spaces, and also works to center the needs of the most marginalized populations (queer, transgender, femme, disabled, fat, womxn, people of color, immigrants, refugees, etc.), critical tenants of critical trans politic (Spade) and intersectional feminism, when developing and implementing initiatives. As community organizers, student staff members are challenged to develop relationships with other students, staff, and faculty to better understand their educational and advocacy-related needs from the WRRC. This might manifest in supporting student advising, accessing meeting spaces, ordering books or resources for the library, or creating programming that relates to issues such as violence in queer and transgender people of color communities or ways to engage in safer sex.

The concepts of critical community, critical trans politic, and intersectional feminism recognize that there is not a monolithic experience around womxnhood, which leaves the WRRC and other womxn's centers to explore "what is womxnhood?" and "who do womxn's centers serve?" The founding and original purpose of many womxn's centers was to eliminate sexism and harassment on postsecondary college campuses. Given the staff dynamics and changing demographics, the WRRC needed to find more expansive answers to these questions, starting with understanding cisgender privilege and gender identities.

As a team, the WRRC defined gender as a social construct to classify a person as a man, womxn, or other identities within, along, outside, or around those binary concepts. Transgender identity might describe a wide range of identities that and experiences of people whose gender identity and/or expression differs from conventional expectations based on their assigned sex and/or gender at birth. Cisgender identity is performance in a gender role that society deems to match the person's assigned sex at birth. The prefix "cis-" means "on this side of" or "not across." Cisgender is a term used to call attention to the privilege of people who are not transgender and, as WRRC staff members develop their critical consciousness through developing baseline context about the center's history and narrative around its founders, it became imperative for staff to recognize ways that their cissexism and internalized transphobia have impacted their ability to advocate with and for community members who identify as transgender, femme gender nonconforming, agender, or gender expansive populations. Cisgenderism and cissexism are terms that reinforce the false binary of genders, and serve to erase the existence of transgender and femme womxn of color experiences with violence. If the staff was to address and begin to dismantle cisgenderism and cissexism, critical reflection and radical praxis must be utilized to create more inclusive and hopefully safer spaces for queer and transgender womxn of color within the UCD community.

The WRRC's staff recognized that if they were to serve people of all minoritized genders, they needed to clarify their mission and values. By defining womxn with an "x" and expanding their focus to "gender equity" versus serving only cisgender womxn through a consensus dialogue, the WRRC developed the following definition of "gender equity" to help guide their practices moving forward:

> The social constructions of gender lead to disparities in social, economic, and political opportunities. To achieve gender equity, disparities specifically impacted by one's other salient identities should be identified and addressed in ways that rectify imbalances between all genders.

By developing a common context, the WRRC staff was able to develop common ground to begin exploring ways that cisgender privilege impacted their biases, services, and ability to develop meaningful relationships with community members of marginalized genders. The following section will provide tactics the WRRC utilized in order to begin addressing and dismantling cisgenderism in traditional womxn's center spaces, in order to embrace and utilize intersectional feminist praxis.

Within the WRRC, defining common context and theoretical foundation was a collaborative process that attempted to recognize the perspectives, identities, and experiences of students, staff, faculty, and community members needing to access services. The postsecondary institutional system is inherently a microcosm of the U.S. white supremacist, heteropatriarchal, cisgenderist, ableist, colonial foundations in its reinforcement of chilly educational environments: lack of accessibility, attrition of students with minoritized identities, exclusionary policies, and financial strain for cultural and identity-based centers and/or academic programs. Collaboration, consensus, and intersectional feminist praxis are antithetical to these practices. White supremacist heteropatriarchy is also disrupted when cisgender, queer womxn of color are leaders who attempt to dismantle exclusive and violent practices, which created conditions for institutionalized homophobia, racism, and sexism to thrive. WRRC staff members were forced to navigate institutional politics and bias when shifting to utilizing a critical trans politic and focusing on creating a more gender inclusive mission and vision. Other administrators would state that by narrowing a focus to serve the most marginalized populations, the center would miss supporting a larger demographic of students, staff, and faculty. However, through dialogue, communication, and aspiring allyship with/from other administrators, affirmative action and equal opportunity offices, human resources, student government, faculty members in gender and womxn's studies departments, and local nonprofit organizations, we were able to help partners understand the importance of the context clarification and shift.

Case study: community organizer educational curriculum

The WRRC selected and hired eight community organizers and one graduate research coordinator for the 2015–2016 academic year. As the WRRC is a confidential resource for sexual harassment, sexual assault, domestic violence, stalking, reproductive health, and other gender-related topics, it is necessary for the undergraduate and graduate student staff to engage in rigorous training to ensure their ability to best serve students, staff, and faculty navigating issues of safety and identity. The undergraduate student staff participate in a ten-week academic, credit-bearing course to learn the WRRC's philosophy, mission, and vision, as well as to create a foundation of theory to practice (praxis) gender equity-related educational and advocacy work, facilitated by the two assistant directors. Each class period is two hours, and focuses on identity, power, privilege, and intersectional feminist current issues. This allows for staff members to begin understanding their initial experiences with gender performance and socialization, particularly as these learned norms connect with race, sexuality, ability, citizenship, class, size, spirituality, coloniality, among other identities and experiences. The class includes mentorship between current staff members and the incumbent staff, to share historical knowledge, practices, and oral tradition of the WRRC. Throughout the ten-week course, staff members were challenged to critically examine their own internalized bias around gender, particularly wrestling with the questions:

- Who is a "womxn"?
- What is "womxnhood"?
- How does the WRRC's history impact our legacy, biases, and who has access to our work?
- Who does the WRRC serve? Who is in the space and who is missing?
- What does it mean to center and serve the most marginalized in our practices?
- How do we enact gender equity in our practices, given our own power and privilege in the spaces we occupy?

There are no correct and clear answers to these questions, and the ten-week academic course allows for staff to question their epistemological roots of gender identity and expression, and is intended to focus on critical community development. By listening, sharing counternarratives and storytelling, building trust, developing accountability and naming privilege, and practicing creativity, the community organizers and graduate research coordinator were able to better understand how their identities impact their ability to serve people with identities and experiences similar and vastly different their own. During class periods, the staff practiced sharing their pronouns and asking others for theirs, inquired about how they learned about their own assumptions around femininity and masculinity, explored and unpacked how gender intersects with their social identities through readings and dialogues (blogs, articles, book chapters, videos, etc.), and how cisgender privilege impacts experiences such as: bathrooms, gyms, medical spaces, shopping, socializing, dating and relationships, reproductive health education, assumptions about other people's pronouns and relationships, among other biases. At the time of the course, there was national publicity about transgender womxn of color being murdered within the United States, and staff intentionally focused on how that impacted their understanding of their roles on campus as confidential resources around violence. The staff were challenged not only to reflect on their cisgender privilege, but also to recognize and own their own mistakes/guilt, interrupt microaggressions and invalidations, and other forms of gender-based violence.

When developing the curriculum, the assistant directors were intentional about understanding how their own cisgender womxn of color experiences have contributed to their own upholding of cisgenderism and cissexism. In creating and facilitating the course content, the assistant directors were intentional about recognizing their power and positionality as career staff members, and attempted to include current student staff members' feedback in the development process. This allows for the opportunity to engage in intersectional feminist praxis by flattening the bureaucratic hierarchy in having students facilitate certain class dialogues and encouraging them to ask follow-up questions to all members in the space, including instructors.

As an instructor and supervisor of the staff, it was vital for me to share times when I made mistakes as a cisgender womxn: when I was well-meaning and wanted to be the "good cisgender person" who tokenizes/d people who identify as transgender, misgendered community members, looked at someone who is more masculine presenting and assumed they were in the wrong-gendered bathroom, when I used derogatory names/phrases that were transphobic or cissexist, when I failed to notice if buildings or venues have gender inclusive bathrooms or spaces, or times when my guilt and shame as a cisgender person caused me to freeze in moments of noticing microaggressions or violence toward people who are transgender and I didn't use my voice to address them. If the WRRC was going to recognize the ways that cisgender womxn were centered in its founding, it was also imperative that I recognized how I also have been complicit in my own life experiences. By role modeling this narrative sharing and ways to improve my own competency around gender, the students, staff, faculty, and community members I was able to work with and for were also able to be vulnerable in re-thinking and re-practicing their performance and assumptions around gender.

After the ten-week academic course, staff continued training over a 40+ hour period over the summer and throughout the year at weekly staff meetings. In these spaces, the original questions posed in class were revisited, particularly when crafting physical and psychological spaces for educational programming. Staff also participated in role plays in ways to interrupt microaggressions and misgendering, questioning assumptions about genders of the people they serve in a confidential resource meeting, and about creating programming that was dynamic and gender inclusive. The following section highlights additional practical applications for utilizing critical trans politic and intersectional feminist praxis in womxn's center spaces, in order to continue to address and dismantle gender exclusive practices.

Center and pay transgender womxn of color

If gender equity is the goal of womxn's center work, and if we are going to center the most marginalized in our work, we must recognize that there are specific white supremacist structures that must be addressed. White supremacy privileges cisgender, white, heterosexual, religious, able-bodied-minded, educated men, and allows them access to job security, housing, leadership and consulting opportunities, and much more. When possible, womxn's centers should find ways to contract transgender womxn of color, femmes, and gender nonconforming educators, artists, vendors, or other speakers for their events. Although it sounds simple, appropriately paying transgender womxn of color for their emotional, psychological, and physical labor is a tactic in practicing critical trans politic through an intersectional feminist lens.

When the WRRC decided to reframe their practices through a gender equity lens, they decided that all major speakers will be trans womxn or femmes of color. For their main conferences, the WRRC contracted Jennicet Gutiérrez (a womxn's rights activist), Hina Wong-Kalu (hula instructor and political activist), and helped bring Laverne

Cox (actress, activist, educator) to address conservative right-wing speakers who were openly anti-queer and trans in their politic. The team created space at each of these events for queer and transgender students of color to access registration first and to attend at little to no cost. Although events weren't always microaggression-free, the WRRC team was able to attempt to provide space for feedback, assessment, processing, support, and to hold ourselves and community members accountable for any transphobic, cissexist, or cisgenderist harm that might have been done. By being transparent about our processes and need for feedback, the team was able to continue to build trust and create more inclusive spaces for people of all marginalized genders to explore their own identities and impacts on their community.

Create gender inclusive spaces and practices

There are no simple action items to create more gender inclusive spaces and practices. Over two years, the WRRC team focused on developing intentional physical and psychological spaces that recognized gender equity as a goal. The team began introducing their names and pronouns (no pronouns, they/them/theirs, zi/zem/zir, xi/hir/hirs, she/her/hers, he/him/his, other chosen pronouns) at every meeting and event; asked community members for their pronouns over the phone, in person, and on forms; and changed all main floor bathrooms into gender inclusive single and multi-stall spaces. On all committees, WRRC representatives were able to name and invite the people whose voices and presence were missing in event planning and policy development/implementation processes. During confidential drop-in appointments, staff members practiced referring to people's partners as "they/them" until they were identified, referred to reproductive body parts and actions as behaviors without gender roles, and provided resources to on-campus and community resources that were known for serving people of all genders in their practices.

Understanding how cissexism, cisgenderism, and transphobia have served as tools to keep transgender womxn of color out of gender-based centers can help administrators reflect on their privilege and guide students toward equity. Womxn's centers can create and implement policy, initiatives, and educational programming that paves the way for gender inclusive practices. Creating gender inclusive bathrooms, asking for pronouns, implementing critical trans politic and intersectional feminism in their curriculum, and engaging in committee work that advocates with and for people with marginalized genders can transform the academy for the better.

New visions for a changing landscape

With budget cuts, institutionalized sexism, and continued violence against womxn, womxn's centers are shrinking in existence in postsecondary education. This is troubling, as these spaces have been necessary to continue to support empower womxn and people with marginalized genders to navigate and persist to matriculation. Although womxn's centers have been sites for empowerment, we, as practitioners, must also recognize how these spaces have been sites of violence against transgender, femme, gender nonconforming, agender, or gender expansive populations.

If administrators are able to truly center people with the most marginalized genders and experiences in their work, they are positioned to engage in radically transformational gender justice work. By addressing institutionalized and internalized transphobic, cissexism, and cisgenderism, administrators are able to unlearn their own biases and create space for re-learning performances of gender. The investment in our critical communities takes work, time, emotional labor, and pushing our limits in ways that are at the ends of our comfort, especially as centers with cisgender privilege deeply rooted in our practices. In this continually changing landscape with more diverse student, staff, and faculty populations, as well as national trends of violence against transgender womxn of color, womxn's centers can provide education and advocacy that practically applies critical trans politic and intersectional feminist praxis to create more equitable and empowering learning environments for all.

Note

1 Womxn is intentionally spelled with an "x" in order to recognize the agency of womxn, individually and collectively, and to challenge the notion that womxn are necessarily defined through their relation to men (i.e., "man" as the universal default, "woman" as a subcategory or afterthought). This spelling is intended to honor anyone who has ever, ever will, or currently identifies as a womxn.

Works cited

Bettez, Silvia Cristina. "Critical Community Building: Beyond Belonging." *Educational Foundations*, vol. 25, nos. 3–4, 2011, pp. 3–19.

Crenshaw, Kimberlé. "Demarginalizing the Intersection of Race and Sex: A Black Feminist Critique of Antidiscrimination Doctrine, Feminist Theory, and Antiracist Politics." *University of Chicago Legal Forum*, 1989, p. 139.

Solórzano, Daniel, et al. "Critical Race Theory, Racial Microaggressions, and Campus Racial Climate: The Experiences of African American College Students." *Journal of Negro Education*, vol. 69, no. 1, 2000, pp. 60–73.

Spade, Dean. *Normal Life: Administrative Violence, Critical Trans Politics, and the Limits of Law*. Durham, NC: Duke UP, 2015.

17 Vision to action
Inside out strategic planning

Karlyn Crowley

Let's be honest – no one ever wrote an ode to strategic planning. Those two words – strategic planning – often strike dread in administrative hearts. You might feel anxious, even resentful, at the undertaking. Benjamin Ginsberg, in the *Chronicle of Higher Education*, names what many feel: "The Strategic Plan: Neither Strategy nor Plan, but a Waste of Time."

All too often we plan for others. We abide by external standards rather than by an inward-driven process. We create plans that remain locked in drawers or on laptops rather than ones that are manageable, or, dare I even say, delightful? What sounds like a recipe for soup – simple, organic – is a recipe for sustainable change. Keep these four key foci in mind – **purpose, connection, vision, action** – to devise a liberating strategic plan from the inside out.

Let purpose through story be your guide

In a pivotal lesson, Jiminy Cricket says to Pinocchio in the movie, "let your conscience be your guide." This is how Pinocchio comes to life and stops performing externally. In social justice work, there are so many problems to solve, so many needs to be met that we lose sight of the purpose and passion we first felt. If we capture "the why," or purpose, of our centers then that is what Simon Sinek in *Start With Why* argues is the most important work of an organization. Purpose and story have many names: mission, core identity, founding principles, etc. Organizations that flourish understand their core story, return to it, and act from it.

Purpose

Opening Questions: What is the purpose of your center? Who is especially purposeful (think passionate and focused)?

I want to tell you the story of Cassandra Voss, the person, after whom the Cassandra Voss Center is named, an intersectional identity center at St. Norbert College in De Pere, Wisconsin. Cassandra was 18 and in my class when I mentioned the suffragist Alice Paul. Cassandra ran up and said, "I am obsessed with Alice Paul and I like to braid my hair back so that I look just like her." Who is this won-drous feminist geek, I thought? Most students don't know who Alice Paul is let alone turn her into their Halloween costume. That story epitomizes Cassandra the person.

Cassandra made things more alive, sunnier, more just. At the end of Introduc-tion to Women's and Gender Studies, she planned a class party in the residence hall with feminist snacks and a gendery soundtrack. On the campus women's center staff, she argued for the first feminist man to work there. Activist and scholar, friend, and daughter, Cassandra made me, and everyone, want to be bet-ter. When Cassandra died in a car accident at 21, our hearts broke. The story of the Cassandra Voss Center is the story of her passion. In turn, that passion fueled her father's determination to raise nearly three million dollars to build the most beautiful gender center in the country (his words). And he did.

This is a hard center story to follow. Others say, "your story is unique; we have nothing comparable." It is a unique story. So is yours. I purposively narrated Cas-sandra's story with careful detail. Can you let it inspire you to tell your center story? The challenge for women's and gender equity centers is to not draw on diffuse passion but to name it, create a specific story, and tell that story again and again. Passion=mission=story: that's how we draw people in, keep them close, and build momentum.

Find your story exercise

Write for ten minutes on these two guiding ideas: (1) name and describe in as much detail as possible the person of passion and purpose related to your center; (2) write down one specific story using the five senses – touch, taste, smell, hear, feel – that captures the personality and vision of that person. Imagine if you had to give a speech and share one story about this person, what would it be? The advanced version of this exercise extracts these and other central themes beyond a single person. The key themes and stories eventually become the core values of your center. Do this exercise a few times with staff/allies/alumni. Find the person to best articulate the final stories in writing; agree on a script and several stories to tell.

Bridge your story

Tie these purposeful stories to staff and board/advisory passions so that people are reminded of their own investment in the center's story. Start a retreat or monthly check-in by having staff share why they got into center work; have them con-nect their story with one of these key stories and values of your center. At the Cassandra Voss Center, we had a wall of pictures and descriptions of "who do you work for?" One staff member worked for her younger self. It's motivating to see the images of the people we do this work for. Staff knew we all worked on behalf of Cassandra; we needed to also remember that we work on behalf of those who make our life worth living now.

Communicate your story

Create space for your key center story in all communications: on your website, in social media, in your center itself. Tell the story at major events – use the story to name and identify what is central. When you do focus groups and assessment, ask for the keywords connected to your center. Do those words reflect the story you tell? If not, recalibrate. Your entire staff should be able to tell the story (and eventually your core values) in a variety of ways: succinct, medium length, and long. First practice the pitch then videotape everyone telling the stories. Hire a consultant or do a trade to give feedback so that a neutral party hones the craft of storytelling. Patrick Reinsborough and Doyle Canning remind us, "Historically, the power of stories and storytelling has always been at the center of social change efforts" (15).

When people are in panic mode about support and resources, they focus on meeting expectations of others rather than clarifying and sharing the core mission. Spending time giving flesh and bone to that story is not a distraction; it's your reason for existing. People respond to specific stories with a compelling plot and rich detail. People do not respond to abstract missions or vague calls. Give people something to love and hope for.

Closing Questions: What is your plan to tell the story of the passion of your center? Visualize its power to transform by imagining audience response. Where will you share that story to inspire and motivate others?

Connection

Opening Questions: What are the most important relationships at your center? Are any relationships surprising? Do you have unlikely allies?

Cassandra Voss and her dad, Kurt Voss, had weekly breakfast at the greasiest spoon in De Pere, Wisconsin. It was across from a paper mill, had orange carpet on the walls, and smelled like 1,000 fried eggs. Every week, Cassandra would talk with her dad about her work at the women's center or in her women's and gender studies classes. As Kurt Voss noted, "Cassandra might say, 'Dad, transgender issues are important.' And I would have no idea what she was talking about. But I listened because I love my daughter. I also debated with her because I equally respected her." Maximizing on the specific visual image of a father and daughter talking about challenging topics softens and disarms naysayers; it welcomes skeptics. People have an emotional rather than purely intellectual response to the idea of dialogue. Thus, we seized on this image as the foundational model of "dialogue across difference."

Can centers model such dialogue across difference? It's an open question. This historical moment of extreme polarization in which every "side" speaks to itself clashes with colleges that are supposed to foster free exchange of ideas. Our centers can be marginal enclaves supporting like-minded ideologies. How do we stretch? One thing is certain: relationships are the bridge. Relationships can be an afterthought when programming for our centers is often job one. Strategic plans are conceived as project-driven rather than relationship-driven. Flip that equation.

The Cassandra Voss Center cultivated an unusual relationship whose effects were surprising. It became clear that there were businesses locally who wanted our programming, even if they didn't realize it. Everyone needs diversity work. Social justice scholars and activists know that better than anyone. Where is the mutual benefit in that equation of need and expertise? As the cliché goes, what would a win-win look like? Many centers are skeptical about working with businesses; some argue they're capitalist sell-outs. Can we push on that easy assumption? No space is pure. Higher education is not pure. While most colleges and universities are nonprofit, they take part in investments, deals, relationships to be viable financially. For centers to flourish, we must strategize better on our own behalf and rely less on others. It's a hard truth. There are ways to do it with integrity.

Here's how we began working with a major insurance company. Employees in this company's diversity and inclusion (D&I) "interest group" wanted our educational programming on issues of difference, equity, and histories of oppressions. In turn, they offered to support us financially. Win-win. We also created "value added" for our college through connections and programming. A cycle of mutual uplift – college to business to center to city – and back again meant that our center is an asset. Our center solves problems. Ideally that's what centers should do. The company was not poised to do the kind and quality of diversity and inclusion programming that our center is trained to do. We elevated their diversity programming. By extension, a number of employees – LGBT, people of color – expanded local friend and colleague networks through the programming. When the company hosted events, with the resources to do so, the company became a hub of diversity connection for the city. Once, the company shared its videographer to tape a critical lecture when we struggled to afford one. They used their resources and we used our knowledge – both for a common goal.

Is there a downside? Other than having to face purist skeptics who wonder if you're less radical because you're working with a for-profit company? It's hard to imagine a downside when this D&I interest group surpassed all expectation as collaborators. Here's why. The Cassandra Voss Center has the great privilege of being a sister center to the bell hooks Institute at Berea College; we have brought feminist scholar and writer bell hooks for several years for a residency. For this programming on bell hooks' work, we planned reading groups and discussions with bell hooks herself. This is how the company did their homework. First, they created and hung posters with bell hooks quotations throughout the workplace; then they used their national video system to have a three-part book discussion; finally they attended all events related to our center's programming. The company participants were more prepared, more authentic, and more vulnerable than any other constituency. One company employee said, "My husband started chastising our grandson for wanting to learn to sew. After reading hooks' *The Will to Change: Men, Masculinity, and Love*, I interrupted him and said, 'No. Our grandson can sew. That is not just women's work. He should be able to express himself however he wants.'" I was floored – my staff was floored. That is model integrated learning: she read the text, understood the concepts, applied it to her life, shared her story, and was changed by the experience. This is social justice transformation.

Women's center director Xenia Markowitt in "Is It My Job to Teach the Revolution?" notes "Many of us have positions that simultaneously require us to represent the institution as one of its officers, even as we hope to use our positions to agitate for social change." Markowitt discusses social change making inside a college. How can such social change making happen in a corporation outside a college? Often for-profit companies are resourced, efficient, less bureaucratic, and quicker to assess initiatives. We may discover how to enact social change differently by learning from them.

Big change exercise

Make three lists that would change your center:

1   List five to ten relationships to cultivate and strengthen.
2   List at least five relationships (people, orgs, areas) that challenge and expand the center.
3   List at least three dream relationships for the future.

Consider your core relationships and communicate what is essential about them. We repeat the father-daughter (Kurt and Cassandra) story at every event and in all our key marketing. We depict this relationship because it moves people – frequently to tears. Don't shy away from cultivating, sharing, and promoting the relationships that make your center possible. A powerful side effect is that others want to be a part of that relational glow. It draws people like a magnet.

Closing Questions: How do you cultivate and foster the relationships that are the foundation of your center? What relationships need repair or change? Where can you concentrate relationship building for maximum results?

Vision

Opening Question: What is your BHAG, or Big Hairy Audacious Goal?

It's hard to dream big when colleges and universities are in a crisis. Women's and gender equity centers struggle with the negative trickle down effects from financial belt tightening. Some centers even face elimination. Centers that started in the 1960s and 1970s, concomitant with the building of Women's and Gender Studies programs, are asked to justify their existence in new ways. Typically, retrenchment means cutting not dreaming bigger. What if having bigger dreams will save us?

Father-donor Kurt Voss, a business person and CEO, drew on the Jim Collins and Jerry Porras classic *Built to Last: Successful Habits of Visionary Companies* that urges companies to have at least one big, hairy, audacious goal, or BHAG. The Cassandra Voss Center was Voss's personal BHAG. Listening and watching someone articulate their BHAG for seven years was humbling. He would say, "I will build the most beautiful center in the country" and "The WMGS program will be the best in the country." Part of me thought – this is crazy. But after hearing it again and again and wanting it to be real, one day I started to believe it.

Social justice colleagues exhibit both more exuberance for our work and also more dejection. How do we maintain a big vision through obstacles? Most strategic plans contain: a vision, a mission, core values, a list of goals, people accountable to those goals with champions and timelines and a facilitator/ coach to hold you to them. But it's vision that is key. Collins and Porras cite "we found more evidence of this powerful mechanism [BHAGS] in the visionary companies and less evidence of it in the comparison companies" (94). So how do BHAGS work?

> Like the moon mission, a true BHAG is clear and compelling and serves as a unifying focal point of effort – often creating immense team spirit. It has a clear finish line, so the organization can know when it has achieved the goal; people like to shoot for finish lines. A BHAG engages people – it reaches out and grabs them in the gut. It is tangible, energizing, highly focused. People "get it" right away; it takes little to no explanation.
>
> (Collins and Porras 94)

A BHAG should be a single sentence, say Collins and Porras (94). They use the moon mission as an analogy because everyone understands it. The goal might be "unreasonable" but could possibly be achieved (97). The BHAG should be uncomfortable; everything in us may fight this suggestion. Why plan when many want us to close? Why dream when many want us to die? Plodding mediocrity is easier but deadly because it's soul killing. And if anyone knows how to reclaim "HAG," it's women's and gender equity center folk!

Magnify vision exercise

Make three lists that magnify vision:

1   Make a list of at least five big center goals.
2   Choose the one goal that is paramount and the biggest stretch.
3   Distill that goal to a few words or a brief statement shorter than one sentence.

Build the BHAG. Start small. Type it on slips of paper. Say it aloud at every meeting. Make it particular and real. Take a month to live with it to distill it to its best version. Then put it everywhere internally. Use visualizations to manifest the BHAG. As staff begin to believe and work toward the dream, slowly start to unveil it to others. Keep it close at first and let momentum build. What is there to lose? At a minimum, you will have the most motivated staff.

Closing Questions: Who would be your dream team to build this BHAG? Where could you share it to seed the reality?

Action

Opening Question: What is the one action, that if you took, would change your center forever?

What are the best strategies to reach your goal? How many people do you know work with a living, breathing strategic plan that produces results? Likely few. Patrick Sanaghan and Mary Hinton state that in higher education strategic planning, "Visionaries are a dime a dozen. Those leaders who can actually execute important things are as rare as blue diamonds."

In consulting, I ask, is there any personal goal you've set and met that you feel proud of? Like a hobby or exercise? A New Year's resolution? One organizational challenge is that higher education is a structure largely built on people who need to be self-motivated. Typically, higher education does not have the same elaborate accountability and goal-setting structures as for-profits do. How do we create an office culture to set our team up for success?

Watching father-donor Kurt Voss overcome obstacles building the Cassandra Voss Center has been extraordinary. He grew his business as a CEO while also fundraising; the two together contributed to the center. He faced naysayers and doubters. He had to manage multiple constituencies, not always in harmony. What kept him going? Accountability, group support, and his faith. Fundamentally his belief in Cassandra. What can we learn from individuals and groups in order to meet goals?

Discover your team's orientation to goal setting. In order to start a self-reflexive conversation about setting goals, leadership and personality inventories can be helpful. They provide a neutral tool to talk about strengths and growth areas when people often find this topic challenging. We all have feelings about our success or lack thereof of setting and attaining goals. For example, Gretchen Rubin in *The Four Tendencies* has a useful quiz about how personality and habits shape goal attainment. Have your staff take the quiz, discuss it, and tailor the goal setting for better results. Sure, there are strong opinions about how these "tests" are flawed. That's not the point. Assessments like StrengthsFinder, Myers-Briggs, Bolman and Deal, etc., help us have self-reflexive conversations that lead to happier performance. That's the point.

Act now exercise

Make three lists that plot action:

1   By now you have a handful of goals that have emerged from the above work. What is most important for the next three years? How does that relate to your BHAG? Who will be accountable for each goal? Who will back plan each goal?

2   Get strategic about goal setting: weekly, monthly, yearly goals must be specific and manageable like SMART goals, a mnemonic for a process to set goals that are specific, measurable, attainable, realistic, and timely. There are many goal-setting strategies so explore. For example, the Pomodoro technique uses timed units to get work done and break through procrastination. Consider how electronic calendars have reminder functions for goal setting that we could use, but might not. In order to thrive, sample some of these strategies while also being honest about staff habits related to goal attainment.

3   Ideally ask/hire someone to hold your entire team accountable on a quarterly basis. If resources are scarce, consider alternative non-monetary bargaining methods like doing a trade or swap; work with another group or organization to help them strategic plan and they can help with yours. Many nonprofits and areas within a college or university want what we want – a flourishing organization. Money is not a barrier to this kind of strategizing.

A caveat on taking action. Frequently, faculty and staff say, "But we're doing branding and marketing – we hang up posters, we put out newsletters, we use social media. It's not helping!" Let me offer an analogy. Becky Bond and Zack Exley in *Rules for Revolutionaries: How Big Organizing Can Change Everything* suggest that new science on voter turnout tactics has yielded surprising results in grassroots organizing. They've learned as campaign strategists that television ads, robocalls, and direct mailing do not have a great yield on return. What does? "The gold standard for moving voters in elections is a volunteer having a conversation with a voter on the doorstep or the telephone" (xiv). This result shocked them; they had to "scale" (or increase in size and scope) this intimate person-to-person communication in our tech-driven moment. This outcome is instructive for a few reasons. First, we need to ask: Is this the most effective strategy to reach this goal? What innovation, new science, or evidence works better? Who can help me know best practice and counter my own biases?

To answer the above plea when asked about marketing effectiveness, which is really a conversation about how we determine and act on "best practice," we have to ask ourselves hard questions: Why do you think what you did should have worked? Did you talk to an expert in X area or non-expert peers? What don't you know about X and who does know something about X? We want effective communication strategy but we don't always ask actual communication experts. Because women's and gender equity centers are often doing triage, we struggle to find time for this research. We can do it: slow down, research, reflect, and plan what "effective" looks like.

Finally, can you align your dream with the institution's dream? Mutual survival is critical. M.L. Santovec says in "Women's Centers: Even More Relevant and Necessary Today," "Look at what's most important to your school's leaders. Align the center's mission to the institutional goals. Tie questions to what your school thinks is important. Search for the questions under the questions and address them" (7). What if gender and equity centers help keep higher education institutions afloat? What if rather than fearing the chopping block, we get ahead of it?

Closing Questions: Do you back plan – plan all necessary steps back to a beginning point – your dreams? A dream often needs one or a few believers. Who are they?

Authentic planning: from the inside out and not the outside in

Purpose. Connection. Vision. Action. Are you ready? We can build centers authentically and without fear. What can you do right now to make a change, however small? How can we avoid staying stuck and beleaguered without resources? What new tactics can we try as women and gender equity centers to flourish in the coming years? As adrienne maree brown in *Emergent Strategy: Shaping Change, Shaping Worlds*, says, "The vision of an organization is the furthest it can see" (238). Let's find out.

Works cited

Bond, Becky, and Zack Exley. *Rules for Revolutionaries: How Big Organizing Can Change Everything*. Chelsea Green P, 2016.

brown, adrienne maree. *Emergent Strategy: Shaping Change, Changing Worlds*. AK P, 2017.

Collins, Jim, and Jerry I. Porras. *Built to Last: Successful Habits of Visionary Companies*. Harper Perennial, 2011.

Ginsberg, Benjamin. "The Strategic Plan: Neither Strategy nor Plan, but a Waste of Time." *The Chronicle of Higher Education*, July 2011, www.chronicle.com/article/The-Strategic-Plan-Neither/128227. Accessed 1 Aug 2018.

Markowitt, Xenia. "Is It My Job to Teach the Revolution?" *The Chronicle of Higher Education*, Oct. 2009, www.chronicle.com/article/Is-It-My-Job-to-Teach-the/48725. Accessed 1 Aug 2018.

Reinsborough, Patrick, and Doyle Canning. *Re:Imagining Change: How to Use Story-based Strategy to Win Campaigns, Build Movements, and Change the World*. PM P, 2017.

Sanaghan, Patrick, and Mary Hinton. "Be Strategic on Strategic Planning." *Inside Higher Education*, July 2013, www.insidehighered.com/advice/2013/07/03/essay-how-do-strategic-planning. Accessed 1 Aug 2018.

Santovec, M.L. "Women's Centers: Even More Relevant and Necessary Today." *Women in Higher Education*, vol. 21, 2012, p. 7. doi:10.1002/whe.10377.

Sinek, Simon. *Start With Why: How Great Leaders Inspire Everyone to Take Action*. Rep. ed. Portfolio, 2011.

18 Setting a transformative agenda for the next era

Research on women's and gender centers

Raquel Wright-Mair and Susan B. Marine

The need for research about Women's Centers is critical to the long-term success of WGCs. Whether it is assessing whether we are improving the campus environment, meeting goals, students are learning, or we are helping develop feminist leaders, we need to know so that we put limited resources to the best use possible.
– Respondent to WGC research survey

Introduction

Women's and gender centers (hereafter WGCs) provide students, faculty, staff, and campus communities with opportunities for personal growth, support, and connection to others concerned about gender equity (Bengiveno; Curry; Davie; Kasper, "Administration, Structure, and Resources"). They also provide meaningful avenues for feminist, womanist, and other theories of transformative praxis to be shared and enacted, creating the foundation for future generations of activists both within and outside of the academy (Lewis et al.; Marine and Lewis; Markowitt). WGCs provide important spaces, and community, for becoming invested in a feminist identity, and practicing feminism by collaborating with others (Davie; Marine and Lewis). Given that the current political climate in the nation is fraught with hostility toward women of all identities, people of color of all genders, and those who are undocumented (Bouie; Conley; O'Connor and Marans), the necessity of such spaces in higher education is more urgent than ever. The energy emergent from WGCs, and the work they do to promote equity and empowerment, continues to foster change, both on the campus and in the world beyond. Given their long and illustrious history in higher education, WGCs and their work are a topic worthy of close examination through research.

Why does research matter for WGCs in the twenty-first century? Admittedly, the realities of neoliberal university policies, with their focus on assessment and accountability, make it difficult for WGCs to engage in transformational work without feeling the effects of these pressures. The neoliberal university's current norms demand that professionals charged with fostering student learning and providing both instruction and co-curricular learning must also provide evidence of their worth, as they relate to the goals of each institution (Morrissey).

Particularly in the realm of the extra- or co-curricular, whose services are typically not conceived of as "essential" to the working of the institution, having to prove that what you do leads to measurable outcomes for students produces anxiety and uncertainty (Berry and Edmond). While endeavoring to measure and document these outcomes may alleviate some of this anxiety, our argument is different. Research on WGCs is valuable because it enables such centers to advance their missions and support the growth of civically engaged students, to foster feminist social change on campuses where WGCs are found, and to contribute to the next generation of social progress for people of all genders/sexes.

In order to advance the specifics of this argument, we must begin by defining what research is. According to Creswell, research intends to explore an issue by gathering data, which is analyzed to contribute to an understanding of the issue (4). Research on WGCs is thus the systematic exploration and documentation of their activities, missions, benefits, and challenges in order to better understand and explain their impact. As this text has demonstrated, WGCs engage in all manner of activities, including community organizing; intentional activities to foster student development, empowerment, and learning; coalition building among disparate groups within an institution; and advocacy for social change. Research, then, seeks to both describe and formally assess these activities, and the differences they make. It allows us to better understand not only the present picture of WGCs but also to plan for their futures. If the purpose of WGCs is to foster the empowerment of those who take part, it is vital to understand how that process takes place, and how it can be more fruitfully accomplished through gathering and analyzing data, toward greater effectiveness and understanding.

Overview of current research on WGCs

Research on women's centers to date has centered on three specific types: (1) descriptive pieces on WGC herstories, functions, purposes, and missions; (2) pieces documenting and analyzing the social change work fomented by WGCs; and (3) pieces (and frameworks for) describing outcomes measurement of the work of WGCs. Each of these forms contributes to the understanding of WGCs and their work in different ways. Each also provides insight into the ways that such work might be leveraged to shift balances of power and to provide important insight for advancing progressive social change on campuses where WGCs exist. At the same time, the extant literature on WGCs suggests much remains to be done to secure their rightful place, to enable their full flourishing and to honor their legacies of participant empowerment, as well as to understand what is "working" about WGCs.

The literature describing WGCs is varied and includes book chapters, journal articles, and full length books. Indeed, the vast majority of the literature was published between the late 1970s and the late 1990s, an era when many centers were founded and especially active in building their identities as centers of social change. The most comprehensive collection of descriptive essays is Sharon Davie's 2002 edited collection, *University and College Women's Centers: A Journey Toward*

Equity. A significant amount of the research (Bengiveno; Byrne; Clevenger; Gould; Kasper, "A Review of Problems and Practices") published to date on women's centers describes the herstory of centers, their purposes and functions, and challenges they have faced. These narratives also provide a sense of the resiliency centers and their staff have developed in the face of such challenges, including expanding programs to serve growing and diverse populations, enlisting the support of faculty, and brokering alumni involvement to advance their visibility.

Research documenting WGCs' efforts to advance social change, along with the challenges and roadblocks to doing so, has provided a vivid picture of what it means to be dedicated to institutional and societal change work. Marine's study of the ways that WGC staff function as "professional feminists" in higher education, encounter challenge, and negotiate for change, is one example of how empirical work provides insight into the daily realities faced by WGC leaders. Kleinman and Ezzell's narrative regarding the push and pull of pro- and anti-choice factions within a women's center provides insight into the ways WGC leader must navigate contested space in politically fraught campus settings. Wies's chapter documents how women's centers function as classrooms for applied feminist theory, enabling deep learning and engagement with theory to practice concepts. WGC responsiveness to the specific needs and concerns of women of color, LGBTQ students, and people of other minoritized genders has also been documented in the literature, as well as the ways that white, middle-class, heterosexual women's priorities are often foregrounded in feminist movements (Bengiveno; Chuang; Marine et al.; Santovec). Researchers (Marine et al.; Nicolazzo and Harris) have also critically explored the broader philosophical issues related to women's centers and inclusion: Who are they for? Who belongs, who is less often included, and how do matters of belonging and inclusion define their work?

Research on outcomes of WGCs' work has been less commonly conducted, perhaps owing to the time intensiveness of outcomes assessment and the limited resources for assessment typically accorded to WGCs. Claudia Curry's 2008 book-length analysis of a women's empowerment program at one women's center located in a community college is one example. This project involved an extensive interview study of women participating in a structured program to enable them to develop voice and empowerment skills, and to enact those skills in their communities. The thoughtful analysis in Curry's study demonstrates the value of extended-length research projects for showcasing the deeply impactful work that happens in WGCs.

Finally, several scholars who are also leaders of WGCs have devoted significant time to naming the roles, purposes, and functions of WGCs in order to create a set of standards for deployment and assessment of those services. The 2015 Council for the Advancement of Standards (CAS) document outlining standards of practice for women's and gender programs, developed by six current and former leaders of WGCs, identified 12 specific domains around which WGC work should be regularly assessed. This document provides a salient, WGC leader-established framework for measuring the implementation and outcomes of WGC work. While published accounts of use of the CAS standards for WGC assessment are hopefully forthcoming, the framework clearly articulates WGCs as centers of student empowerment and social change – a theme running throughout the literature on WGCs.

Center perspectives on research

In order to remain nimble and responsive to the advancement of WGCs and their continued growth and visibility, setting a research agenda for the next two decades is essential. Arguably, this research agenda must emanate from the needs of the leadership of these centers, be attentive to primary functions and purposes, and must be strategic with respect to increasing their visibility and a shared understanding of their "value-added" work in higher education. To this end, we developed and conducted a survey of WGC leaders to determine (1) what kinds of research they are already undertaking, (2) the desired areas for further development of research and assessment, and (3) current barriers and catalysts to conducting research. The survey was distributed to all members of the WRAC-L (women's resources and action centers) listserv in December 2017; 42 respondents participated in the survey, the results of which are depicted in Table 18.1.

Table 18.1 Survey of WGC leaders' perspectives on research (n = 42)

Question	Responses
Topics of interest	Learning outcomes for students (83%)
	Implementing anti-racist practices (81%)
	Navigating institutional politics (79%)
	Leadership development outcomes (74%)
	Anti-sexual violence prevention efforts (64%)
Most urgently needed research topics	Learning outcomes for students (65.9%)
	Effects of anti-sexual violence programming (49%)
	Anti-racist practices outcomes (45%)
Willing to partner with researchers?	Yes (84%)
	No (16%)
If not, why not?	Feeling too pressed for time (50%)
	Uncertainty about usefulness of results (13%)
	Navigating institutional politics (13%)
Is research on WGCs important to do?	Yes (86%)
	No (14%)
What would make conducting research more appealing?	Outcomes would benefit my center (54%)
	Minimal investment from WGC staff (56%)
	Researcher involved students in the process (51%)
	If funding was available (18%)
Have you previously conducted research?	Yes (37%)
	No (47%)
How would you describe the research process?	Beneficial to my learning (59%)
	Beneficial to my WGC (59%)
	Interesting (60%)
	None of the above (11%)

Note that totals for responses do not equal 100% as we allowed participants to select multiple responses for each question.

The results of this study indicate numerous areas of inquiry that require urgent attention in respect to the growth and development of WGCs. Of those listed, the top research areas identified were (1) learning outcomes for students who participate in WGC programs, (2) effects of anti-sexual violence prevention efforts at WGCs, (3) outcomes of implementing anti-racist practices at WGCs, and (4) navigating institutional politics at WGCs. Respondents overwhelmingly agreed that conducting meaningful research on WGCs was not only necessary, but also crucial to benefitting their respective centers. While 86% of respondents reported valuing research on the work of WGCs, only 37% of respondents had actually participated in research studies on their centers to date. This illustrates there is a gap to be filled in conducting research that can be applied to WGCs. Additionally, those respondents that did participate in research conducted on their centers posited that those studies benefitted their centers, their students and also their own professional development and experience. Therefore, we believe that research conducted on WGCs has been largely well received and appears to have been beneficial to centers across the US.

Research is also strategically positioned to bring together campus and community members involved in WGCs, in order to amplify the positive work already happening there. One respondent mentioned the benefit of collaboration in WGCs, as a means to help to demystify the research experience. In an effort to gain a better understanding of the research process, a larger conversation needs to be had around how research connects to practice. One suggestion for bridging the gap between research and practice is that research should not solely be conducted by scholars, but should also include the participation of those that may be impacted by the research process or are designed to benefit from further understanding of WGCs. Specifically, for maximal effectiveness, research teams should be composed of various community members – staff, students, and other WGC stakeholders – working alongside researchers. This is intended to incorporate a stronger understanding of WGCs from various perspectives and their multiple positionalities. Respondents proposed conferences or summits to provide space for discussions about the benefit of applied research on WGCs, to strengthen the process and understanding of applying research to practice.

Respondents also pointed out that conducting and prioritizing research can be extremely complicated, depending on the politics of their specific institutions, and how WGCs are situated within them. For example, respondents noted that limited resources and time in administrative roles made it more difficult for WGC staff, some of whom already possess the credentials to serve as researchers, to actively engage with the process of conducting and executing research in meaningful ways. One respondent commented, "as staff in WGCs often tasked with a huge mission without adequate institutional support, it is so difficult to make meaningful time to conduct proper research without taking away from other critically important needs of our constituents."

Given the feedback of WGC leaders, we have surmised that future efforts to conduct research focused on WGCs should prioritize the following: (1) measuring and documenting the outcomes of WGC work (including student learning outcomes, outcomes of activist efforts, and outcomes of enacting anti-racist practices in WGCs; and (2) strategies for effectively navigating politics at WGCs. Survey data indicate that WGC leadership are indeed motivated to partner with researchers to conduct further explorations of the work and its impact. Given that the paucity of research on WGC outcomes, coupled with the fact that the leadership are most interested in measuring these outcomes (see Table 18.1), we propose that research issues should be decided upon with WGC constituents and that research conducted should maintain reciprocity with the communities they engage with. Outcomes measurement was described as crucially important to WGCs, especially focused on student learning outcomes, activist efforts, and navigating politics. Measuring learning outcomes is an area where researchers – those whose work is focused on developing tools for measurement and deploying research activities – could be most useful to WGCs. Together, researchers and center staff (who may already, themselves, be skilled researchers) could partner to define these outcomes and develop methodological approaches that center participant voices and perspectives. It is important to note also that research is in fact not valued in every context. As one participant lamented, "[there is] no clear message that conducting research at my Center is valued at my institution, which makes it a difficult time/money/and student ask."

Measuring centers' overall impact and effectiveness could be accomplished in any number of ways, but we principally suggest that WGCs consider the use of the 2015 CAS Standard frameworks in this work. This framework, developed by WGC leaders, provides a streamlined way to determine if centers are meeting their goals across a range of important domains, including how they are organized and led; how they deploy human and other resources; and how they advance diversity, equity, inclusion, and access for a wide variety of different constituencies. Perhaps the most appealing feature of the CAS Standards is that WGCs can use them to conduct their own internal assessments, reducing the need for outside assistance and support, which can be costly and time-consuming. WGC leaders could also create a system whereby three to four staff of a given center might volunteer to use the standards to conduct assessments with other "sister centers," in exchange for having those centers' leaders assess their own. This would enable centers to receive objective feedback from others who are familiar with and invested in the success of their work.

More than 75% of respondents shared that they wanted to see research conducted on the institutional politics of WGCs. Specifically, respondents expressed interest in needing research on strategies for effectively navigating politics at WGCs. The politics experienced by WGCs are important area of investigation due to their impact on how WGCs function. WGCs can be contextualized by understanding institutional politics and require specific attention. These strategies could be multifaceted and include understanding how WGCs advance their purpose and mission, how WGCs advocate for resources, and how WGCs collaborate with other entities to pursue institutional change. These strategies would help better the understanding of the positioning of WGCs at college campuses and how they function within the institution.

Future directions for WGC research

In conclusion, there is a large push for more research to be conducted on WGCs. In order to advance gender equity, especially during politically turbulent times when campus environments may not necessarily be inclusive to those from minoritized identities, research should focus on the outcomes of WGCs, their impact on varying populations, and their ability to serve as transformative spaces. It is important to note that this research should center the perspectives of those that work in these centers, as well as who they serve campus-wide. The involvement of various constituents is beneficial to research due to its purposeful engagement of those who interact with WGCs. Additionally, participants involved in research conducted on WGCs have noted that their participation has been a beneficial experience that has contributed to the development of their voices and empowerment skills. Therefore, the reciprocity of research on WGCs should be maintained and considered of high importance. By creating opportunities for multiple perspectives to be included, community-engaged research welcomes and values participation from stakeholders across the board. With these collective efforts, WGCs can expand and refine their already impressive work to achieve transformative praxis.

Works cited

Bengiveno, Teri Ann. "Feminist Consciousness and the Potential for Change in Campus Based Student Staffed Women's Centers." *Journal of International Women's Studies*, vol. 1, no. 1, 2000, pp. 1–9.

Berry, Jon, and Nadia Edmond. "Discourses of 'Equivalence' in HE and Notions of Student Engagement: Resisting the Neoliberal University." *Student Engagement and Experience Journal*, vol. 3, no. 2, 2014, pp. 1–19. doi:10.7190/seejv3i2.90.

Bouie, Jamelle. "State Actors: President Trump Used People of Color as Cover for His Anti-immigrant Policies." *Slate*, 31 Jan. 2018, https://slate.com/news-and-politics/2018/01/trump-uses-people-of-color-as-cover-for-his-anti-immigrant-policies.html. Accessed 2 Feb. 2018.

Byrne, Kelli Zaytoun. "The Roles of Campus-Based Women's Centers." *Feminist Teacher*, vol. 13, no. 1, 2000, pp. 48–60.

Chuang, I-Chen. "Asian Women Students' Group: Success through Mutual Support." *Women in Higher Education*, vol. 19, no. 7, 2010, p. 19.

Clevenger, Bonnie Mason. "Women's Centers on Campus: A Profile." *Initiatives*, vol. 51, no. 2/3, 1988, pp. 3–9.

Conley, Julia. "Women's March: After First Year of Trump's Anti-woman Agenda, Marches Mobilize Voters." *Common Dreams*, 21 Jan. 2018, www.commondreams.org/news/2018/01/21/womens-march-after-first-year-trumps-anti-woman-agenda-marches-mobilize-voters. Accessed 2 Feb. 2018.

Council for the Advancement of Standards in Higher Education. *CAS Self-assessment Guide: Women's and Gender Programs and Services.* Council for the Advancement of Standards in Higher Education, 2015.

Creswell, John W. *Qualitative Inquiry and Research Design: Choosing among Five Approaches.* SAGE Publications, 2013.

Curry, Claudia H. *Understanding the Empowerment Phenomenon: Effects of a Pilot Women's Empowerment Program on Female College Students.* Verlag, 2008.

Davie, Sharon L., editor. *University and College Women's Centers: A Journey toward Equity.* Greenwood P, 2002.

Gould, Jane S. "Personal Reflections on Building a Women's Center in a Women's College." *Women's Studies Quarterly,* vol. 25, no. 1/2, 1997, pp. 110–19.

hooks, bell. *Teaching to Transgress: Education as the Practice of Freedom.* Routledge, 1994.

Kasper, Barbara. "Campus-based Women's Centers: A Review of Problems and Practices." *Affilia,* vol. 19, no. 2, 2004, pp. 185–98.

Kasper, Barbara. "Campus-based Women's Centers: Administration, Structure, and Resources." *NASPA Journal,* vol. 41, no. 3, 2004, pp. 337–499.

Kleinman, Sherryl, and Matthew B. Ezzell. "Opposing 'Both Sides': Rhetoric, Reproductive Rights, and Control of a Campus Women's Center." *Women's Studies International Forum,* vol. 35, no. 6, Pergamon, 2012.

Lewis, Ruth, et al. "'I Get Together with My Friends and Try to Change It.' Young Feminist Students Resist 'Laddism', 'Rape Culture' and 'Everyday Sexism.'" *Journal of Gender Studies,* vol. 25, 2016, pp. 1–17.

Marine, Susan B., et al. "Gender-inclusive Practices in Campus Women's and Gender Centers: Benefits, Challenges, and Future Prospects." *NASPA Journal about Women in Higher Education,* vol. 10, no. 1, 2017, pp. 45–63.

Marine, Susan B., and Ruth Lewis. "'I'm in This for Real': Revisiting Young Women's Feminism." *Women's Studies International Forum,* vol. 47, 2014, pp. 11–22.

Markowitt, Xenia. "Is It My Job to Teach the Revolution?" *The Chronicle of Higher Education,* 11 Oct. 2009, www.chronicle.com/article/Is-It-My-Job-to-Teach-the/48725.

Morrissey, John. "Regimes of Performance: Practices of the Normalised Self in the Neoliberal University." *British Journal of Sociology of Education,* vol. 36, no. 4, 2015, pp. 614–34.

Nicolazzo, Z., and Crystal Harris. "This Is What a Feminist (Space) Looks Like: (Re) conceptualizing Women's Centers as Feminist Spaces in Higher Education." *About Campus,* vol. 18, no. 6, 2014, pp. 2–9.

O'Connor, Lydia, and Daniel Marans. "Here Are 16 Examples of Donald Trump Being Racist." *Huffington Post,* 16 Feb. 2017, www.huffingtonpost.com/entry/president-donald-trump-racist-examples_us_584f2ccae4b0bd9c3dfe5566. Accessed 2 Feb. 2018.

Santovec, Mary Lou. "Addressing Privilege in Today's Women's Centers." *Women in Higher Education,* vol. 17, no. 5, 2008, p. 21.

Wies, Jennifer R. "The Campus Women's Center as Classroom: A Model for Thinking and Action." *Empowering Women in Higher Education and Student Affairs: Theory, Research, Narratives, and Practice from Feminist Perspectives,* edited by Penny A. Pasque and Shelley Errington Nicholson, Stylus Publishing, 2011, pp. 255–69.

Index